ELIZABETHAN REBELLIONS

*For everyone out there facing trials that get
in the way of your dreams.*

ELIZABETHAN REBELLIONS

CONSPIRACY, INTRIGUE AND TREASON

HELENE HARRISON

PEN & SWORD HISTORY

AN IMPRINT OF PEN & SWORD BOOKS LTD.
YORKSHIRE – PHILADELPHIA

First published in Great Britain in 2023 by
PEN AND SWORD HISTORY
An imprint of
Pen & Sword Books Ltd
Yorkshire – Philadelphia

Copyright © Helene Harrison, 2023

ISBN 978 1 39908 199 3

The right of Helene Harrison to be identified as Author of this work has been asserted by her in accordance with the Copyright, Designs and Patents Act 1988.

A CIP catalogue record for this book is available from the British Library.

All rights reserved. No part of this book may be reproduced or transmitted in any form or by any means, electronic or mechanical including photocopying, recording or by any information storage and retrieval system, without permission from the Publisher in writing.

Typeset in Times New Roman 12/16 by
SJmagic DESIGN SERVICES, India.
Printed and bound in the UK by CPI Group (UK) Ltd.

Pen & Sword Books Limited incorporates the imprints of Atlas, Archaeology, Aviation, Discovery, Family History, Fiction, History, Maritime, Military, Military Classics, Politics, Select, Transport, True Crime, Air World, Frontline Publishing, Leo Cooper, Remember When, Seaforth Publishing, The Praetorian Press, Wharncliffe Local History, Wharncliffe Transport, Wharncliffe True Crime and White Owl.

For a complete list of Pen & Sword titles please contact
PEN & SWORD BOOKS LIMITED
47 Church Street, Barnsley, South Yorkshire, S70 2AS, England
E-mail: enquiries@pen-and-sword.co.uk
Website: www.pen-and-sword.co.uk

Or
PEN AND SWORD BOOKS
1950 Lawrence Rd, Havertown, PA 19083, USA
E-mail: Uspen-and-sword@casematepublishers.com
Website: www.penandswordbooks.com

Contents

Acknowledgements — vi
Illustration Credits — viii
Preface — x
Introduction — xii

Chapter 1 Earlier Tudor Rebellions — 1
           'Rebels, enemies and traitors'

Chapter 2 Northern Rising 1569 — 29
           'Seek nothing so greedily as to subdue the realm'

Chapter 3 Ridolfi Plot 1571 — 56
           'Who was to the queen so dangerous an enemy'

Chapter 4 Throckmorton Plot 1583 — 83
           'To remove her Majesty from her Crowne and state'

Chapter 5 Babington Plot 1586 — 111
           'Devilish and wicked-minded subjects'

Chapter 6 Essex Rebellion 1601 — 138
           'What is allotted to us by destiny cannot be avoided'

Chapter 7 Elizabeth and Rebellion — 165
           'Deprive the same Elizabeth of her pretended title to the crown'

Epilogue — 191
Endnotes — 197
Bibliography — 209
Index — 217

Acknowledgements

I would like to thank Pen & Sword for giving me this incredible opportunity to publish my work; to everyone there who has been a part of this journey so far and in the future – Sarah-Beth Watkins, Claire Hopkins, Laura Hirst, Chris Cocks, and Lucy May for being so supportive and answering all of my questions without judgement. Your guidance has been invaluable, and you made me feel confident in the fact that I could do this, and I am looking forward to hopefully writing much more.

I would also like to thank my family and friends for being so supportive during this whole process. Mum, Dad, and Matilda for just being there for me in your own unique ways. Special thanks to Mark. Only you know what you have done for me over the years and particularly through this lockdown. I definitely could not have done this without you, you amazing human being. Huge thanks to Laura for reading through my drafts and making sure everything made sense. It got to the point where I could not quite tell myself and I definitely owe you a drink or three! You're a fabulous friend. Also, thanks to Ben, Emily, and Hattie. I could not have done it without you all, keeping me calm and making me believe that I could do it even when I doubted myself. You are all brilliant people and I feel so grateful to have you in my life. A mention also has to go to Leigh and Aaron at the Wheelhouse Coffee Bar for keeping me in tasty treats and plenty of hot chocolate during the writing process.

A special shout out to Gaby, my dissertation supervisor for both my BA and MA History qualifications at Northumbria University. You kept encouraging me through my dissertations when I thought I could not do it, and you gave me lots of new ideas which I am still building on today. Thank you so much for believing in me when I did not believe in myself. In the future I am hoping to build on what we started in my master's dissertation, so thank you for helping me develop those ideas and giving such excellent feedback. You started me on this journey and I'm so grateful.

A huge thanks to all you wonderful historians out there who have provided such a wealth of information and opinions for me to get my teeth into. Lockdown has not been easy in a lot of ways but losing myself in Tudor history has helped massively. The works of Anne Somerset, Lisa Hilton, Susan Doran, Stephen Alford, John Cooper, and Antonia Fraser in particular have been a godsend.

Big thanks go to the Wellcome Collection and Creative Commons for images used in this book. These are invaluable resources with plenty of scope and clear instructions for copyright. It stopped my head feeling quite so bamboozled! Thanks also to the Yale Center for British Art, Wikimedia Commons, the Metropolitan Museum of Art, the National Gallery of Art in Washington D.C., and Rijksmuseum in Amsterdam. All are invaluable resources for historical images and sources. Many I had not realised had Tudor images and sources, but I will certainly be using them in future. Thank you also to The National Archives at Kew for providing documents such as the Babington cipher and the Gallows letter.

Lastly, a big shout-out to the #HistoryGirls community on Instagram. I had so many lovely messages from you all when I first released the news of this book and you have all been following my progress since, boosting my morale when I feel low and pushing me by your own amazingness to be the best that I can be. There are too many of you to list by name but just know that you're all fantastic people with so many interesting things to say and I look forward to continuing to be a part of this growing community.

To all of those aspiring writers out there who think that publication will never happen for you. I never thought in a million years it would happen for me, but it has. It can happen for you too. As someone wise keeps saying to me, kindly keep going.

Illustration Credits

1. Familia Regia: Henry VIII, Henry VII, Elizabeth of York, Jane Seymour by George Vertue / Yale Center for British Art, Paul Mellon Collection
2. Anne Boleyn, Queen of England, by Jacobus Houbraken, 1738, after Hans Holbein the Younger / Wellcome Collection, Public Domain
3. An Allegory of the Tudor Succession, 1590, Unknown Artist, 16th Century, after Lucas de Heere 1534–1584 / Yale Center for British Art, Paul Mellon Collection
4. Edward VI as a child, c.1538 by Hans Holbein the Younger / National Gallery of Art in Washington D.C., Andrew W. Mellon Collection
5. Mary I, Queen of England, Engraving by G. Vertue, 1736, after Hans Eworth / Wellcome Collection, Public Domain
6. Elizabeth I, Queen of England, Unknown Artist / Rijksmuseum, Amsterdam, on loan from the Cultural Heritage Agency of the Netherlands, Amersfoort
7. Mary, Queen of Scots, Unknown Artist c.1610–15 / Wikimedia Commons, Creative Commons Attribution-Share Alike 4.0 International
8. Elizabeth I, William Cecil, and Francis Walsingham by W. Faithorne / Wellcome Collection, Creative Commons Attribution 4.0 International (CC BY 4.0)
9. William Cecil, 1st Baron Burghley; from the picture in the Bodleian, Unknown Artist / Wellcome Collection, Creative Commons Attribution 4.0 International (CC BY 4.0)
10. Sir Francis Walsingham by John de Critz c.1589 / Yale Center for British Art, Paul Mellon Collection

Illustration Credits

11. Robert Dudley, 1st Earl of Leicester, by Steven van der Meulen, c.1565 / Yale Center for British Art, Paul Mellon Collection
12. Thomas Howard, 4th Duke of Norfolk, by Jacobus Houbraken, 1735 / Yale Center for British Art, Yale University Art Gallery Collection
13. Memorial to Thomas Howard, 4th Duke of Norfolk on Tower Hill / Photograph is Author's Own
14. Queen Elizabeth I in Parliament, Unknown Artist, 1682 / Metropolitan Museum of Art, Gift of Henry W. Kent, transferred from the Printing Office
15. Babington Cipher, Signed by Anthony Babington / The National Archives at Kew, SP 12/193/54
16. White Tower at the Tower of London / Photograph is Author's Own
17. Graffiti left by John Ballard in the Beauchamp Tower at the Tower of London / Photograph is Author's Own
18. 'Gallows Letter' written by Mary Queen of Scots to Anthony Babington / The National Archives at Kew, SP 53/18/53
19. The Death of Mary Queen of Scots (from *the European Magazine and London Review*, volume I) by William Walker, 1782 / Metropolitan Museum of Art, gift of Susan Dwight Bliss, 1958
20. James I of England (and VI of Scotland) by Paul van Somer c.1618 / Yale Center for British Art, Paul Mellon Fund
21. Philip II of Spain by Giulio Bonasone c.1554 / Metropolitan Museum of Art, Rogers Fund, 1922
22. Naval Reward Medal of Elizabeth I, 18th century, aftercast of a model from 1588, bronze / Metropolitan Museum of Art, Gift of Assunta Sommella Peluso, Ignazio Peluso, Ada Peluso and Romano I. Peluso, 2007
23. Robert Cecil, later 1st Earl of Salisbury, by Jacobus Houbraken after John de Critz / Wellcome Collection, Public Domain
24. Robert Devereux, 2nd Earl of Essex 1596/1601, Unknown Artist / National Gallery of Art in Washington D.C., gift of Mrs Henry R. Rea

Preface

My initial interest in the Tudor period was in fact based around the infamous Anne Boleyn, second wife to Henry VIII and mother to Elizabeth I. This is who my university dissertations were based on. Through Anne I began to read more about Elizabeth and then Mary Queen of Scots. My interest in Tudor rebellions was first aroused when studying the Pilgrimage of Grace and the Essex Rebellion for my A Level module on Tudor Rebellions. I remember being so intrigued about the whole subject, because they were so different, but equally enthralling. Over the years I have engaged more with rebellions and the reasons behind them. Why would people risk a horrible death to rebel against their monarch? The Essex Rebellion especially caught my attention because it was such a selfish revolt without wider aims, so unlike the others of the period.

I was so thrilled that I got to visit the British Library during the writing of this book. They put on a wonderful exhibition called 'Elizabeth and Mary: Royal Cousins, Rival Queens' which I saw with a really good friend who completely indulged me in the time I wanted to spend there. Being so close to those documents like the Babington cipher, the Tide letter, and the Gallows letter really brings it all to life somehow and I got goosebumps standing there and seeing the signatures of Elizabeth I, Mary Queen of Scots, William Cecil, and Francis Walsingham among others on documents which changed the face of English history. It was so poignant and managed to make me understand and appreciate things in a way I had not done before. It just worked out to be absolutely perfect timing.

What I have tried to do with this book is to pull together the strands of the plots in chronological order, intertwined with different historiographical viewpoints and contemporary accounts, letters, and pamphlets of the time. Historians often disagree as to the importance of Mary Queen of Scots in the earlier plots, and the extent to which Francis Walsingham manipulated plots around Mary to lead to her execution, specifically with the Babington Plot of 1586. I have attempted to amalgamate these opinions into one cohesive narrative to give a complete picture of what we know and what the different arguments are, so that you can make up your own mind. I am hoping that each chapter can stand as an essay on its own so each one can be read without you needing to read the rest to put it in context.

I already have plenty of ideas for my next book, and I hope to keeping reading and writing plenty more, expanding my huge collection of history books on the Tudors and the Wars of the Roses, and exploring new people and periods.

Being approached by Pen & Sword Books and asked to write this book was such a privilege and I really hope I have done it justice. There are no books focusing on Elizabethan rebellions, only textbooks focusing on Tudor rebellions more generally. Rebellions in Tudor England were a product of the times in which the people lived. This was a period of great change in terms of dynasty and succession, socio-economic conditions, and religion. The Tudors were still a relatively new dynasty when Elizabeth succeeded to the throne in 1558, plagued by pretenders and claimants who believed they had a better right to the throne than Elizabeth I, of which Mary Queen of Scots was the most dangerous.

Without Mary Queen of Scots in England there would not have been so many plots against Elizabeth I as an alternative claimant, arguably even a stronger claimant, was within arm's reach and willing to engage in conspiracy, intrigue, and treason.

Helene Harrison, December 2021

Introduction

Elizabeth I had to deal with a number of rebellions during her reign as Queen of England between 1558 and 1603. She had not had a very easy or pampered life as might be expected of the daughter of a king. These early experiences shaped her both as a person and as a ruler, so it is important to understand what happened to her, how it could have affected her emotionally, and in how she approached and dealt with problems during her life and reign. This book intends to examine the rebellions of Elizabeth's reign, and how she dealt with them. In order to do this, we need to understand how her early experiences shaped her and how her predecessors' attempts to deal with rebellion influenced her own approach.

What is particularly interesting is that there were no real rebellions against Elizabeth until 1569, eleven years into her reign. This was just a year after the flight of Mary Stuart, Queen of Scots, from Scotland to seek support from Elizabeth in England to regain her throne and power. Mary had been ousted by Protestant lords and imprisoned in Lochleven Castle. She was forced to abdicate the Scottish throne on 24 July 1567 in favour of her 1-year-old son, who became James VI of Scotland and later, on the death of Elizabeth I, James I of England. James Stewart, 1st Earl of Moray, was made regent. He was the illegitimate son of Mary's father, James V. He would be assassinated in 1570, and three further regents would follow: Matthew Stewart, 4th Earl of Lennox, John Erskine, 1st Earl of Mar, and James Douglas, 4th Earl of Morton.

There were five major rebellions under Elizabeth which will be examined here – the Northern Rising, the Ridolfi Plot, the Throckmorton Plot, the Babington Plot, and the Essex Rebellion – and

Introduction

all except the Essex Rebellion, which happened after her execution in 1587, involved Mary Queen of Scots in some way. This demonstrates just how much threat it took for Elizabeth to actually act against Mary. Although in the end she would try to wash her hands of any responsibility, blaming others for her execution and grieving in public for her royal cousin.

*

The future Elizabeth I was born to Henry VIII and his second wife, Anne Boleyn, on 7 September 1533. Her birth was a disappointment to both her mother and father. Henry VIII had annulled his marriage to his first wife, Katherine of Aragon, because she had failed to give him a son; only a daughter who would become Mary I. This annulment had taken nearly seven years to achieve, and he expected Anne to give him a son and heir as she had promised, so Elizabeth's birth was a blow to both of them. Anne would go on to have a further two, or possibly three, miscarriages.

Elizabeth's early years would have been happy and luxurious. She was given her own establishment at Hatfield House at the end of 1533 and Anne lavished new clothes and gifts on her. Both parents visited her regularly and showed her off at court. However, things changed dramatically for the young princess in May 1536 when Anne Boleyn was arrested and accused of adultery, incest, and treason with five different men including her own brother, George Boleyn, Lord Rochford. When Anne was executed on 19 May 1536, Elizabeth was not yet 3 years old. She was made illegitimate when Anne's marriage to the king was annulled, probably on the grounds of Henry's prior relationship with Anne's sister, Mary Boleyn. It has been suggested that Mary's children, Catherine and Henry Carey, were fathered by Henry VIII during this affair.

After her mother's death, Elizabeth had a succession of stepmothers. The first of these was Jane Seymour, formerly a lady-in-waiting to both Anne Boleyn and Katherine of Aragon. She finally gave Henry VIII the much-waited-for son and heir, who would become Edward VI. At the time of her greatest triumph, she tragically died from puerperal fever just days after the birth in October 1537. Jane was responsible for welcoming Elizabeth back to court after her mother's disgrace. Anne of Cleves became Henry VIII's fourth wife and Elizabeth's second stepmother in 1540, but Henry divorced her just six months later to marry her attendant, Katherine Howard. Anne would remain a part of Elizabeth's life, dying in 1557. Katherine Howard was cousin to Elizabeth's mother, Anne Boleyn, so was a direct relation of Elizabeth. Katherine was aged around 17 when she married the nearly 50-year-old king. Just a year and a half later she would be executed for adultery just like her cousin, Anne Boleyn.

Elizabeth's fourth and final stepmother was Katherine Parr. She was probably the most influential woman in Elizabeth's early life. Katherine married Henry VIII at Hampton Court Palace on 12 July 1543 and immediately made overtures to the king's children, although sources suggest she had known Princess Mary for a few years and had served in her household. Katherine was made regent when Henry VIII went to fight in France the following year, so Elizabeth had a positive female role model who proved that a woman could rule, even just temporarily, in the absence of a king. This likely had a huge impact on Elizabeth as she was at an impressionable age anyway, and her previous stepmothers did not really have any noticeable influence on her. Henry VIII was quite open about the fact that he believed women could not rule and that is why he needed a son. This had been drilled into him by his father, Henry VII, who wanted to avoid another Wars of the Roses where the succession had constantly been open to question, battles fought, and monarchs overthrown and replaced. Katherine showed Elizabeth that it was possible for a woman to rule a country successfully.

In the 1544 Act of Succession Elizabeth and her half-sister, Mary, the daughter of Katherine of Aragon, were added back into the succession after Edward VI and his heirs. The likelihood that

Elizabeth would succeed to the throne still seemed to be slim, as there was no suggestion that Edward VI would not live a long life, marry, and have children. Some historians imply that Edward VI was a sickly child but there is not really any evidence of this in the contemporary sources. Ambassadors would report home to their masters Edward's accomplishments, but there was no mention of poor health until the last six months of his life, apart from a quartan fever aged four. Mary was also ahead of Elizabeth in the succession as the eldest daughter. Mary was still young enough to marry and have children of her own as well, which would push Elizabeth further down in the line of succession.

After Henry VIII's death on 28 January 1547 Elizabeth moved into the household of her stepmother, Katherine Parr, at Chelsea. Within months of Henry's death, Katherine married her former suitor, Thomas Seymour, the brother of Henry VIII's third wife, Jane Seymour. Elizabeth continued to live with them and was joined at Chelsea by Lady Jane Grey, her cousin. Jane's wardship had been purchased by Thomas Seymour who told Jane's parents he would marry her to Edward VI. The pair were both Protestant and intelligent, but Elizabeth was more socially adept than Jane and enjoyed socialising more than Jane did. The relationship between Elizabeth and Seymour is very controversial, both at the time and in the centuries since. This is probably the time in her life when Elizabeth was most influenced in how she dealt with men and the idea of marriage. What Elizabeth experienced with Seymour would have had a serious impact on anyone; she was only 14 in 1547.

Various reports, including confessions and letters, describe what happened between Elizabeth and Seymour in 1547 and 1548. It has been hinted that Katherine Parr joined in on various occasions when Seymour entered Elizabeth's bedroom in the morning and tickled her, only partially dressed and she still in her nightgown. David Starkey reports one instance where in the garden Katherine held Elizabeth still while Seymour cut her dress to ribbons.[1] It is said that Elizabeth was sent away from Chelsea to Cheshunt under the wardship of Sir Anthony Denny in May 1548 after Katherine Parr discovered Elizabeth and Seymour alone in the garden in an embrace. Katherine Parr had fallen pregnant towards the end of 1547 and possibly this pregnancy made Katherine see Seymour's behaviour towards Elizabeth in a different light. Katherine sent Elizabeth away to Cheshunt to protect her reputation and the two unfortunately would not meet again. They did correspond, however, and in a letter from June 1548, Elizabeth wrote, 'I was replete with sorrow to depart from your highness.'[2] This suggests that Elizabeth regretted what had happened between her and Seymour because it was the cause of her being separated from Katherine, whom she seems to have been very close to prior to this. Elizabeth seems to have been grateful for Katherine's care of her, and her appointment of William Grindal as her tutor. Katherine gave birth to a daughter, Mary Seymour, on 30 August 1548 but she barely survived a week past the birth, dying of puerperal fever on 7 September, like Jane Seymour before her.

After Katherine's death, Thomas Seymour seems to have hoped to marry Elizabeth, and thus get closer to the throne. It also seems that he approached Princess Mary as a possible bride at this time, as she was ahead of Elizabeth in the line of succession. There were even rumours that he had approached Mary regarding marriage before he had married Katherine Parr. If this were true, Katherine was the second choice. Marrying the heir would have got Seymour closer to the throne than marrying the dowager queen. Seymour was jealous of the power of his brother, Edward, Duke of Somerset, and Earl of Hertford, who was Protector of Edward VI, and wanted some of that power for himself. Seymour overreached himself by criticising his brother's policies with regards to the war in Scotland, and he then risked everything with a daring plan to gain control of the young king in 1548, ostensibly by kidnapping him. However, the plan was foiled when one of the king's spaniels was woken up when Seymour entered his apartments, and Seymour shot and killed it. He was then arrested and taken to the Tower for questioning.

Introduction

Everyone connected with Seymour, including Elizabeth, was questioned about what they knew, regarding his thoughts and actions. Elizabeth's servants, Sir Thomas Parry, her cofferer, and Kat Ashley, her chief lady who would remain with her until her death in 1565, both revealed what they knew about the relationship between Elizabeth and Seymour and that there had been some talk of a marriage between them. Elizabeth wrote to Protector Somerset to explain herself and on 28 January 1549, she said that Ashley had told her that 'they say [in London] that your grace shall have my lord admiral [Seymour]'.[3] Elizabeth had replied, however, that she would not marry without the consent of the king and council. Had she married without consent she would have been removed from the succession as per the Act of Succession of 1544 enacted by Henry VIII. There were also rumours that Elizabeth was pregnant by Seymour, and she asked to be allowed to come to court to disprove the rumours. This request was denied her.

Being this close to a traitor, as Seymour was found to be, no doubt affected Elizabeth. After this point she seemed to be more careful in her dealings with men, possibly with the exception of Robert Dudley, 1st Earl of Leicester, later in her life. When rumours spread that Dudley had been involved in the death of his first wife, Amy Robsart, Elizabeth sent him away from court until he was cleared. She had obviously learnt from the Seymour incident that she needed to distance herself from anything that could damage her reputation. The Seymour episode also helps to explain Elizabeth's leniency towards Mary Queen of Scots until there was damning evidence against her. Elizabeth knew what it was to be used and perhaps believed to some extent that Mary was being used by the plotters to gain power and favour. This will be explored in later chapters. Seymour was executed on 20 March 1549 on Tower Hill for treason and Elizabeth is alleged to have said, 'this day died a man of much wit and very little judgement.'

Elizabeth seems to have retired to her residence at Hatfield House in Hertfordshire for the remainder of her brother's reign. She appears to have avoided the controversy surrounding the nine-day reign of

Lady Jane Grey after Edward VI's death in July 1553. Edward VI, through his Device for the Succession, had attempted to change the succession to the throne to stop his Catholic half-sister, Mary, from succeeding him. Edward worried, rightfully as it turned out, that Mary would return England to Rome and undo his Protestant reforms. He claimed that Mary had been declared illegitimate by their father, Henry VIII, so was ineligible to inherit the crown. By this logic, Elizabeth was ineligible as well. Edward intended the crown to pass through the line of his aunt, Henry VIII's sister, Mary Tudor, Queen of France and Duchess of Suffolk. Lady Jane Grey was Mary's granddaughter, through Frances Brandon and her husband, Henry Grey, 1st Duke of Suffolk.

However, Mary was determined that she was the rightful Queen of England. She gathered her forces at Framlingham Castle in Suffolk, intending to march on London to depose Jane Grey and take the throne herself. The council quickly came over to Mary's side and there was no need for her to march out with an army. Elizabeth entered London at the side of her triumphant sister on 3 August 1553 to popular acclaim. As the historian Laura Brennan has noted, this would have shown Elizabeth that the people acclaimed Mary as the true heir by right of being her father's daughter. The same logic applied to Elizabeth who was now heir apparent to the English throne.[4] This gave Elizabeth hope that, should Mary die childless, she could expect a similar reaction on her accession. In the event, Elizabeth's acclamation was greater than Mary's as Mary had made an unpopular foreign marriage and burned hundreds of Protestants, earning her the epithet of 'Bloody Mary'.

Elizabeth probably faced one of the biggest personal crises of her life during the reign of her sister, Mary I. She was accused of being involved in the rebellion of Sir Thomas Wyatt the Younger in 1554. The rebellion was to protest against the proposed marriage of Mary to Philip II of Spain as there were concerns that England would become an outpost of Spain, involved in Spanish wars, and would lose her independence. Wyatt intended to depose Mary and replace her with Elizabeth, married to Edward Courtenay, 1st Earl of Devon. This rebellion is discussed further in Chapter 1. Elizabeth was questioned at her home at Hatfield House, and she was forced to travel to court, although she was unwell at the time and claimed she was not well enough to travel. Wyatt admitted under questioning that he had written to Elizabeth, but only to warn her to get away. Elizabeth had written nothing to Wyatt or the other rebels, but she did send a verbal message saying that she would act as she thought best but would not commit to anything. On 16 March 1554, Elizabeth was told that she was suspected of involvement in the plot and would be taken to the Tower of London. There was no evidence that Elizabeth had done anything to incriminate herself and she was never charged. She was released from the Tower to house arrest at Woodstock Palace on 19 May 1554, the eighteenth anniversary of her mother, Anne Boleyn's, execution on Tower Green. Wyatt was executed affirming that Elizabeth was not involved in the plot.

Wyatt's Rebellion had proven to Elizabeth that the heir to the throne would naturally be a focal point for opposition, whether they desired it or not and whether they were actually involved or not.[5] This is an absolutely key point as it can help to explain Elizabeth's later reluctance to act against Mary Queen of Scots without concrete evidence, despite her name consistently cropping up linked to various rebellions against Elizabeth. She knew from personal experience that people could use Mary's name as heir to act against her, even if Mary herself was not involved. Elizabeth gave Mary too much leeway as she appears to have been more involved in rebellions against Elizabeth than Elizabeth ever was against her sister. Elizabeth appeared to have more of an instinct for self-preservation than Mary Queen of Scots.

Elizabeth stayed away from court as far as possible while her sister reigned. She remained under house arrest at Woodstock until April 1555 when she was summoned back to court to attend the final stages of Mary I's supposed pregnancy, which turned out to be a phantom pregnancy. Mary had allegedly wanted Elizabeth to be there when she was unseated as heir to the throne, to witness her sister's triumph. Elizabeth then moved to her residence at Hatfield, and it was at Hatfield that Elizabeth learned of her sister's death and her own accession to the throne on 17 November 1558.

*

Examining Elizabeth's experiences before she came to the throne in 1558 can help us to understand some of her decisions and motivations during her reign, and especially when dealing with some of the hardest and most controversial issues. She experienced several rebellions during her -year reign, but there were no rebellions until Mary Queen of Scots fled to England in 1568, so the first eleven years of her reign were relatively quiet. The main issues of these years were the question over Elizabeth's marriage, Elizabeth's relationship with Robert Dudley, Earl of Leicester, and the Religious Settlement.

Of the five key rebellions under Elizabeth I, only one of them had nothing to do with Mary Queen of Scots: the Essex Rebellion of 1601, fourteen years after Mary's execution. This suggests that Mary was the catalyst for revolt in England under Elizabeth. There were no rebellions between the Babington Plot in 1586 which led directly to Mary's execution the following year, and the 1601 Essex Rebellion. This is significant, as there were rebellions in 1569, 1571, 1583, and 1586 while Mary was imprisoned in England, but only one after Mary's execution. The Essex Rebellion was more of a selfish form of rebellion rather than the more popular revolts of people grouping together to rebel against a social or religious cause, or in favour of an alternative monarch or successor. The Essex Rebellion is the only selfish uprising of the whole Tudor period, as the majority focused on social issues, religion, or possible alternate successors to the throne.

Elizabethan rebellions are particularly interesting because there were so many plots and conspiracies focused on the same person. This is unusual among other rebellions, particularly under the Tudors who were so focused on keeping the throne stable and securing the succession so as to avoid a repeat of the Wars of the Roses. Henry VIII in particular seems to have executed anyone who had a claim to the throne, like Edward Stafford, 3rd Duke of Buckingham, Margaret Pole, Countess of Salisbury, her son Henry Pole, 1st Baron Montagu, and Edmund de la Pole, 3rd Duke of Suffolk. Elizabeth does not seem to have taken the same route as her father, allowing Mary Queen of Scots more chances than her father would have.

Chapter 1

Early Tudor Rebellions

'Rebels, enemies, and traitors'[1]

The Tudor dynasty suffered a number of rebellions and each monarch of the dynasty had at least one major revolt to deal with during their time on the throne. As Henry VII had seized the throne on the battlefield at Bosworth in 1485, perhaps this was understandable. Not all of the citizens, especially the nobility, accepted the Tudors as rightful kings and queens. there were surviving Plantagenet heirs who were preferable to many. The monarchs' responses to these rebellions can also be understood in the context of the Wars of the Roses which were still in living memory, even to a few when Elizabeth I came to the throne in 1558, though more so in the reigns of Henry VII and Henry VIII. Perhaps because the Tudors seemed to have a problem in providing male heirs the dynasty was seen as unstable which may have prompted at least some of the rebellions against them.

The rebellions under the Tudor monarchs seem to mainly fall into two categories: succession and religion. These were the main issues that the Tudor monarchs were preoccupied with, particularly Henry VIII, whose reign was hugely affected by both issues, though Elizabeth I was also affected by both as will be seen. Henry VIII divorced his first wife, Katherine of Aragon, and beheaded his second, Anne Boleyn, in order to get a son by his third wife, Jane Seymour. Because Henry VII had seized the throne on the battlefield, he had drilled into his son how vulnerable the Tudor dynasty was and Henry VIII had taken that to heart. Henry VIII also knew from first-hand experience that one son was not enough to secure the succession; his elder brother, Arthur, had died in 1502, leaving him unexpectedly as heir to the throne. This explains Henry's further three marriages after Jane Seymour's death in 1537, just days after the birth of their son, the future Edward VI. Henry VIII's children were also very aware of potential succession issues. Edward VI took steps to try and exclude his half-sisters from the throne, and Mary I was determined to have a son of her own to prevent Elizabeth from succeeding her. There were religious issues after the Break with Rome, known as the mid-Tudor crisis, as each monarch had a very different belief of what the religion should be in England. Tensions between Catholicism and Protestantism dominated much of the sixteenth century across Europe, not just in England. However, England and Scotland seem to be some of the only countries where religion was used as an excuse to overthrow the monarch. There was also concern over England becoming an offshoot of another country and losing its independence, as evidenced mostly by Mary I's marriage to Philip II of Spain and the question over who Elizabeth should marry at the beginning of her reign.

The rebellions under Henry VII focused on pretenders to the throne and the right of Henry VII and the Tudor dynasty to rule; namely Lambert Simnel in 1487 and Perkin Warbeck who dominated the 1490s. There was only one major rebellion under Henry VIII which was focused on religious issues in the aftermath of the Break with Rome, called the Pilgrimage of Grace. Edward VI had to deal with two rebellions at the same time in 1549 – the Kett Rebellion and the Western Rebellion, the first of which focused largely on social issues like enclosure and poor economic conditions, and the second of which rebelled against the introduction of the new Protestant prayerbook, called the *Book of Common Prayer* which was introduced that year. It could be argued that there was a rebellion between the reigns of Edward VI and Mary I in 1553 with the nine-day reign of Jane Grey, which actually technically lasted thirteen days, before Mary succeeded in taking the throne from her. This was the only real 'successful' rebellion under the Tudors, though it resulted in a Tudor taking the throne. Mary I had to deal with a rebellion against her proposed marriage to Philip II of Spain, led by Sir Thomas Wyatt the Younger, who was worried that England would become an outpost of Spain as a result. This is different to many of the other rebellions as it focused on foreign interference in English affairs, which were part of many other rebellions in some ways, but not the sole focus.

An understanding of these earlier Tudor rebellions can help us to understand Elizabeth's reactions to the rebellions that she had to deal with during her reign. Elizabeth herself was rumoured to be involved in the Wyatt Rebellion under her half-sister, Mary I, though nothing was ever proven. She was imprisoned in the Tower of London as a result and came close to execution. Her early experiences of rebellion shaped her own reactions when she had to deal with revolts against her own claim to the throne and controversial decisions she made.

*

The first major rebellion of the Tudor dynasty was under Henry VII in 1487 and concerned a young boy by the name of Lambert Simnel. Henry VII had only been on the throne for two years; and the Wars of the Roses were not known to be over as Henry VII could have just been another king who took the throne by force and could be overthrown at any moment. It is only with hindsight that we can see that the Wars of the Roses were effectively over, and that Henry VII had founded a dynasty that would reign for over a hundred years. There would not be another violent change of ruler until the English Civil War in the seventeenth century when England changed, temporarily, from a monarchy to a republic under Oliver Cromwell and Charles I was executed.

The English people did not really know Henry VII. He had grown up in exile in France in the Duchy of Brittany where he had escaped to with his uncle, Jasper Tudor, Earl of Pembroke, and later 1st Duke of Bedford, in the aftermath of the Battle of Tewkesbury in 1471. Tewkesbury marked the defeat of the Lancastrian dynasty and the restoration of the Yorkist Edward IV to the English throne. It also marked the beginning of fourteen years of exile for the future Henry VII. Why is Henry VII's exile important to the rebellions he struggled with during his reign? The English people did not really know much about him because he had not been in the country and the two major rebellions he had to tackle were to do with the succession and promoting candidates who were more well known in England: namely Richard, Duke of York, younger of the Princes in the Tower, and Edward Plantagenet, 17th Earl of Warwick.

Lambert Simnel was a pretender. The surviving Yorkists believed that, if no Yorkist claimant to the throne existed, one had to be created.[2] Simnel was the son of an Oxford man who pretended to be Edward, Earl of Warwick, son of George, 1st Duke of Clarence, and nephew to both Edward IV and Richard III. The real Warwick was born in 1475 so was aged 12 in 1487, and Simnel was said to be around aged ten. This would not necessarily have been a problem if Simnel looked older than his years, or it could be claimed that Warwick looked younger than his years due to his imprisonment in the Tower. Polydore Vergil reported that rumours spread of Warwick's death in prison in 1487 and when the priest Richard Simons learned this, he changed Simnel's name to Edward and crossed to Ireland, where many disaffected Yorkists had fled to after Bosworth.[3] Simons spread a rumour that Warwick had escaped from the Tower and was under his guardianship. Yorkists claimed rather that they had rescued Warwick from the Tower themselves and brought him to Ireland.[4] It is unlikely that it was intended for Simnel to remain on the throne once Henry VII had been overthrown. It seems probable that John de la Pole, 1st Earl of Lincoln, would rule and that Simnel was just a figurehead for the rebellion; essentially expendable. Lincoln was the son of Edward IV and Richard III's sister, Elizabeth, Duchess of Suffolk, and so had a claim to the throne himself, though this descended through the female line, rather than Warwick's through the male line.

Along with the Earl of Lincoln, Simnel also had the support of Francis, Viscount Lovell, who was in touch with Irish lords like Gerald Fitzgerald, 8th Earl of Kildare. Simnel travelled to Burgundy and met Duchess Margaret of Burgundy, sister to Edward IV and aunt to the Earl of Warwick. Lovell had fled to join Margaret in Burgundy after a previous failed attempt at uprising against Henry VII. Margaret accepted Simnel as her nephew, Warwick. She also provided 5,000 mercenary soldiers to aid Simnel and Lovell to take the English throne, but she expected a return on her investment. Whether Margaret really believed Simnel to be the Earl of Warwick is unknown, and historians are divided. Some believe that Margaret really did believe the charade, but others suggest that she knew it was a pretence but was willing to go along with it in order to put a Yorkist on the throne again after the death of her brother, Richard III, at the Battle of Bosworth in 1485.

Lambert Simnel arrived in Dublin, Ireland, in 1487 with Richard Simons and Lord Lovell. He was received as the rightful King of England and on 24 May 1487 Simnel was crowned as Edward VI at Christchurch Cathedral by the Bishop of Meath. He was paraded through the streets on the shoulders of Sir William Darcy, who is known to have been exceptionally tall. The Irish added a further 4,000 to 5,000 men to those supplied by Margaret of Burgundy for the invasion. When Henry VII learned of Simnel being accepted in Burgundy and Ireland as the rightful King of England he had the real Earl of Warwick taken from the Tower of London and paraded through the streets of London. This did not dissuade the rebel leaders from continuing their charade.

The rebels left Ireland and sailed for England, landing on 4 June 1487. On 16 June, the army of Simnel, Lincoln and Lovell met with the royal army under Henry VII at Stoke. There is no surviving report of the battle, but it is said that the rebel army numbered around 9,000 men and the royal army around 12,000 men, so the rebels were critically outnumbered. Henry VII himself took no part in the battle and it is said that only the advance guard of 6,000 men in the royal army led by John de Vere, 13th Earl of Oxford, engaged the rebels. After a couple of hours of fighting the tide of the battle turned in favour of the king. After a further hour or so the rebel troops broke and fled. Many retreating soldiers drowned in the River Trent, and around half of the rebel army ended up dead. Polydore Vergil notes that around 4,000 men were killed,[5] which might be a conservative estimate, although different accounts offer different estimations of the battle casualties. With hindsight, the Battle of Stoke is often seen as the last battle of the Wars of the Roses. This is because it effectively defeated the only really valid alternate claims to the throne in the persons of the Earl of Lincoln and the Earl of Warwick, though the Princes in the Tower and other potential claimants would continue to haunt the Tudor throne in the coming years. Others see the Battle of Bosworth in 1485 as the final battle of the Wars of the Roses. It is personal opinion.

Lovell and Sir Thomas Broughton were the only rebel leaders to survive, and they escaped to the court of James III of Scotland before vanishing from the historical record. Henry VII was merciful to those who fought against him and most got off with fines. This made people grateful that they were not imprisoned or executed, and also put more money into the royal treasury. The king regretted that the Earl of Lincoln had been killed in the battle as he wanted to know how far the conspiracy went and who at court had supported it. He had given orders that Lincoln was to be taken alive but in the heat of battle this order was ignored. Richard Simons, the priest who had taken Simnel under his wing, could not be executed as he was a religious man, but he was imprisoned. Simnel himself was treated relatively leniently and was sent to work in the royal kitchens, eventually rising to the role of royal falconer, dying sometime around 1534, aged approximately fifty-seven. This leniency was perhaps because of his youth. It seems likely that Henry VII accepted that Simnel was a pawn in the machinations of others like Lincoln, Lovell, and Margaret of Burgundy.

Henry VII worried that Simnel was merely a figurehead, and the intention was to replace him with one of the surviving Princes in the Tower, who would be kept out of harm's way until the rebellion was successful. Bertram Fields believes that this scenario makes more sense than the idea that either Warwick or Lincoln would take the throne.[6] Warwick's claim was questionable because he descended from the Duke of Clarence who had been executed for treason in 1477, and thereby his children could not inherit the throne. Lincoln was in the succession but descended from an inferior female line. As the children of the male lines – Edward IV, Clarence, and Richard III – were all unavailable (assuming that the Princes in the Tower were really dead, and Warwick was excluded), then Lincoln would be the next heir as the first male child from the female lines of Edward IV and Richard III's sisters. Lincoln was descended from the third sister. The eldest, Anne, died with only surviving daughters and the second, Elizabeth of York, was married to Henry VII. As the intention was to overthrow Henry, Lincoln disregarded their son, Arthur.

There was also a suggestion that Elizabeth Woodville, the Queen's mother, was involved in the rebellion. She was stripped of many of her privileges and retreated to a convent at Bermondsey, dying there five years later, in 1492. This idea has been questioned, as why would Elizabeth support an imposter with her daughter, Elizabeth of York, already on the throne and her grandson, Prince Arthur, to follow his father? This could only make sense if Elizabeth knew that one of her sons was still alive and safe, and intended to take the throne in place of his brother-in-law, Henry VII. It is often difficult to sort out what the overall intention of the rebellion was. The rebels wanted to overthrow King Henry VII, but it is not clear exactly whom they intended to replace him with.

*

The Perkin Warbeck Rebellion, although still a rebellion headed by a pretender to the throne, posed more of a threat to the English throne than the Lambert Simnel Rebellion. The Warbeck Rebellion lasted over a longer period of time than the Simnel Rebellion, and it came closer to success in many ways. Unlike the Earl of Warwick in the Simnel Rebellion, Richard, Duke of York could not be paraded through the streets of London to prove the pretender was a fake. No one knew with confidence whether the Princes in the Tower were dead, and no bodies had been recovered that we know of for certain, or that have made it into the records. Skeletons recovered in the Tower of London in 1674 which had been buried under a staircase in the White Tower were placed in an urn on the orders of Charles II and interred in Westminster Abbey. These were assumed to be the remains of the Princes in the Tower but there is no evidence, and the remains have not been examined.

Perkin Warbeck was the son of a Tournai man, John Osbeck, and his wife, Katherine de Faro, and was said to have a striking resemblance to Edward IV, the father of the Princes in the Tower. His own confession given at the time of his capture by Henry VII's troops, suggests he was born into an educated family, comfortably off if not wealthy, in the French town of Tournai.[7] His father was described as the comptroller to the city of Tournai. His name is sometimes spelt as Pierrechon de Werbecque, but the English seem to have changed it to Perkin Warbeck. Warbeck's confession was obtained under duress, so the veracity of what he said cannot be guaranteed.

Warbeck arrived in Cork, Ireland, in the employ of a Breton merchant called Pregent Meno. He was parading around advertising some of his employer's wares when the citizens declared him to be Edward, Earl of Warwick. He had to swear an oath to refute this. It was then thought that he was a bastard son of Richard III, which would not have made him a legitimate claimant to the English throne anyway. Warbeck later claimed that it was against his will that some Yorkist adherents, including the former mayor of Cork, John Atwater, declared him to be Richard, Duke of York, younger of the Princes in the Tower, and made him learn English, royal history, and manners.

Warbeck's arrival on the international scene shocked Henry VII as, at first, he seemed like a legitimate claimant to the throne. He gained the backing of James Fitzgerald, 8th Earl of Desmond, and Gerald Fitzgerald, 8th Earl of Kildare, while in Ireland. Letters were written to James IV of Scotland to try and garner his support, but the biggest vote of confidence came from the French king, Charles VIII. Between March and November 1492 Warbeck was a guest at the French court, until Charles made peace with the English and he and his followers were forced to move on. They travelled then to the court of Margaret, Duchess of Burgundy, who had also been involved in the Simnel Rebellion five years earlier. Margaret greeted Warbeck as her long-lost nephew, Richard, and sent letters to different heads of state declaring his authenticity as her nephew and the rightful King of England. Warbeck travelled to Vienna and attended the funeral of Holy Roman Emperor, Frederick III, and met the new Holy Roman Emperor, Maximilian who recognised him as King of England. Whether Margaret and Maximilian truly believed in Warbeck's identity is unknown. It is quite possible they were using him for their own ends to try and unseat Henry VII in favour possibly of the Earl of Warwick, Margaret's nephew, who was imprisoned in the Tower of London.

Polydore Vergil recounts that Henry VII sent spies to try and find out who the pretender really was, and they discovered him as Perkin Warbeck, 'born of low degree', though from Warbeck's later confession this was not entirely true.[8] Perhaps Henry VII doctored the real story for propaganda purposes. Henry VII published the news across England and abroad. Henry also declared that the boy could not be Richard, Duke of York, because he and his brother, Edward V, had been killed in the Tower of London by their uncle, Richard III, which was widely believed but not likely to be proven without bodies. On 1 November 1494, Henry VII created his second son, Henry, Duke of York, to counteract the pretender, who was claiming to be Richard, Duke of York. As there can only be one of each dukedom at any one time, Henry VII was dealing directly with the claims of Perkin Warbeck, that he did not believe Warbeck was the true Duke of York.

Henry VII then offered pardons to some men in Flanders who were supporting Warbeck and they agreed to turn spy for the king and gave him the names of people who were supporting Warbeck, even in Henry's own court. Sir William Stanley, brother to the king's own stepfather, Thomas Stanley, 1st Earl of Derby, was one of those implicated and he was executed on 16 February 1495 for his support of the conspiracy against the king. Henry had initially been inclined to spare Stanley, given his links to his mother, Margaret Beaufort, and his vital assistance at the Battle of Bosworth in 1485 which had given Henry the throne. Stanley had brought his men in to fight for Henry at a crucial moment at Bosworth which meant that Henry's forces had the advantage of numbers. However, Henry would not let Stanley act against him and jeopardise the security of the throne.

Margaret of Burgundy promised Warbeck that she would fund an expedition to England, aiding him in his attempt to take the throne. An agreement was signed which meant that Warbeck would have to repay Margaret the loan, return her trade licences which Henry VII had revoked for her support of Warbeck, and give her Scarborough. The Holy Roman Emperor, Maximilian, also provided financial assistance. The *Parliament Rolls* from October 1495 state that Warbeck came to England accompanied by 'rebels, enemies and traitors' in ships and landed at Deal in Kent on 3 July 1495 and 'waged battle and war'.[9] Warbeck remained on board his ship for this first attempt as the advance party went ashore. They were overwhelmed by the locals and Warbeck could only watch as 163 of his men were captured and a further 150 were killed on the beach. He could not do anything but turn and sail again for Ireland.

On 23 July 1495, Warbeck, along with the Earl of Desmond, tried to take Waterford but failed. In England the rebels captured at Deal were tried and executed between the 16 and 24 July. The invasion scare lasted around three weeks, but it was a bit of an anti-climax. Ireland did not seem to support Warbeck anymore, so he travelled to Scotland, where he was received by James IV of Scotland at Stirling Palace on 27 November 1495. He had travelled to Scotland to ask for assistance, both financial and military, and had to plead his cause. James became convinced that Warbeck was in fact Richard, Duke of York, and pledged to aid him in taking the throne of England. In December 1495, Warbeck married Lady Catherine Gordon, daughter of the Earl of Huntley, and great-granddaughter of James I of Scotland. This marriage suggests that James IV really did believe in Warbeck as Richard, Duke of York, as it is difficult to imagine him allowing Warbeck to marry Catherine Gordon, such a high-born young lady, without believing in the deception.

By the end of summer 1496 James IV of Scotland was preparing for war with England. It was reported that a Scottish army would assemble at Ellam Kirk on 15 September 1496 for an invasion intended to go ahead two days later. The Scots crossed the border into England on 17 September and burned and looted as they headed south. When they heard that an English army of 4,000 men was headed north to meet their army of fewer than 1,500, they retreated back over the border, having covered just four miles. It became clear that the people would not rise for Warbeck, and the Scottish political position was compromised as a result of the failure of the invasion on Warbeck's behalf. This made the Scots rethink their promise to assist Warbeck.

The people of Cornwall rose in revolt against the taxes which had been raised to fight against the Scottish invasion. Had Warbeck landed at this point on the south coast of England and joined the rebels, who had volunteered to support him, he might have triumphed. However, Warbeck likely did not receive the letter from the rebels as he had sailed again for Ireland. Warbeck sailed from Ayr in July 1497 with his wife and child and landed in Ireland on 25 July, either in Kerry or West Cork.

Warbeck sailed from Ireland heading for the Cornish coast in September 1497 and landed near Land's End at Whitesand Bay on 7 September with 300 supporters. Within a week Warbeck had an army of 3,000 men gathered behind him at Castle Kynnock near Bodmin. Warbeck, however, had left it too late, and many of his followers were poorly armed. The Cornish Rebellion had petered out and most of the rebels had dispersed. Warbeck later admitted when questioned that as soon as he landed, he knew that his cause was doomed. The local sheriff tried to attack the rebel camp but was repulsed and many of his troops deserted and joined the rebels, whose army now numbered 8,000 men. Edward Courtenay, 1st Earl of Devon, was sent to subdue the rebels, but he failed and withdrew to Exeter.

The rebels arrived at Exeter on 17 September 1497 and tried to take the city. Around 200 were killed before the attack was called off. A truce was negotiated as both sides were exhausted and could not push on. Shortly after midnight on 21 September Warbeck fled with sixty followers and that morning the Cornishmen gave up and went home. Warbeck headed for Beaulieu Abbey, hoping that a boat could be found to take them back to France. Warbeck was recognised at Beaulieu and a message was sent to the king, whose forces surrounded the abbey. Warbeck was told he would be spared if he surrendered to the king. He begged for mercy and admitted that he was not really Richard, Duke of York.

At the end of November 1497 Henry VII returned to London with Warbeck, having questioned him at Exeter on 5 October 1497 where he made a full confession. Through November and December Warbeck was paraded through London where some people threw abuse at him as he passed. Warbeck signed a confession declaring that he had been forced to impersonate Richard, Duke of York, and this was printed and circulated. This was intended to disillusion those who still believed that Warbeck was the Duke of York. On 9 June 1498 Warbeck escaped from the court where he was kept close and fled to Sheen where he threw himself on the mercy of the prior of the Carthusian monastery.

The prior begged for Warbeck's life, but Warbeck was taken back to London on 15 June and put in the stocks at Westminster Hall before being imprisoned in the Tower of London. The Spanish refused to conclude marriage negotiations between Prince Arthur and Katherine of Aragon until both Warbeck and the Earl of Warwick were dead. This would eradicate two threats to the throne and make the future more secure for Arthur, who would not then have to worry about these threats, or any children and descendants.

In the Tower, Warbeck's cell was directly below Warwick's so the two could communicate through a hole in the ceiling or floor respectively. Allegedly Warwick said he would help Warbeck to take the throne if he really was Richard, Duke of York, otherwise he would take the throne himself. On 3 August 1499, the plot was betrayed, but no arrests were made for a further three weeks, suggesting that the plot had already been discovered, and perhaps had even been manipulated from the beginning. Warbeck was tried on 16 November 1499 at Westminster Hall and was condemned to a traitor's death of hanging, drawing, and quartering. The former mayor of Cork, John Atwater, was also tried and found guilty. Edward, Earl of Warwick, was tried on 21 November, accused of plotting a rebellion with Warbeck and found guilty. On 23 November 149,9 Warbeck was drawn on a hurdle to Tyburn with a halter round his neck, where he was hanged until dead rather than suffering the full traitor's death. His head was then displayed on London Bridge. Atwater's death followed. The Earl of Warwick was beheaded on Tower Hill on 28 November 1499.

The stated intent of the invasion was to overthrow Henry VII.[10] As Warbeck was said to be Richard, Duke of York, it seems likely that he would sit on the throne. Unlike the Simnel Rebellion, there were not really any other claimants, like the Earl of Lincoln, who had their liberty. The Earl of Warwick was the other most likely viable claimant, but it was well known that he was imprisoned in the Tower of London at the time of the Warbeck Rebellion. As this was the second pretender to the throne to emerge within the first ten years of Henry VII's reign perhaps that explains the king's more violent reaction to this rebellion than the previous one. He wanted to make sure it would not happen again, and it did not. There would not be another rebellion over the succession until 1553 on the death of Edward VI, and the contested reign of Lady Jane Grey.

What is learnt from this rebellion is that, if you have a pretender or even someone, like Warwick, with a genuine claim to the throne, they will constantly be a focus for rebellion, as Elizabeth became under her half-sister, Mary, in the 1550s. Henry VII learnt from the Lambert Simnel Rebellion that he could not afford to be lenient towards these rebels when the English throne and his own life were at stake. This was a lesson that Elizabeth would struggle to learn during her own reign when dealing with Mary Queen of Scots. As Nathan Amin brutally puts it, the Yorkists believed that 'the Tudor usurper had to fall'.[11] This could also be applied to how supporters of Mary Queen of Scots felt about Elizabeth in later years.

*

There was a quiet period with no real rebellions for the end of Henry VII's reign and well into Henry VIII's reign. This was when religion became a key part of uprisings against the crown, when Henry VIII broke with the Church of Rome in 1532 in order to divorce his first wife, Katherine of Aragon, and marry his second, Anne Boleyn. This Break with Rome led directly to the Pilgrimage of Grace in 1536, which sought to halt the dissolution of the monasteries and return some of the Catholic rites which had been banned in England. The rebels also wanted rid of reformist ministers like Thomas Cromwell and the Archbishop of Canterbury, Thomas Cranmer. A secondary aim was to restore Princess Mary to the succession, from which she had been barred as illegitimate on the marriage of her father, Henry VIII, to Anne Boleyn and the birth of Princess Elizabeth in 1533.

The Pilgrimage of Grace came out of the earlier Lincolnshire Rising, which was a fairly brief revolt which aimed to halt the dissolution of the monasteries. It had begun on 1 October 1536 at Louth after their abbey was closed down. This short-lived rebellion was halted when the rebels had to choose between dispersing, or facing the forces of Charles Brandon, 1st Duke of Suffolk. The rebellion effectively only lasted three days and the ringleaders, Captain Cobbler, and the Vicar of Louth, were executed shortly after at Tyburn. This revolt helped to inspire the much larger and more dangerous Pilgrimage of Grace.

Like the Lincolnshire Rising, the rebels of the Pilgrimage of Grace wanted to halt the dissolution of the monasteries. The north was still largely Catholic in spite of the changes being pushed through Parliament in London. Reformist advisors to Henry VIII like Thomas Cromwell and Archbishop Thomas Cranmer were seen to be at the root of these changes, so one of the aims of the rebellion was to force Henry VIII to oust these radical advisors and replace them with more conservative men. There had also been a poor harvest and the people were struggling to survive in some areas. The rising in Yorkshire was more of a threat than the one in Lincolnshire, largely because of the leadership.

The leader of this 'pilgrimage', as it became known, was Robert Aske, a Yorkshire lawyer from Aughton in the Derwent Valley, and dependent of the Percy family, the Earls of Northumberland. It has been suggested that he was naïve and too trustful of others like the Duke of Norfolk and the king, which may account in part for the terrible fate which befell him. It was Aske who chose the title 'Pilgrimage of Grace' and led the rebels south. He claimed that they were pilgrims who wanted to defend the Church and rescue the king from his advisors, but Aske did not have complete control.

All 'pilgrims' had to swear an oath to maintain God, the King, the Commons and the Church. They believed that wicked counsel had misled the king and that is why things had gone wrong in England – Anne Boleyn, the Break with Rome, and the economic hardships the general populace were now battling with. The rebels wore the badge of the Five Wounds of Christ and called it a religious pilgrimage, almost a crusade. The badge was to represent the wounds received by Christ at the time of the crucifixion, giving the rebellion a very definite religious bent. Not all of their demands were religious, but the bulk of their grievances were related to the religious changes of the recent years.

The scale of this rebellion had not been seen since the Peasants' Revolt of 1381. On 6 October around 10,000 rebels occupied Lincoln then, on 15 October, 20,000 rebels approached the city gates of York.[12] By 19 October 1536 one report said that there were 30,000 rebels at Hull, too many to be defeated.[13] Another report said that, by the end of November 1536, there were 40,000 rebels at Doncaster.[14] The rebel numbers were dramatically increasing each week and month to a level that the royal army could not destroy. The emissaries whom the king sent north to deal with the rebels did not really have a choice but to negotiate because they were so outnumbered. Almost all of England north of the River Trent was under rebel control in autumn 1536, and the rebels had reopened some northern monasteries as they made their way south.

After taking York, the rebels continued on to Pontefract Castle. Thomas, Lord Darcy, invited Aske into the castle to debate with him and two days later Darcy surrendered to the rebels and joined their cause. Whether his surrender was really under duress is debatable as he certainly sympathised with the rebels' demands and did not seem to put up too much of a fight when they requested his allegiance to their cause. In a letter of 11 November 1536 written to the Duke of Norfolk, Darcy said that he did not have the fuel, ordnance, or artillery to resist the rebels, so did not have a choice but to join them, in fear for his own life.[15] In the same letter, Henry VIII seems to have asked Lord Darcy to find a way to kidnap or kill Aske, but Darcy refused. The letter does not show Darcy as begging for his life exactly, but more exhorting his loyalty to the king and trying to explain exactly what had prompted him to join the rebels and that his loyalty now prevented him handing Aske over.

A royal army under George Talbot, 4th Earl of Shrewsbury, gathered just twenty-five miles from Pontefract. It was decided that thirty men from each side would meet at Doncaster Bridge to discuss demands and negotiate. Thomas Howard, 3rd Duke of Norfolk, had been appointed Royal Lieutenant to negotiate with the rebels and, as he only had 7,000 men under his command at this time, he knew he could not beat them. A truce was agreed if the rebels dispersed and on 2 November 1536 a general pardon was issued for rebels north of Doncaster excepting Robert Aske and nine others who were considered to be the ringleaders and guilty of inciting the others to rebellion.

Demands were formulated in the Pontefract Articles which said that the monasteries should be saved, the Royal Supremacy repealed, base-born councillors should be replaced, and Princess Mary restored to the succession. Mary was seen as the true heir to her father, Henry VIII, and she embodied the 'old' religion of Roman Catholicism which she stuck to in spite of the Reformation going on around her, determined to remain with the religion of her mother, Katherine of Aragon. In the petition the pilgrims refer to Cromwell as 'the said traitor' who, while he lives, 'none of us who are gentlemen or head yeomen can trust to any pardon'.[16] Norfolk received the Pontefract Articles from the rebels on 4 December 1536 at Doncaster.

The king promised a pardon to all rebels and an inquiry into their grievances based on their petition. However, this was likely just a stalling tactic to get the rebels to disperse and to allow the royal army time to equip and move north. Aske travelled to London to discuss the rebels' grievances with Henry VIII who allowed him to return home with assurances that satisfied the rebels. The king had promised to call a parliament at York to deal with the rebels' demands, but this was a promise that he had no intention of keeping. Henry had told Norfolk to promise whatever he needed to in order to get the rebels to disperse and it worked. Had the parliament at York gone ahead, Henry would likely have had to sacrifice Cromwell but, as it is, it does not seem that Cromwell lost any power, though he did keep a low profile during the rebellion.

There was a fresh uprising, however, in February 1537 when Sir Francis Bigod attacked Hull. In the eyes of Henry VIII, this new rising effectively nullified the pardon offered to the original rebels. Norfolk proceeded against the rebels from the original rising, though they had not taken part in the second rising. Aske, Lord Darcy, and Sir Thomas Constable were escorted to London, confident that their pardons would be upheld. It was not to be and all three were confined to the Tower of London. The idea of a northern parliament to discuss the grievances of the north was dropped.

By May 1537, after the attempted rising by Francis Bigod, Robert Aske was in prison in London and sentenced to be hanged, drawn and quartered. The king used this second rising as an excuse to act against the leaders of the original Pilgrimage. Henry VIII had determined that all prisoners should be executed in their own counties, likely to put the fear into others who might be considering rebellion. Aske was taken to York and hanged until dead before being disembowelled. Lord Darcy and his cousin, John Hussey, 1st Baron Hussey, were tried in front of a jury of their peers and found guilty on 15 May 1537. Francis Bigod was executed at Tyburn on 2 June, Hussey was beheaded in Lincoln on 29 June, Darcy on Tower Hill on 30 June, Constable was executed in Hull on 6 July, and Aske at York on 12 July 1537.

There were over 144 executions in London itself from the rebellions in the north in 1536 and 1537 and even more were carried out in the northern counties. The executions included six abbots and thirty-eight monks.[17] The triumph over the Pilgrimage emboldened Henry VIII and Thomas Cromwell to continue the destruction of the monasteries, so perhaps the rebellion did the opposite of what was intended and encouraged the king and government to perhaps go further than was initially intended. The pilgrims reinforced Henry VIII's belief in his own religious policies. Even in the executions carried out, the Pilgrimage of Grace was very obviously a religious rebellion, and the first religious rebellion of the Tudor period, though certainly not the last.

*

Again, there was a break between rebellions. Perhaps the sheer number of people who had been involved and the executions carried out in the aftermath of the Pilgrimage of Grace in 1536 had scared people. Or perhaps there needed to be a major change in policy to light the fuse to rebellion. The next set of two rebellions were during the reign of Edward VI in 1549. Henry VIII had died in 1547 and the throne passed to his only son, Edward. Edward had been raised in the Protestant religion and was determined to turn England further away from Rome, assisted by his uncle and Lord Protector, Edward Seymour, 1st Duke of Somerset. The reigns of Edward VI and Mary I are often referred to as the mid-Tudor crisis, with the pair being polar opposites in religion, and the people of England unsure as to what was legal or illegal from one moment to the next. These 1549 rebellions can be seen as the first physical manifestations of this crisis.

In 1549 there were two almost simultaneous rebellions in England, one in Devon and Cornwall, known as the Western Rebellion, and one in Norfolk, known as Kett's Rebellion. The Western Rebellion happened between June and August, while Kett's Rebellion was in July and August. Although Kett's Rebellion lasted for a shorter amount of time it is often the better known of the two, perhaps because it was more well organised and managed to take Norwich. The new *Book of Common Prayer* had just been introduced into England that year and was much more Protestant in its outlook than the existing prayerbooks. Many people took exception to this more radical religious stance. However, religion was not the only issue.

Social and economic factors were also crucial, particularly the issue of enclosure, complaints about taxes and food prices, and the gentry abuse of power. These more general issues are often overlooked in favour of a religious stance.

Robert Kett sent a list of demands to Protector Somerset, largely based around enclosure, which hugely affected the general population. Enclosure meant that land was being fenced off, or 'enclosed' by landowners and was not free to use for common grazing anymore. This made life harder for those who depended on the land for their livelihoods. This was largely a socio-economic revolt, rather than the religious revolt in the west, although there were still some religious demands made in the Mousehold Articles. Several articles to do with rents and money wanted things returned to as they were at the beginning of the reign of Henry VII, nearly sixty-five years earlier. However, inflation and the debasement of the currency under Henry VIII made this demand at least unachievable. Not for nothing was Henry VIII known as 'Old Coppernose'; it was said that, by the end of his reign, the coinage was more copper than anything else and that the tip of Henry's nose on the coins was where you could see the copper shining through. These coins were still in circulation in 1549, and no doubt were part of the reason why the people suffered such economic hardship.

At the beginning of July 1549, a group of around 2,000 rebels marched on Exeter, protesting over the new *Book of Common Prayer*. In the second week of July in Norfolk, around 16,000 rebels led by Robert Kett made camp on Mousehold Heath outside Norwich. The rebellion began in Wymondham in Norfolk, which is where a branch of Kett's family was based and Kett actually held the manor of Wymondham from the Earl of Warwick, who would later put down the rebellion. Kett had a longstanding feud with John Flowerdew. Flowerdew's fences, which he had erected to enclose land, were pulled down by rebels, and he bribed them to do the same to Kett's fences. Around 9 or 10 July 1549, Kett let the rebels back to Flowerdew's property to enact reprisals; thus he only became the leader of the revolt by accident and not by design.

Martial law was declared on 18 July and Edward VI's bodyguard was increased, but the rebels proclaimed that they were loyal to the king. Arrangements were also made to protect Windsor Castle. On 1 July, a summons was sent out to nobles and gentlemen to attend the king at Windsor with as many horsemen and footmen as could be arranged.[18] There were fears that the rebels would try to seize the king to force the government to grant their demands. As the king was underage, power in England lay with the Protector. Protector Somerset seemed sympathetic to the rebels, but other councillors were much less so. Perhaps it was Somerset's sympathy with the common people that earned him the nickname 'the Good Duke' where his successor as Protector, the Duke of Northumberland, was 'the Bad Duke'. When it became obvious that military intervention was required, Somerset dithered over how many men to send and who to put in charge.[19] He did not want to admit that it was his policies that had led to a breakdown of public order. Somerset offered concessions to the rebels, saying that if they laid down their arms and sent a couple of men to London with a list of their grievances that he would listen, and even invited them to participate further in the political process.[20] This is quite astounding. Henry VIII had offered some concessions to the rebels in 1536, but he never had any intention of following through with them. Somerset, it seems, did intend to follow through on these. Of course, because of his fall, we will never know what might have happened in the aftermath of the rebellion had Somerset remained in power, but the reprisals against the rebels likely would not have been so harsh as they actually were in the end.

On 31 July 1549, William Parr, 1st Marquis of Northampton, went with 1,500 men to Norwich to attempt to cut off the rebels' supply lines, but he fled when faced with the sheer number of rebels. Kett was now guilty of treason for striking against the king's army.[21] However, in the camp on Mousehold Heath order seemed to be maintained, with temporary law courts set up and prayers said each morning. Kett ordered that justice was dispensed under an oak tree in the camp. The tree became known as the Tree of Reformation. Kett's rebels were actually fully supportive of the new *Book of Common Prayer*, which is often misunderstood;[22] it was the rebels in the west whose rebellion was against the new religious order. If you did not know better, you would not have thought it was a rebel encampment on Mousehold Heath. John Dudley, 1st Earl of Warwick and later 1st Duke of Northumberland, was dispatched with an additional army of 6,000 foot soldiers and 1,500 cavalry to defeat Kett and the Norfolk rebels. Kett offered to meet Warwick to talk, but his soldiers would not let him, fearful that Kett would be arrested or killed on sight. Dudley opened fire in Norwich and forty-nine rebels were promptly hanged. Kett moved to Dussindale, taking hostages with him. A pardon was offered to the rebels and rejected, but as Warwick's army advanced, Kett and others fled.

Most rebels fought to the death with around 2,000 lying dead on the battlefield. German and Italian mercenaries had been deployed against the rebels who therefore had no possibility of succeeding; certainly not without noble leadership did they have any chance of victory. Kett had fled and hidden in a barn eight miles away from the battlefield, but he was found and captured. He was taken back to Norwich where 300 rebels were hanged and, after a trial in London, Kett himself was hanged in chains from Norwich Castle, the scene of his crimes and, ironically, his greatest triumph.

In the Western Rebellion, Exeter was liberated on 6 August 1549 by Lord John Russell and his forces (Russell would be made 1st Earl of Bedford in 1550 in recognition of his service to Edward VI). Somerset had lost any patience with these rebels and his tone towards them had changed. Russell initially believed that the rebels had been defeated, but he then received word that they were in fact regrouping at Sampford Courtenay. Russell's army was strengthened when reinforcements arrived under Sir Anthony Kingston, leading to a royal army now numbering 8,000 men, far more than the surviving rebels. William Grey, 13th Baron Grey de Wilton, and William Parr, 1st Marquis of Northampton, led the attack in the Battle of Sampford Courtenay. It was said that between 500 and 600 rebels were killed in the battle, and that the rebels would not give up until most of their number were dead. More rebels were killed in the retreat.

The most remarkable consequence from the 1549 rebellions was the toppling of Edward Seymour, 1st Duke of Somerset, from the Protectorship over his nephew, Edward VI. This was a coup d'état orchestrated by John Dudley, 1st Earl of Warwick, who would become 1st Duke of Northumberland and Lord Protector after Somerset's fall. It was said that Somerset had sympathised with the rebels, and had even colluded with them, failing to suppress the revolt speedily and promising the rebels that they would not be punished for their uprising.[23] Somerset was removed from the Protectorship and imprisoned in the Tower, though he would later be released and even readmitted to court and the council. Northumberland then accused Somerset of plotting against him, he was again imprisoned in the Tower, and eventually executed on 22 January 1552 on Tower Hill.

*

The Wyatt Rebellion of 1554 was the most important event of Elizabeth's life before she became Queen of England. It put her in the most perilous position of her life, imprisoned and in fear of execution in the same place that her mother, Anne Boleyn, had been executed by her father, Henry VIII, eighteen years before. There is no real evidence that Elizabeth was actually involved in the plotting, but her name was used by the plotters, so she was investigated, along with members of her household. Edward VI had died in 1553, and had tried to alter the line of succession to put his cousin, Lady Jane Grey, on the throne rather than allowing it to pass to his Catholic half-sister, Mary I. However, Mary triumphed, and Jane was imprisoned in the

Tower of London. Mary was determined to marry and produce an heir to stop her half-sister, Elizabeth, from inheriting the throne. Mary knew that Elizabeth tended towards the Protestant faith as she refused to hear Mass and was educated by reformist tutors. This meant that Mary needed a husband and the husband that she chose was Philip II of Spain, the son of the Holy Roman Emperor, Charles V. Mary's decision probably had its roots in the fact that her mother, Katherine of Aragon, was Spanish, and Charles V was Katherine's nephew.

The spark to rebellion was the fact that Philip was Spanish, and not in fact his religion, although the rebels were not particularly happy about that either. There were serious concerns that Philip would, as Mary's husband and king, take over control of England and that the country would effectively become an outpost of Spain, and involved in Spanish wars. This xenophobia was at the heart of the Wyatt Rebellion of 1554, led by Sir Thomas Wyatt the Younger, son of the Sir Thomas Wyatt who had once wooed Anne Boleyn. The aim of the rebellion was to overthrow Mary I to prevent Spanish influence in England and put Elizabeth on the throne in her place.[24] Wyatt was initially approached about joining the rising by Edward Courtenay, 1st Earl of Devon, who hoped to marry Elizabeth when the plot was successful and rule England alongside her. Courtenay was involved in the plotting at first, but then he revealed what he knew about the plot to the council.

The revolt was initially planned for March 1554, to coincide with the arrival of Philip in England, but it was uncovered early, around 21 January 1554. When Courtenay confessed what he knew, rebels were forced to act precipitately. The idea was that Cornwall would rise first, and then Henry Grey, 1st Duke of Suffolk, the father of Lady Jane Grey, was supposed to raise the Midlands, but failed. Sir Thomas Wyatt the Younger was the only leader who managed to raise any men, in Kent, and marched on London, taking Rochester on 26 January. Thomas Howard, 3rd Duke of Norfolk, set out with the royal army to quash them. By 30 January the rebels were camped at

Blackheath outside London. Their terms included custody of Queen Mary I and the Tower of London, and the removal of some of her councillors, replaced by men of their own choosing.[25] With Mary in their custody the Spanish marriage would not go ahead, and they could replace her councillors who were Spanish or who had Spanish leanings with others.

The rebels issued a proclamation that the Spanish were coming to invade, hoping to provoke a general rising across the country to join the rebels Wyatt had already gathered in Kent. The King of France, Henry II, had promised eighty ships to assist the rebels: France did not want England allied to Spain either. If England was allied to Spain they would likely make war on France, which Henry II wanted to avoid. Thomas Wyatt and his rebels reached Southwark on 3 February, but the bridge was closed to them. By 7 February there were scuffles between the rebels and royal forces around Whitehall, St James's, and Charing Cross. Wyatt was declared a traitor for rising against his rightful queen. Some of the London militia had even defected to join the rebels, largely out of xenophobia and fear of Spanish influence. Wyatt made it as far as Temple Bar and onto Fleet Street but surrendered at Charing Cross. Royal troops under the command of William Herbert, 1st Earl of Pembroke, and Edward Clinton, 9th Baron Clinton (later 1st Earl of Lincoln) had secured London and defeated the rebels.

Mary had been advised to flee London and save herself, as some councillors believed that the rebels would succeed in reaching the palace. However, Mary refused to leave and instead made a rousing speech at the Guildhall on 1 February 1554, claiming that she would not marry without the consent of Parliament, so her marriage was put into their hands. This speech persuaded the people of London to stand against the rebels. Some 25,000 armed citizens of London came to Mary's aid, though she initially only had 500 men from the city bands to defend her.[26] This demonstrated just how popular Mary was, at least at the beginning of her reign, as the daughter of Henry VIII and rightful queen. Elizabeth would have similar skills of oratory, as when she addressed the troops at Tilbury in 1588 under threat from the Spanish Armada.

Lady Jane Grey had been imprisoned in the Tower of London since July 1553 and the failed attempt to seat her on the English throne in Mary's place. She was finally executed after the failure of the Wyatt Rebellion, on 12 February 1554 on Tower Green within the Tower, being spared a public execution. Before her death, Jane had refused to convert to Catholicism, despite repeated attempts from Mary I, and died a martyr to her Protestant faith, reciting the 51st psalm. Her husband, Guildford Dudley, son of the executed Duke of Northumberland, had been executed the same day. Jane had not been involved in the rebellion as she had been imprisoned, but her father, Henry Grey, 1st Duke of Suffolk, had risen in revolt. Mary I realised that Jane would always be a figurehead for rebellion against her as long as she remained alive.

The Spanish ambassador, Simon Renard de Bermont (often just seen as Renard), was pushing for the execution of Princess Elizabeth after the rebellion, even going so far as to suggest that Philip's arrival in England was dependent on it. Elizabeth was questioned over her involvement in the Wyatt Rebellion at her residence of Hatfield House in Hertfordshire and then told to travel to London for further questioning. Elizabeth claimed she was too ill to travel, and indeed she was sick, suffering from one of the maladies which hit her throughout her life at times of great stress and anxiety. She was made to travel to London and travelled in a litter with the curtains open so that the people could see her looking wan, ill, frightened, and innocent.

Elizabeth was taken initially to the royal court at Whitehall, passing the rotting bodies of traitors on her entry into London. Her servants and attendants were taken from her, and she was faced with, not her sister, but Stephen Gardiner, Bishop of Winchester. Elizabeth was questioned closely but denied any involvement with Wyatt or his rebellion. Her requests to see Mary were consistently refused.

She was, however, allowed to write a letter to her sister to protest her innocence and loyalty. She wrote, 'I protest afore God … that I never practised, counselled, nor consented to anything that might be prejudicial to your person any way or dangerous to the state by any mean.'[27] Elizabeth could not have made her position clearer: she was completely innocent of any wrongdoing in her eyes. She went on to 'pray God as evil persuasions persuade not one sister against the other'. Elizabeth was concerned that Mary's advisors were trying to turn Mary against her, as the Spanish ambassador, Renard, especially was attempting to do. Elizabeth obviously did not trust others not to insert things onto the end of her letter and so she filled the page with diagonal lines to prevent unwanted insertions. She signed off, 'Your highness' most faithful subject that hath been from the beginning and will be to my end'.[28] Elizabeth was playing on familial loyalty and affection, that Mary had been loving and kind to her when she was a child. Elizabeth did not honestly believe that Mary wanted to kill her, but that she might if she felt threatened by her.

Elizabeth had been told she was to be sent to the Tower of London, hence her desperation and pleading that is evident in the letter, as she writes of her fear of the Tower and how the Tower is for the guilty and not the innocent. Few who went into the Tower would emerge again unless it was to attend their own executions. She arrived at the Tower on 17 March 1554 and would stay in the Bell Tower. She would remain there until 19 May, just over two months later. The Bell Tower was where Sir Thomas Wyatt the Elder was imprisoned in 1536, accused of adultery with Elizabeth's mother, Anne Boleyn, although he was never charged and was eventually released. It was possibly cruelty and revenge on Mary's part to send guards to Elizabeth's room on 19 May, the anniversary of her mother's execution. But the guards were there to take her away from the Tower to house arrest at Woodstock.

On 11 April 1554, Sir Thomas Wyatt the Younger was taken to his execution on Tower Hill. He was permitted to make a final speech, in which he continued to deny that Elizabeth was involved in the rebellion at all. The only evidence of contact between the pair was that Wyatt had sent Elizabeth a letter telling her to get away for her own safety. Elizabeth had replied only to say that she would do as she thought fit. All through his questioning, Wyatt would deny Elizabeth's involvement, and assert her innocence. Elizabeth would do the same. Wyatt also spoke of Edward Courtenay, 1st Earl of Devon, saying that he had nothing to do with the rising either.

In the Wyatt Rebellion it was the outcomes of the rebellion that had wider-reaching consequences than the events of the rebellion itself. The rebellion led directly to the execution of Lady Jane Grey, and the imprisonment of the heir to the throne, Princess Elizabeth, in the Tower of London under threat of execution herself. Elizabeth would never forget her time in the Tower, and it has been suggested that it was during this time of great stress and danger that she formed her close bond with Robert Dudley, later 1st Earl of Leicester, which would endure until his death in 1588.

*

What can be understood from examining these earlier Tudor rebellions is just how often they were provoked by one single event or change in government – the Lambert Simnel and Perkin Warbeck rebellions were prompted by a change of monarch who had taken the throne by force, the Pilgrimage of Grace was prompted by the dissolution of the monasteries, the Kett Rebellion by enclosure and rising prices, the Western Rebellion by the introduction of the new *Book of Common Prayer*, and the Wyatt Rebellion by Mary I's proposed marriage to Philip II of Spain.

As we will come to see, rebellions under Elizabeth I were also prompted largely by one major event, but of the five rebellions, four of them were prompted by the same event: the arrival of Mary Queen of Scots to England in 1568, having fled from Scotland after abdicating the throne.

Chapter 2

Northern Rising 1569

'Seek nothing so greedily as to subdue the realm'[1]

The Northern Rising of 1569/70 was the first major rebellion against Elizabeth. The origins lie in the arrival of Mary Queen of Scots in England in 1568 when she fled from Scotland having been forced to abdicate the Scottish throne in favour of her son, James VI. There were no real rebellions against Elizabeth prior to this point, which suggests that Mary was the catalyst to revolt, largely as a Catholic heir or alternative queen to Elizabeth. Mary was not just a threat because of the succession, but also because of her religious affiliation to the old religion of Roman Catholicism. She would die as a Catholic martyr to her faith. Her arrival in England provided a focal point for Catholics and foreign sympathisers.

The 1560s had been a quiet decade in England with no wars or civil unrest to disturb these years. When Elizabeth I ascended to the throne in 1558 it was thought that there would be all kinds of problems regarding a female ruler, religious reform, and the legitimacy of the succession as Elizabeth was, by English law and in the eyes of Catholic Europe, illegitimate. However, none of these problems appeared. Towards the end of the 1560s there were some poor harvests and increasing enclosure which agitated the lower classes, and religious reforms moving either too quickly or too slowly to disturb others.[2] As the historian K.J. Kesselring explains, the rebellion grew from 'a complex blend of aristocratic intrigue, regional grievances against an aggressively centralising state, and a widespread if inchoate dissatisfaction with ongoing Protestant reform'.[3] These problems were enhanced by the arrival of Mary Queen of Scots in England which added possible political turmoil to the economic and religious issues which were beginning to make themselves known. After a peaceful first decade of Elizabeth's reign, the problems were just beginning.

In the late 1560s the main threat to Elizabeth's throne was Mary Queen of Scots, although by the will of Henry VIII, Elizabeth's successor would be Katherine Grey, sister to the ill-fated Lady Jane Grey. Henry had overlooked the line of his elder sister, Margaret, Queen of Scotland, whose descendants were Mary Queen of Scots and James VI of Scotland, in favour of the line of his younger sister, Mary, Queen of France and Duchess of Suffolk, whose descendants were the Grey sisters. Margaret had been married into the Scottish royal family so possibly Henry VIII was influenced by wanting an English-born heir rather than a foreign-born one. At the time of Henry VIII's death there was still a hope that Henry's son, Edward VI, would marry Mary Queen of Scots, and unite the English and Scottish thrones with an heir, though this came to nothing. However, there were not any rebellions in favour of Katherine Grey or her son during Elizabeth's reign, with many people still favouring the elder line of succession from Margaret Tudor in spite of Henry VIII's will. Perhaps the fate of Jane Grey had soured the prospect of another Grey queen. In the end, the line of Mary Queen of Scots through Margaret Tudor would prevail with the accession of Mary's son, James VI of Scotland (James I of England) in 1603. Mary seemed the natural successor to Elizabeth and her claim was strengthened by her marriage to Lord Darnley, also descended from Margaret Tudor, and the subsequent birth of James VI in 1566. Mary had an heir of her body where Elizabeth did not.

William Cecil, Baron Burghley, would use the Northern Rising and the Duke of Norfolk's conspiracies with Mary Queen of Scots to press home his point and have Mary put on trial for the murder of her husband, Henry Stuart, Lord Darnley, before she fled Scotland for England. Darnley was found murdered at Kirk o' Field in Edinburgh.

While Mary was away at Holyrood, around 2 a.m. on 10 February 1567, there were two explosions at Kirk o' Field. The bodies of Darnley and his valet were found outside the house. It looked as though Darnley had been smothered as there were no marks on the body. It is likely that the pair were woken by the explosions and made it outside before being killed. Mary was suspected of colluding in his death, along with James Hepburn, 4th Earl of Bothwell, and Archibald Douglas. After Darnley's death Mary would go on to marry Bothwell, although it would not be a happy marriage and Bothwell would fail to come to Mary's aid. It has been suggested that Bothwell kidnapped Mary after Darnley's death, having had designs on the Scottish throne, and raped her; Mary then married him to protect her reputation. The other suggestion is that Mary went with Bothwell willingly and they concocted the rape story together so Mary's reputation would not be besmirched by her marriage to a man suspected of murdering her previous husband. After this scandalous marriage the Protestant lords and people of Scotland had had enough. Mary was imprisoned in Lochleven Castle and was forced to abdicate the Scottish throne on 24 July 1567 in favour of her son, James VI, just days after miscarrying Bothwell's twins.

On 2 May 1568, Mary escaped Lochleven Castle and managed to flee across the Solway Firth and into England on 16 May by fishing boat, landing at Workington on the coast of Cumberland. On 18 May she was taken into what was described as protective custody, becoming in effect a political refugee, at Carlisle Castle. When she first landed in England, Mary had hoped that Elizabeth would help her to regain the Scottish throne by giving military and financial aid, as well as her political backing. However, Elizabeth ordered an inquiry into the conduct of the Scottish lords and whether Mary was in fact guilty of her husband, Darnley's, murder. She could not be seen to be helping a murderess and, if Mary was guilty, would Elizabeth want to put a murderess on the Scottish throne? It was a unique, and could have been perilous, situation had Elizabeth acted inappropriately or impulsively at this point. Mary refused to attend the inquiry and it ended with an inconclusive verdict against both Mary and the Scottish lords. James Stewart, 1st Earl of Moray, was made regent in Scotland for the baby James VI and Mary remained in custody in England.

Sir Francis Knollys, a close advisor to Elizabeth and married to Elizabeth's cousin, Catherine Carey, was sent to Carlisle to tell Mary that she was to be put into the charge of George Talbot, 6th Earl of Shrewsbury, and his wife, Bess of Hardwick, initially at Bolton Castle in Yorkshire, before being moved to Tutbury Castle in Staffordshire, further south. Shrewsbury's properties were all in the 'interior' of England, far from both London and Scotland as well as being distant from the coast. Elizabeth considered Mary to be enough of a threat to her own power to want to keep her confined and out of trouble, away from anywhere from where she might affect an escape. Perhaps this was as much for Mary's sake as her own, as Mary was the favoured heir to the English throne and might be used as a figurehead for rebellion, as indeed she would be over the years of her imprisonment in England up to her execution in 1587. Elizabeth understood the peril of an heir to the throne in a way that no one else could. Mary's arrival in England also coincided with a difficult time in English political affairs for Elizabeth and Cecil, so keeping Mary confined was also paramount to protect negotiations and double-dealing.

There were problems between Spain and England at this time as England had seized Spanish ships and Spain had retaliated by doing the same to English ships. There were concerns that this could escalate into all-out war between the two. In 1568, Chatham Dockyard was established for the Royal Navy to build new ships, so it seems as though Elizabeth was making preparations in case of a war with Spain. England was also faced with revolt in Ireland as the first Desmond Rebellion broke out in 1569 and would last until 1572. The Irish did not like increased English control of their territories and so James Fitzmaurice, cousin to Gerald Fitzgerald, 14th Earl of

Desmond, seized Tracton and would not leave without the custody of Lady Ursula St Leger and Lady Mary Grenville, wives of two of the English colonists in Ireland. This had the possibility of erupting into a war as well; Desmond himself would lead a second revolt in 1579. Elizabeth had also dissolved Parliament without naming a successor, so there was still uncertainty over that issue which was exacerbated by the arrival of Mary in England. Mary Queen of Scots was seen as a legitimate Catholic claimant in contrast to Elizabeth as an illegitimate Protestant Queen. Mary's presence in England seemed to offer a legitimate justification for rebellion.

In early 1569 rumours spread of a proposed marriage between Mary Queen of Scots and Thomas Howard, 4th Duke of Norfolk. This marriage would have meant the union of the Scottish throne to the premier Duke in England with a claim to the English throne. It could have been the light to the touchpaper for rebellion against Elizabeth I and her overthrow. It would have demonstrated an alternate claim to the throne with an English husband and the possibility of a half-English heir if they had a child. Norfolk denied the planned marriage, but Elizabeth only half-believed him. Mary was in the process of divorcing the Earl of Bothwell who would die as an exile abroad in Denmark in 1578. The historian Susan Doran expresses the opinion that the scheme to marry Mary Queen of Scots to the Duke of Norfolk was harmless in itself, but it did explode in Elizabeth's face by triggering a major Catholic rebellion in the north in 1569.[4] This rebellion would be the major citizens' revolt of Elizabeth's reign. The rebels claimed that they aimed to release Mary from her imprisonment and ensure her nomination as Elizabeth's heir to the English throne. However, the likelihood is that, had the rebels secured Mary's release, they would probably have deposed Elizabeth and set Mary in her place in spite of their protestations. The rebellion was prepared to call in foreign support from Spain to ensure a Catholic succession in England. This was at least the thinking of Elizabeth, William Cecil, and other advisors at court, although it was not stated as one of the aims of the rebellion. The marriage was Mary's route out of captivity and, for the Privy Council at least, it was a plausible chance for a peaceful union with Scotland if Elizabeth died without heirs, as seemed increasingly likely, as she refused to marry.

*

Elizabeth put a stop to the marriage plans between Mary Queen of Scots and the Duke of Norfolk, although the council itself was not opposed. Robert Dudley, 1st Earl of Leicester, and close friend and advisor to Elizabeth, was known to support the union. The marriage was seen as a way to possibly convert Mary Queen of Scots to Protestantism. Leicester confessed all to the queen in September 1569. Perhaps Elizabeth was angry that the succession issue had been debated behind her back, seeing it as a breach of trust, or perhaps she was concerned that the marriage would actually be an increased threat to her own position and power. Some people saw this marriage as a way of containing Mary, securing the succession, and making peace with both France and Spain. Norfolk fled to his estate at Kenninghall, pleading illness, and hoping to rise in conjunction with the earls of Northumberland and Westmoreland who were planning an uprising. Had Norfolk not left court so suddenly and suspiciously the uprising probably would not have happened as it was seen in the north as the signal for rebellion. Norfolk had retired without the queen's permission which was seen as an admission of guilt. The Earl of Northumberland may not have supported the marriage between Mary and Norfolk as Norfolk was Church of England and thus a heretic by Catholic standards. Norfolk was, however, supported by Henry Fitzalan, 12th Earl of Arundel, and they saw William Cecil as an upstart who had usurped their noble and God-given right to advise the queen. Cecil was seen as someone of low birth, not worthy to advise royalty, rather like Cardinal Thomas Wolsey and Thomas Cromwell, who had advised Henry VIII forty years earlier. The earls of Northumberland and Westmoreland assumed that Norfolk's flight was the signal for rebellion, so had he not fled, rebellion likely would not have broken out.

In September 1569, Norfolk was summoned to London to answer questions regarding his activities around Mary Queen of Scots. He knew he had been discovered in his marriage plans and confessed what he knew, sending a message north to his brother-in-law, Charles Neville, 6th Earl of Westmoreland, advising him that they had been discovered and not to rise against the queen and government. It was out of his hands, however. The following month Norfolk was imprisoned in the Tower of London. He remained imprisoned for nine months before he was released and thus was unable to get involved in the Northern Rising. Had Norfolk been free at this point, he likely would have been involved in the uprising and executed in 1569 or 1570 rather than 1572. He would go on to participate in the Ridolfi Plot in 1571 which would lead directly to his execution. Perhaps Norfolk was a suspicious figure to Elizabeth anyway as his father, Henry Howard, Earl of Surrey, and his grandfather, Thomas Howard, 3rd Duke of Norfolk, had been imprisoned in the Tower of London in 1546 by Henry VIII for treason. Surrey was executed on 19 January 1547, just nine days before Henry VIII's death. The 3rd Duke of Norfolk was spared execution only by the king's death, remaining imprisoned during the reign of Edward VI and only released when Mary I succeeded to the throne in 1553. He only survived a year after his release, dying aged 80 in August 1554. This family history may have prejudiced Elizabeth towards the 4th Duke of Norfolk, although the evidence suggests he was indeed plotting against her.

Plans were in place for a rising in the north even before Norfolk's arrest and incarceration. Norfolk wrote to Elizabeth on 24 September 1569 asking her pardon, and he also wrote to the conspirators to try and dissuade them from taking any action that might place him or them in peril. Elizabeth's hold over the north was 'precarious'.[5] The Council of the North was the authority in the area, but it was comparatively lawless when contrasted with the south of England, with London and English government at its centre. Elizabeth had never travelled north, and her advisors seemed to be alarmed at the very idea of it, as it was known that the north was still largely Catholic and resented many of the changes of the past half-decade and more. This was evidenced with the Pilgrimage of Grace in 1536 under Henry VIII. Henry VIII had never travelled further north than York which he visited in 1541. The people of the north generally wanted a return to the ancient rites and ceremonies of the Roman Catholic Church.

Through Roberto Ridolfi, a Florentine merchant and banker, the Norfolk faction had approached Guerau de Spes, the Spanish ambassador, with suggestions for the overthrow of William Cecil, the subjugation of Elizabeth I to their will, the restoration of Roman Catholicism including Papal obedience, the release of the Duke of Norfolk, and the restoration of Mary Queen of Scots to the Scottish throne as well as a declaration of her position as heir to the English throne. This latter point might well have depended on Mary's marriage to the Duke of Norfolk going ahead, although this is not specified. It seems like a lot to achieve, and it is unlikely it could have been achieved without the complete overthrow of Elizabeth. Perhaps the rebels would have done better to focus on one point and look for gradual change, though it is still unlikely that this would have been successful. Elizabeth had inherited her father's stubbornness and temper which would not have inclined her towards the rebels. Norfolk was all too ready to enter into secret plots and machinations, but he also deserted in a panic when things went too far, or he feared he was close to discovery.[6] When he suspected that his plotting had been unearthed, he confessed and threw himself on the queen's mercy. Ridolfi had been acting as a go-between between the English nobility and the Pope. De Spes seemed confident about the success of any rebellion in England against Elizabeth and her advisors. This contact with the Spanish was later kept secret from many of the rebel followers, who might have deserted their cause through xenophobia and a fear of a foreign takeover of England.

In early October 1569, Sir Francis Walsingham had been instructed to detain and interrogate Ridolfi who was suspected of plotting with Mary Queen of Scots and the Pope, along with the Spanish. Ridolfi was kept in custody at Walsingham's house on Seething Lane in London, during which time he admitted, at least in part, to his associations with Mary's agent, John Leslie, Bishop of Ross, and his knowledge of the proposed Norfolk marriage. On the basis of Walsingham's intelligence, Ridolfi was set free in November, possibly because Walsingham had reported that Ridolfi had been turned and was prepared to act as a double agent for Elizabeth, though there is no written evidence of this. The later Babington Plot would be uncovered and manipulated through the use of secret agents like Gilbert Gifford and Robert Poley. This appears to be the first instance of the Elizabethan government making use of double agents to uncover plots against the crown and government. Ridolfi would be part of another rebellion two years later which would take his name. This suggests that Ridolfi had not really been turned at all but was just biding his time until a better opportunity presented itself.

On 9 November 1569, Thomas Radcliffe, 3rd Earl of Sussex, Lord President of the Council of the North, sent a summons to Thomas Percy, 7th Earl of Northumberland, and Charles Neville, 6th Earl of Westmoreland, at Topcliffe, one of Northumberland's residences in North Yorkshire just south of Thirsk. They were expected to travel to court in London and explain what had been happening as rumours had been swirling that they were gathering troops for rebellion. One of the triggers which lit the fuse to rebellion was that the Earl of Northumberland resented his loss of a valuable copper mine to the queen, and his loss of the wardenship of the East Marches. This severely decreased his income. He believed that William Cecil would soon act against him now that he was weakened. The Earl of Westmoreland felt that Neville influence was fading but he may have remained loyal to the crown had it not been for his wife, Jane, who was sister to the imprisoned 4th Duke of Norfolk. She pushed him into action on her brother's behalf. Both Northumberland and Westmoreland had lost land and wealth to the so-called 'new men' whom Elizabeth had promoted. The sons of northern families were detained, possibly to deter their relatives from rebelling. Preliminary measures were taken to defend York, Hull, Pontefract, and Knaresborough, which were key coastal towns and would be primary landing points for any potential foreign invasion. This demonstrates that the threat of rebellion was being taken very seriously by the government.

The rebels hoped to draw on the powerful Catholic feelings of the people in the north to end religious reform and restore England to Papal obedience, rather as the leaders of the Pilgrimage of Grace had hoped to do in 1536. It was also in the same northern areas of England as the Pilgrimage had been and the rebels again marched under the banner of the Five Wounds of Christ, symbolising the presence of Christ in their midst. Soldiers, priests, and horses were dressed in tabards painted with a red cross, reminiscent of the crusades centuries earlier.[7] Elizabeth had hoped that her Church of England could contain both Catholics and Protestants but the radicals on each side were not willing to accept this compromise and the radical Protestants were often the most visible by destroying imagery (known as iconoclasm) which turned the Catholics against them. They wanted to slow the absorption of the Church by the state while theoretically remaining loyal to the crown. Loyalty could be subjective; the rebels believed they were still loyal to the crown but wanted some changes, while the crown and government believed that the rebels were being disloyal. Again, this is very similar to what happened in the Pilgrimage of Grace, where the Earl of Northumberland's father, Sir Thomas Percy, had been executed for his involvement in the rebellion.

Once the royal messenger left Topcliffe, the bells were rung in the local church as a call to rebellion. Northumberland and Westmoreland had no intention of travelling south to explain themselves, fearing that they would be arrested and imprisoned, as Norfolk had been when he was summoned to London under a similar pretext. This fear revived the idea of rebellion, but the leadership was not united. This created problems, along with their wide range of aims and objectives. Many northern lords like Henry Clifford, 2nd Earl of Cumberland, refused to join the revolt and remained loyal to the crown. The day after this summons, Elizabeth wrote to Sussex to say that, if Northumberland and Westmoreland refused to travel south and explain themselves at his command, he should give them letters written in the queen's own hand.[8] The suggestion seems to be to see if they would dare to disobey a summons written in the queen's own hand, rather than relayed by a loyal subject. They could not then doubt that the summons was real and quite serious. Given what was to come, this did not work. Northumberland and Westmoreland quite possibly believed that the queen was being manipulated by her advisors into acting against the old nobility.

The Earl of Sussex had suspected what might happen by giving the rebel earls a summons to London, but he did as he was bid. Elizabeth became suspicious of Sussex due to his reluctance to act against the rebel earls. Sussex was friendly with the Duke of Norfolk and had known about his proposed marriage to Mary Queen of Scots. He had also been hunting and hawking with Northumberland and Westmoreland that summer. Elizabeth, however, would have done well to heed Sussex's advice and leave the earls alone for a while.[9] She could have headed off the rebellion before it even began. She was right to mistrust the earls as they had contemplated rising against her after Norfolk's arrest. The summons from the queen only spurred them on to revolt. Sussex advised that Elizabeth should delay sending the summons until winter so that the roads north would be blocked, and they could not summon their tenants for rebellion. This would have been a more sensible course of action, but Elizabeth did not want to wait and possibly believed that Sussex was urging her to wait to give the earls more time to arm. However, Sussex was completely loyal, and Elizabeth did him a disservice by doubting him.

Rather like the Duke of Norfolk, the Nevilles and the Percys found it insulting that Elizabeth had dismissed a number of noblemen from her council and replaced them with people they considered to be 'nobodies'. This had rankled with them for many years. They felt marginalised by Cecil, threatened by the Religious Settlement, which was too Protestant for their liking, and could not accept the lack of resolution over the status of Mary Queen of Scots. They played on the wounded pride of the northern families who felt ousted from government and power. These were the issues which pushed them over the edge into rebellion in 1569. When the earls resorted to revolt, they did so in the name of protecting Elizabeth from her so-called heretical advisors. They were unhappy but it might not have turned into open revolt without a group of anti-Cecil activists including Richard Norton, the Sheriff of Yorkshire, who had been involved in the Pilgrimage of Grace in 1536, Thomas Hussey, and Robert Tempest.[10] They claimed that they had the support of Fernando Álvarez de Toledo, 3rd Duke of Alba, a Spanish nobleman and Governor of the Netherlands, who would land troops at Hartlepool to aid the rebellion.

Sussex had the earls of Northumberland and Westmoreland declared traitors on 13 November 1569. This single action coalesced 'what had been an incoherent reaction to general discontent into a specifically focused conflict'.[11] In other words, this declaration meant that the earls would be punished no matter what they did so they may as well go the distance and orchestrate a full rebellion to make their feelings known and, hopefully, invoke some change in the country based on their aims. The main core of those willing to take up arms against the government during the Northern Rising came from the lands and manors of the Earl of Westmoreland and those gentry who supported him, but the bulk were not actually tenants of the earls. It seems that they responded to the muster when the earls decided to take up arms. It was not a case of people blindly following their lord as they were told, but a more widespread feeling of discontent in the region with religion as the focus. The centres of rebellion were Thirsk, Northallerton, Richmond, Yarm, Darlington, and most of County Durham.[12] The north was in uproar, rebelling against the government's reformist slant, the queen's choice of advisors, and supporting Mary Queen of Scots as heir to the English throne. At this point there was no stated intention to overthrow Elizabeth, although this would feature heavily in later Elizabethan rebellions. There was also a sense of the north seeking revenge for years of southern interference in their affairs. What they did not realise was that this rebellion would effectively end separate northern rule and meld it more firmly with the central government in London, the very opposite of what was wanted by the northern lords and families.

Mass was celebrated wherever the rebels went. This initial reaction seemed to confirm the earls' belief that promising to restore Catholicism and Papal authority in England would prove an important rallying cry to rebellion. At Kirkbymoorside in North Riding the plain communion table and prayerbook were symbolically cast aside while in Sedgefield the altar was rebuilt, and Protestant books were burned. On 14 November 1569, the earls of Northumberland and Westmoreland along with Richard Norton, Sheriff of Yorkshire, entered Durham with 300 armed horsemen. They tore down the communion table in the cathedral, which had replaced the Catholic altar, ripped up Protestant and English bibles and prayerbooks, and had Mass said. Historian A.N. Wilson records that 794 people were recorded entering the cathedral to hear Mass celebrated that day.[13] This was a huge show of support for what the rebel earls and their supporters were hoping to achieve by this revolt. It was thought that, by promoting religion as the cause of rebellion, it would make their uprising more attractive to the northern population. Their promise to restore Catholicism seemed to act as a rallying cry. There was concern in London that the rebels would gain a larger following if they portrayed their rebellion as a holy war or a crusade of sorts. G.R. Elton argues that religion was, in fact, a cloak, however, rather than the main reason for the rebellion.[14] If this is true then what was the main reason for the rebellion? The succession? This seems to be premature, as there was still every hope in 1569 that Elizabeth would marry and have an heir, unlike in later plots where her age was against her in this. Religious wars had already erupted in Scotland and France; it was not beyond the realms of possibility that the same could happen in England, especially with a figurehead like Mary Queen of Scots in England for the Catholic cause.

The following day, 15 November 1569, the rebels began to march south. As they marched, the earls and their supporters issued a proclamation stating that her advisors had isolated Elizabeth from her nobility, and that they had introduced harmful laws which were not doing any good for the country. The earls made it clear that their hostility was not directed towards the queen but at her advisors. Much of the nobility believed that they should be the ones advising the queen, and not the likes of the Cecils (William, Baron Burghley, and later his son, Robert) who were low born in their eyes and not worthy to advise a monarch. As the rebels marched further south their power base was weaker. Their support was largely in the north which was more inclined largely towards the Catholic religion. The Protestant reforms had more of an impact and more of a following in the south of the country, so people were less likely to rise up in the south in support of Catholic earls with a religious agenda. Mary Queen of Scots also seemed to have less of a support base in the south, possibly because of the zealousness of her religion.

On 18 November 1569, Elizabeth again wrote to the Earl of Sussex regarding the rebellion, stating that the rebels 'seek nothing so greedily as to subdue the realm under the yoke of foreign princes.'[15] Perhaps Elizabeth intended to play on the natural xenophobia of the English people; there had been rumours of Spanish soldiers en route to aid the rebels, which many of the English did not want. Philip II of Spain had involved England in foreign wars when he had been married to Mary I, which had led to the loss of Calais in 1558, England's last foothold in France. Mary Queen of Scots could also be seen as a foreign prince, being the former Queen of Scotland and France, and raised largely in France. This only added to English xenophobia. By this point the rebels were at Boroughbridge on the Great North Road and numbered around 6,000 men, many of whom were yeomen farmers rather than labourers.[16] Elizabeth noted that religion seemed to be the main focus of their rebellion, recounting events in Durham such as the destruction of the communion table and tearing up of English bibles. She instructed Sussex to deal with the rebels as soon as possible, but if he did not have enough men, to wait until Henry Carey, 1st Baron Hunsdon joined him with more. Elizabeth was clearly being kept up to date with what was happening in the rebellion and was guiding the crown's response to the crisis. She decided to dispatch more soldiers than were strictly necessary to deal with the rebels, possibly in fear of foreign reinforcements. Sussex, Hunsdon, and Sir Ralph Sadler had requested to be reinforced with 500 cavalrymen and better weapons to deal with the rebels. They were authorised to muster 10,000 men instead. Elizabeth wanted to be sure there were enough men to deal with the rebels and any foreign troops who came to assist them.

Now a key point was reached. On 22 November 1569, George Talbot, 6th Earl of Shrewsbury, the gaoler of Mary Queen of Scots since she had arrived in England the previous year, was ordered to move his prisoner south to Coventry. She was put in the charge of Henry Hastings, 3rd Earl of Huntingdon during the rebellion. This move was in order to minimise the risk that she would be freed by the rebels and declared queen in Elizabeth's place. The rescue of Mary Queen of Scots was one of the stated aims of the rebels. The same date was when the pardon offered to the rebels was due to expire. Any rebels who returned home by this date would not be punished. The earls and their supporters numbered over 5,000 men by this point (1,600 horsemen and 4,000 foot soldiers)[17] and they reached Clifford Moor in Yorkshire, which lies between York and Leeds. Richard Norton, Sheriff of Yorkshire, had written to the Earl of Northumberland to say that Spanish troops were on their way to support the rebellion, but these soldiers never materialised. It is possible that this news was merely intended to boost the morale of the rebels and worry the government, as Norton knew that the letter was likely to be intercepted by the government. It is conceivable and even likely that Norton wanted the letter intercepted so that the government would split their resources to watch the ports as well, giving the rebels an easier march south. The Spanish involvement was a farce as Philip of Spain did not want Mary Queen of Scots (daughter-in-law of the Guise family, whom he hated) as Queen of England, though in 1588 he would use Mary's execution as an excuse to launch his Armada against England.

By 24 November the rebels began to retreat as the plot collapsed, despite the fact that they had around 10,000 men supporting their cause. They passed through Richmond, Ripon, Wetherby, Knaresborough, Tadcaster, Cawood, and got as far as Selby, the southernmost point reached by the rebels. They had taken Barnard Castle in County Durham but were unable to hold it. Their chances of success were diminished by their lack of funds; the Earl of Northumberland, for example, had to pawn part of his Garter insignia in a bid to raise money.[18] The rebels dispersed without a fight when they saw that their cause was lost. Emergency musters had been gathered to march north to put down the rebellion, of around 15,000 men. The rebels reached Bramham Moor, within fifty miles of Tutbury, where Mary Queen of Scots was being held before she was moved to Coventry. The rebels discovered, when they reached Tadcaster, that Mary was not there anymore and inferred that she had been moved into closer confinement to prevent them from rescuing her. Whether a raid was made on Tutbury is unknown, but very unlikely. At this point, it became obvious that their cause was doomed. The rebels retreated to Richmond by 28 November, and Brancepeth by 30 November.[19] Mary was more concerned about being freed from her confinement than taking the English throne in 1569, and she still hoped that Elizabeth would assist her in regaining the Scottish throne.

This would change as it became apparent that Elizabeth would rather keep Mary under lock and key than assist her to regain her power. Mary's liberty would mean that a rival for Elizabeth's throne was free and unable to be controlled or manipulated.

Government propaganda which said that religion was being used as an excuse for civil disobedience was beginning to have an effect. The rebels were disbanding and returning home. By 11 December 1569 the Earl of Sussex had decided that he had a sufficient number of troops to set out against the rebels, but the rising had effectively ended already as they realised that Mary Queen of Scots had been moved beyond their reach. The rebels had 4,000 soldiers and 1,800 horsemen compared to the 12,000 men of the royal army commanded by Ambrose Dudley, 3rd Earl of Warwick, and Edward Clinton, 9th Baron Clinton (later 1st Earl of Lincoln). Elizabeth had been warned that she could not trust the loyalty of the north, hence her decision to send an army from the south. York accommodated 3,000 of the 14,000 soldiers who were sent to suppress the rebellion and loaned more than £1,000 (over £200,000 in today's money) to supply soldiers' wages. By 16 December the earls had told their followers to fend for themselves, and fled north into Scotland from Durham, hoping to get protection from the Scottish king, James VI, the son of Mary Queen of Scots, and his regent, James Stewart, 1st Earl of Moray. The earls headed first for Hexham, then to Naworth, and reached Liddesdale on 20 December 1569. Scottish border families assisted in their flight into Scotland and their escape from justice (temporary in the case of the Earl of Northumberland who would be apprehended).

Richard Norton, Sheriff of Yorkshire, suffered a traitor's death at Tyburn for his involvement in the plot. Hundreds of rebels would be hanged under martial law as a result of the uprising. Historian Anne Somerset declares that the rebellion was a 'pathetic fiasco'.[20] This is a very apt description of a rebellion where there was poor leadership, not enough funds to support it, and no clear stated objectives that all rebels adhered to. It was the poorer followers who seemed to suffer most after the rebellion as the earls of Northumberland and Westmoreland had managed to escape into Scotland so were out of Elizabeth's grasp. Elizabeth sent a command north that the more prosperous rebels should be kept in prison until tried at the assizes, the insinuation being that, if convicted, their property would be forfeit to the crown. The commoners could be dealt with by martial law and executed without delay. There was no material benefit in delay to the executions of the commoners. Elizabeth had been cheated of her biggest prey so made an example of the small fry.

Exactly how many suffered as a result of this rebellion is unclear. It appears that the death penalty was enacted in at least 500 cases, though some estimates put this slightly lower and others a little higher. Historian Susan Doran claims that 500 of the 6,000 rebels were hanged under martial law; 200 more were condemned but then reprieved through the compassion of men on the spot.[21] It has been claimed that Elizabeth wanted more rebels to suffer than actually did. Had she had her way, everyone whose loyalty was suspect would have been punished. Elizabeth was severely shaken by the rebellion. It was the first time that the people had risen against her, and it was a shock. Communications were poor and allegedly the queen complained that not enough was being done to chastise the north and that her commanders were not keeping her informed. There is not any evidence that Elizabeth felt any remorse for the numbers of people who died. She wanted people to be tried and executed, those who had stayed at home when the Earl of Sussex tried to call them up to fight against the rebels, because she felt this was a dereliction of duty. Officials at York who were trying some of the wealthier rebels asked whether some of those condemned could be reprieved as they had been forced to join the rising against their will, but the queen did not want to spare them. Those who avoided the death penalty for their involvement were only pardoned after paying heavy fines, totalling £4,800, around £1.14 million in today's money. The crown also acquired forfeited lands, valued at approximately £2,500 a year (about £600,000 today). Elizabeth made it very clear that she was against extending mercy to those who had rebelled against her or had failed to try and quell the rebellion. She saw them as equally culpable.

*

As far as the rebellion of the northern earls ended in December 1569, despite the fact that the two major perpetrators (Northumberland and Westmoreland) had not been caught, there was further intrigue to come. On 13 January 1570, Elizabeth ordered the arrest of Leonard Dacre, who sympathised with the plight of Mary Queen of Scots; she then ordered demobilisation on 16 January 1570. After the northern rebels had retreated, Leonard Dacre had fortified Naworth Castle, his own property, and gathered 3,000 men, supposedly to protect Elizabeth from said northern rebels. Dacre had been in a dispute with the 4th Duke of Norfolk over the Dacre inheritance, which had been granted to Norfolk rather than Dacre himself. It is possible Dacre's men had been assembled to deal with that dispute and he used the excuse of tackling the rebellion as a cover, despite the fact that Norfolk was in the Tower. When he realised that his cover was blown, Dacre summoned Scots from the border regions to his aid.

Dacre had been corresponding with Mary Queen of Scots since 1566, but he was with Elizabeth at Windsor Castle when the rising began and travelled north as a loyal subject to his queen. The rebel earls had initially been betrayed by Leonard Dacre who had encouraged the rebellion and then gave names to the council.[22] However, once he reached his seat at Naworth he began to attract Mary Queen of Scots' supporters to his side. Had he intended to do this from the first and join the rebellion? Or was it a spur of the moment decision? We will likely never know for sure, although his continuing correspondence with Mary over the previous three years would suggest a deep loyalty to her and he may well have intended to join the rebels in releasing her from her captivity. Other evidence suggests that, as early as June

1569, Dacre had sent word to Philip of Spain that if he wanted to send an army to England, he, Dacre, could raise an additional 15,000 men to support the invasion. This certainly points to the fact that Dacre was in sympathy with the rebels against Elizabeth and her government. As Dacre was at court when the Northern Rising began, he was too late to help the earls, but decided to start a private rebellion of his own.

To try and quell this new upswell of revolt, Lord Hunsdon, Governor of Berwick, set out from Hexham with his small army of around 1,500 men on 19 February 1570. Lord Darcy was holding Doncaster for the queen. The following day Hunsdon and his men were ambushed by Leonard Dacre with 3,000 men. Hunsdon was en route to meet up with Henry Scrope, 9th Baron Scrope of Bolton, who had been gathering more men to quell the new uprising. Hunsdon was victorious, despite being outnumbered two to one by Dacre's men. Hunsdon's infantry resisted the charge of the rebel horsemen, while his cavalry attacked the rebel flank. Four hundred rebels were killed, 300 were taken prisoner and Dacre himself fled to Liddesdale. This became known as the Battle of Gelt Bridge and was the one 'brief but ferocious' military encounter in the whole of the Northern Rising.[23] Dacre managed to make it to Scotland and then across to the continent. He would die in 1573 in Brussels, having continued to urge Philip of Spain to act against Elizabeth. The Northern Rising could have flared up again had Hunsdon not stood his ground against Dacre. There was no need for heavy reprisals as the rebels had been trounced so completely. Elizabeth had asked that 600 northerners be hanged as punishment for the rising, but Hunsdon ensured that far fewer than this actually died. Rebels who were to be pardoned had to attend a sermon detailing their sins and then swear an oath of loyalty to Elizabeth, before receiving mercy. They had to agree that Elizabeth was the Supreme Head of the Church and that the Pope had no jurisdiction in England.

Elizabeth wrote to Hunsdon on 26 February 1570 to thank him for his actions to defeat 'that cankered, subtle traitor Leonard Dacre'.[24]

Dacre had fled rather than finish the fight. Elizabeth expresses her disappointment that Dacre was not captured to be punished for his rebellion but is happy that the revolt has been successfully put down. Elizabeth possibly calls Dacre 'subtle' because he had at first claimed that he was raising men to help put down the earls' rebellion, but then used them to foment a rebellion himself. This could also explain her use of the word 'cankered', as it must have felt like she had nurtured an ulcer in her kingdom: she could not trust those who were supposedly her loyal subjects and who were supposed to keep order in her kingdom. Critically, Elizabeth acknowledged that this was the first time that an army had to be raised in her reign against any rebels. This was eleven years into her reign and, as has been seen, in a reign lasting just six years Edward VI dealt with two rebellions, and in a reign of five years Mary I dealt with one. Elizabeth seemed to be doing rather well at this point in comparison to her half-siblings.

Despite the fact that Dacre escaped, there was some good news for Elizabeth in June 1572 when John Erskine, 1st Earl of Mar, the new regent for James VI of Scotland, handed over to the English government Thomas Percy, 7th Earl of Northumberland. He had fled to Scotland in December 1569 along with Charles Neville, 6th Earl of Westmoreland. At the time it was thought that they would wait out the winter in Scotland and then return south with another army in the spring to 'revive their revolt in a new place and a new guise' after the excommunication of Elizabeth I which occurred in 1570.[25] This excommunication would have given them a religious imperative from the Pope to overthrow the heretic Elizabeth and replace her. The Earl of Westmoreland and his wife (who was sister to Thomas Howard, 4th Duke of Norfolk) had escaped to the Netherlands and never returned to England. He received a small pension from the Spanish king, Philip II. Westmoreland was attainted in Parliament in 1571, lost his earldom, and died penniless in 1601 on the continent. The Earl of Northumberland was executed on 22 August 1572 by Elizabeth and was ultimately beatified in 1895 by Pope Leo XIII.

Before his execution he was questioned by Lord Hunsdon and denied that the rebels had ever intended to depose Elizabeth, but he admitted to Mary's importance as her heir.

Around eighty men, most of little account, died as a result of Dacre's revolt. Many rebels were publicly hanged, and their rotting bodies were displayed as a deterrent to others who might think about rebelling against the queen. Both Westmoreland and Dacre escaped, and Northumberland was only executed in 1572, so it was mainly their followers who were punished, at least in the immediate aftermath of the revolt. Some rebels fled abroad to the Low Countries after the rebellion, afraid of being punished for their involvement. Edward Clinton, 9th Baron Clinton, helped to suppress the Northern Rebellion and punish the rebels and as a result was made 1st Earl of Lincoln in 1572. He had previously served Henry VIII, Edward VI, and Mary I so had a long history of royal service. Lincoln, along with Ambrose Dudley, 3rd Earl of Warwick, brother to Robert Dudley, Earl of Leicester, had raised an army to deal with the rebellion, but the revolt had already petered out by the time that the army was assembled and ready to march.

Every bell tower that had sounded its bell in support of the rebellion was stripped of its bell, with only one bell remaining to remind the north of their disobedience, and as a warning to others who would rise in revolt against their queen. Walsingham had initially been reluctant to act too soon against the rebels, but his source in Paris had insisted that Spain and France wanted to undermine English security. This could also explain the size of the army that was sent north. The government wanted to be prepared in case the rebels did receive foreign aid, as had been rumoured. The crown spent around £42,300 to suppress the rebellion itself. A further £52,608 was spent on the army pursuing rebels into Scotland, resulting in a total spend of nearly £95,000 (around £22 million today).[26] Luckily for Elizabeth, this foreign aid did not materialise to help the northern rebels, though the Spanish would become more deeply involved in English plotting as time went on, culminating in the Babington Plot of 1586, the execution of Mary Queen of Scots the following year, and the English defeat of the Spanish Armada in 1588. The Northern Rising proved that Walsingham and Cecil did indeed have reason to be concerned.

*

The Northern Rising was the first and only serious civil disturbance of Elizabeth's reign. What we can take from the Northern Rising is the idea that, if an alternative claimant to the throne existed, they would be used as the face of rebellion, whether actually involved or not. Mary was the focus of the rising but not the instigator.[27] There is no real evidence to suggest that Mary Queen of Scots was actually directly involved in this rebellion, as she was in the later Ridolfi, Throckmorton, and Babington Plots, but her name was certainly used to try and attract Catholic rebels to the cause in acting against Elizabeth and her Protestant advisors. On 26 November 1569, Elizabeth had written to Mary's gaoler, the Earl of Shrewsbury, to say that, although she would appreciate his assistance in putting down the rebellion, she required him to be 'looking to the person of her whom the world beholdeth to be the principal hidden cause of these troubles'.[28] Although Elizabeth knew that Mary was not the architect of the rebellion, she understood that Mary's name was being used to bring the rebels together, and that they might hope for more than just Mary's release. There was not enough evidence to link Mary directly to the Northern Rising. However, as long as Mary was in England there was the concern that she would replace Elizabeth and return England to Papal obedience. This would have meant that most of Elizabeth's advisors would also have been in fear of their lives, hence they worked so hard against Mary, and eventually brought her to the scaffold in 1587.

The earls of Northumberland and Westmoreland had been involved in politics for years and had experienced periods of disfavour with the queen but had never been tipped over into open rebellion before. It was political miscalculations and a sense of dissatisfaction that pushed them over into revolt.[29] Tenants no longer offered complete loyalty to a feudal lord and times were changing irrevocably. Perhaps this lack of loyalty to a feudal lord can assist to explain why many tenants of the earls did not rise in their support. They realised that the time of noble power was past, and they would do better to support their queen. The northern lords probably found this harder to deal with, being more isolated from the central government in London. The ordinary people were not entirely happy at being at the beck and call of a feudal lord and wanted more freedom and control over their own actions. This had to have frustrated and perhaps even angered the northern lords which may have led in part to their act of rebellion. The earldoms were broken up by confiscations and the property was redistributed to those loyal to Elizabeth.

The rising effectively ended feudalism in the north.[30] Feudalism was the idea of land held in exchange for homage, legal and military service to a liege lord. This was the way that the north had been run, almost as its own kingdom prior to this point. The government was far away in London and travel was not always easy in the sixteenth century, so the north was largely left to its own devices. The south was more solidified into one kingdom, but monarchs rarely travelled north so the lords in the north had largely been left to run the area as they saw fit. With the Northern Rising this ended. The government in the south took more of an interest in the ways of the north and tried to meld its inhabitants to the ways of the south and a more central government. Northern power was limited by both conflict and consensus, as well as financial penalties such as fines and forfeiture of lands. Limiting wealth also limited the ability of the northern lords and families to raise private armies and attract a following for rebellion in the first place.

Henry Hastings, 3rd Earl of Huntingdon, was made President of the Council of North in 1572; he had taken over the guard of

Mary Queen of Scots during the Northern Rising from the Earl of Shrewsbury temporarily. He was considered to be a Puritan and the north was still largely Catholic in its beliefs. Huntingdon's task was to amalgamate the north with the south and make England more of a united country with one seat of government and no regional power bases. He set about wiping out the line formed by the River Trent which separated England into two very different halves and uniting her under one government and one system of religious beliefs set out by the Elizabethan Religious Settlement of 1559. The Northern Rising had clearly demonstrated how divided the north and south were, and how dangerous this could be.

The Northern Rising of 1569 and the Pilgrimage of Grace of 1536 had a lot of things in common. The crown and government believed that the rebels were being disloyal because they did not agree with their monarch's policies, especially towards religion. However, the rebels believed that they were being loyal to the crown but were expressing their grievances in a way that the government had to listen to them as they felt they were being ignored in expressing them in other ways. The two rebellions also had largely religious aims, though sometimes hidden under the guise of wider social discontent. The Pilgrimage of Grace rebels did not call themselves rebels, but pilgrims, giving it a distinctly religious tone. The Northern Rising did not go so far, though their actions in Durham in particular definitely suggest a religious overtone to the revolt. In the later Babington Plot of 1586, it was believed by the conspirators that the north would rise in support of their plot to avenge the harm that had been done to the region after the 1569 rebellion. However, the rebellion in 1586 did not get far enough along before the conspirators were arrested to know whether the north would have risen in conjunction with Anthony Babington and the other conspirators.

This rebellion would be the first time that Elizabeth would contemplate executing Mary Queen of Scots. She had a death warrant drawn up so that Mary could be killed in haste if the rebellion looked like it would succeed. When the rising failed, talk of executing Mary stopped. The government knew that Mary would be a problem while she was in England, but at this point she had not done enough to warrant a death sentence, and Elizabeth was hoping that they would be able to reach an agreement with the Scots to return Mary to them and to her throne. Even if the issue of Mary was resolved in some way the Northern Rising had revealed that there were still religious divisions in England and fervour that could erupt again into rebellion at any time.

Pope Pius V published the Papal bull, *Regnans in Excelsis*, in 1570, intended to give the rebels in the north a legal and religious backing, but it came too late to help them. However, it would give encouragement and a tacit backing to future rebellions which intended to unseat Elizabeth and replace her with Mary Queen of Scots, declaring Elizabeth to be 'deprived of her pretended title to the aforesaid crown'.[31] The Pope was thus encouraging loyal English Catholics to rebel against their heretic sovereign and physically overthrow her, backing up the religious and moral overthrow that the bull was intended to do. A ballad written by Thomas Preston describes 'how the Pope doth bewayle, that the rebelles in England cannot prevayle', as 'the Rebelles they weare put to flight'.[32] The Pope bemoaned the rebel failure on this ballad, but the Papacy would never provide any military or financial aid to achieve Elizabeth's overthrow, however. Their support was purely moral.

There was another ballad written around the same time by Thomas Bette who was trying to tamp down on rumours surrounding the rebellion, telling people to pray and ask for forgiveness:

> Wherefore let vs with one accorde,
> Fall all to fast and praye:
> And Pardon craue now of the Lorde,
> To kepe vs from decaye.[33]

There was a fear of divine retribution from God for rebellion against a lawful sovereign, and that is the tone of this ballad entitled 'Agaynst

Rebellious and False Rumours'. Bette is asking the people to come together and support their queen in order to stop the country falling apart and falling prey to others who would take advantage of England's weakness to gain power over her.

Although the rebellion had a limited lifespan and, superficially, it did not seem to achieve any of its aims, it influenced the Elizabethan administration for years to come. They realised they had to deal with Mary Queen of Scots and, over the following years she would be involved with several more rebellions against the English crown, becoming more reckless and desperate in her attempts to escape captivity and take the English throne. The Northern Rising had demonstrated that swift action could put a halt to rebellion, and that Elizabeth commanded great love from her people, especially in the south. There was not really any proper planning by the rebel leaders and so it was relatively easy for the government to make a show of force and wait for the rebellion to fall apart. What was learnt from the Northern Rising was that there were those in England who would rebel against the Protestant Tudor queen in favour of a Catholic Stuart one, and that those plotters would not give up easily. Until there was no Catholic Stuart queen left to fight for.

Chapter 3

Ridolfi Plot 1571

'Who was to the Queen so dangerous an enemy'[1]

Roberto di Ridolfi is an intriguing but shadowy figure in Elizabethan history. He had been involved previously in the Northern Rising in 1569, but then gave his name to another plot in 1571 which aimed to rescue Mary Queen of Scots from her imprisonment at Sheffield Castle and put her on the English throne, aided by a foreign invasion from Spain. This plot did not gain as much traction as the earlier Northern Rising as it was uncovered before any real action could be taken. It was largely plotting behind closed doors, but it did reveal Elizabeth's vulnerability. It also lacked the popular support of the Northern Rising, although the Ridolfi Plot did emerge directly as a result of that earlier rising combined with Spanish animosity.[2] The Ridolfi Plot also had more money and better organisation behind it. The Northern Rising had demonstrated that there were people willing to rise against the government for a cause they believed in. The Ridolfi Plot aimed to provide that cause.

The 1571 Ridolfi Plot was the first real conspiracy that aimed to replace Elizabeth on the English throne with Mary Queen of Scots. Up to this point, any aims with regards to Mary were to have her established as Elizabeth's successor rather than to replace Elizabeth as queen. However, a tract published in London after the Ridolfi Plot claimed that Mary was the 'greatest cause of the Rebellion lately in the North'.[3] This implies that perhaps Mary was not quite as innocent as one might suppose. However, it might have meant that her name was used to inspire the rebels to revolt, and one of the stated aims was to rescue Mary from her imprisonment. It does not necessarily mean that she was physically involved. The aims of the Ridolfi Plot were to get rid of Elizabeth, marry Mary Queen of Scots to Thomas Howard, 4th Duke of Norfolk, and put Mary on the throne through a concerted effort between the continental powers of France and Spain, and English Catholics. This plot set a precedent for those which followed – by Francis Throckmorton and Anthony Babington in the 1580s – to overthrow and assassinate the Protestant Elizabeth and replace her with the Catholic Mary.

However, eminent Tudor historian Susan Doran argues that Mary's primary objective was not to take the English throne from Elizabeth but to escape her captivity and assist her allies in Scotland to retrieve the Scottish throne for herself from her son, James VI, who was ruling through a regency.[4] This is possible. Mary had been forced to abdicate the Scottish throne following the death of her second husband, Henry, Lord Darnley, and scandalous third marriage to a man suspected of involvement in his murder, the Earl of Bothwell. This could explain Mary's actions and her assertion that she wasn't committing treason. If she wanted her liberty rather than to overthrow Elizabeth this would not be treason unless she acted against the monarch to achieve it. Perhaps Mary wanted to escape from her captivity, but it was the others involved, like Roberto di Ridolfi, Pope Pius V, and the Spanish, who wanted to overthrow Elizabeth and replace her with Mary to return England to Roman Catholicism, because they saw the Church of England as heretical. Mary could have been guilty by association at this point. However, Mary certainly endorsed later plots which aimed to overthrow and assassinate Elizabeth, even if the exact aims of the Ridolfi Plot are not entirely clear.

Roberto di Ridolfi (sometimes spelled Ridolphi) was a Florentine merchant who had settled in England during the reign of the Catholic Mary I, Elizabeth's half-sister, around 1555. He established a reputation as a banker and became connected with many of the leading Catholic families in England. Even into Elizabeth's reign he managed to keep up correspondence with both the Spanish and French ambassadors in England, both of whom represented staunchly Catholic nations. This alone could have been seen as a threat to Elizabeth. He was also a Papal agent from 1566 onwards, just before Mary Queen of Scots' flight into England, but was rather an inept conspirator in many ways, which has led to several historians suggesting that he may have been a double agent actually working for Walsingham. He had no real diplomatic skills and did not understand English minds, despite having lived in England for over a decade. The Duke of Alba described Ridolfi as lightweight and a chatterbox with an inability to carry out a practical scheme.[5] He talked about grand plans but did not know how to actually carry them out. If he was really conspiring against Elizabeth then, according to Alba at least, he had absolutely no chance of success. Ridolfi was receiving large amounts of money from abroad, including from the Pope and was distributing it to supporters of Mary Queen of Scots, like John Leslie, Bishop of Ross, and the Duke of Norfolk's servants. It was intended to fund political Catholicism in England. This brought him to the attention of William Cecil and Sir Francis Walsingham. Cecil received information about the plot from various sources including Scotland and Tuscany, so it was not by any means a secret across Europe that there was a plot to rescue Mary, depose Elizabeth, and return England to the Roman Catholic fold. We still cannot be sure whose side Ridolfi was actually on during the plotting, which makes this conspiracy murky and complex to decipher. Ridolfi had been involved on the periphery of the Northern Rising, but it is uncertain whether he had been turned as Walsingham's agent or not.

The Ridolfi Plot was the first real example of the incredible working relationship that would develop between Sir Francis Walsingham and William Cecil, Lord Burghley, and how they came to create such a cohesive and successful partnership which would last for two decades. Cecil had been in the service of Edward Seymour, 1st Duke of Somerset, Protector to Edward VI, but on his fall switched into the service of John Dudley, 1st Duke of Northumberland, the new

Protector. Cecil had been with Elizabeth since the reign of Mary I in administering her lands and was appointed Secretary of State by Elizabeth on her accession. He would have tight control over crown finances and the leadership of the Privy Council until he resigned from royal service in 1598, just a few months before his death. Sir Francis Walsingham began in royal service when he became English ambassador to France in 1570, though he had been working with Cecil since the previous year. Walsingham would have control over an intelligence network which would protect the Queen and uncover many plots against her life. Together Walsingham and Cecil aimed to protect Elizabeth from what they thought was the principal threat to Elizabeth's person and the Protestant regime in England: Mary Queen of Scots and the plots that she became involved in against Elizabeth. Mary Queen of Scots and Thomas Howard, 4th Duke of Norfolk, were involved in what became known as the Ridolfi Plot, along with John Leslie, Bishop of Ross (who was Mary's agent), Philip II of Spain, Pope Pius V, and Fernando Alvarez de Toledo, 3rd Duke of Alba (Philip's representative in the Netherlands). Alba seems to have been the only one who was the least bit sceptical about the plot and whether it was even possible for it to succeed. In the end, nearly all of those who were involved in the conspiracy tried to pin the blame on someone else.

By February 1571 Mary Queen of Scots had come to believe that it was foolish to look for better or fairer treatment from Elizabeth. Excuses had constantly been put forward since Mary arrived in England in 1568, to explain why she was still a prisoner and so she came to believe that her liberation would not be achieved through diplomatic channels, only through plotting and intrigue.[6] Negotiations with the Scottish government were ongoing but would ultimately break down. This led to Mary deciding to put her trust in Elizabeth's enemies abroad, rather than in the negotiations that were taking place between England and Scotland to allow Mary to return to her throne, possibly sharing it with her son who had acceded to the Scottish throne, backed by a regent, on her forced abdication in 1568. Mary did not believe that the negotiations would bear fruit. She complained about the state of England, the cruelty of her own position as a prisoner in England, the persecution of Catholics, threats to her claim to the English throne, negotiations with the Pope to annul her marriage to the Earl of Bothwell, and a plan to send her son, James VI of Scotland, to Spain to marry a Spanish princess.[7] Mary seemed to resent the fact that things were being decided without her, and that she was being left out of major decisions. Her world had crumbled around her as she had lost her throne, custody of her son, and even her liberty. Complaints were all that were left to her in a way. The negotiations between Scotland and England would indeed break down and it has been suggested that this may have been, at least in part, as a result of the Ridolfi Plot. Mary's involvement in this plot showed her to be unworthy to rule. Had she been allowed to regain her throne in Scotland, would it have stopped her plotting to take the English throne? Unlikely. The English government believed that it was better to have Mary in captivity in England than free and with an army in Scotland, able to act against Elizabeth and England.

*

The Ridolfi Plot was uncovered in 1571, but it had been the background to Anglo-Spanish relations since 1569 and the Northern Rising discussed in the previous chapter.[8] Roberto di Ridolfi had been involved in that rebellion as well, though in a minor way as he spent much of the time the rebellion was in progress imprisoned in England. In September 1569, it was discovered that Ridolfi had made bills of exchange worth £3,000 available to John Leslie, Bishop of Ross, who was a close advisor to Mary Queen of Scots and was working on her behalf to release her from captivity. Today this would be worth over £700,000, a substantial sum. The intent was to try and restore her to the Scottish throne which she had been forced to abdicate the year before. It was through the Bishop of Ross that Mary first made contact with Roberto di Ridolfi and the Spanish ambassador, Guerau de Spes. The French and Spanish ambassadors had already met and wanted to remove William Cecil, agreeing to sink their own differences to do so. De Spes claimed he knew of no greater heretic than Cecil.[9] Cecil was known to support wider Protestant reform, although he did adhere to Roman Catholic practices in the reign of Mary I, probably simply to survive. This earlier plot against Elizabeth was aimed more at removing her advisors rather than the queen herself, much like the Northern Rising two years earlier, though the Ridolfi Plot was in some ways more dangerous and more of a threat to the throne.

Ridolfi was arrested by Sir Francis Walsingham the following month, on 7 October 1569, and questioned at Walsingham's home on Seething Lane in London, suspected of engaging in plotting with Mary Queen of Scots and the Pope. The Duke of Norfolk was already in the Tower but, at this point, there was little hard evidence against him. His imprisonment at this time stopped his involvement in the Northern Rising. Ridolfi was kept in custody for about a month before being released on 11 November. The intelligence network around Elizabeth had been keeping an eye on Ridolfi as he was a suspected Papal agent, and the Spanish ambassador, Guerau de Spes, was known to be in touch with him. This was enough to make Walsingham and Cecil wary of him, keep an eye on him, and eventually prompted his arrest. Some historians believe that Walsingham thought he had turned Ridolfi to his man and that he would spy on Mary and the Spanish for the English government, otherwise it is difficult to understand the leniency displayed towards him. Why was he given his liberty if there was any chance that he would act against the queen? There has also been a suggestion that Elizabeth offered leniency to him in exchange for full disclosure of what he knew.[10] It is almost inconceivable that Ridolfi could have hoped to successfully deceive Walsingham, Cecil, and Elizabeth. They were all experienced in conspiracy and manipulation so it seems unlikely that they would have been easily hoodwinked. Ridolfi's activities confirmed Cecil's fears for Elizabeth's security and the security of the state.

Pope Pius V finally issued the bull of excommunication against Elizabeth, which had been threatened for the last decade, and almost since the beginning of her reign, on 25 February 1570: *Regnans in Excelsis*. The Pope declared Elizabeth 'to be deprived of her pretended title to the aforesaid crown and of all lordship, dignity and privilege whatsoever'.[11] All of her subjects were absolved of their loyalty to her as a result. This had been rumoured for a while, but perhaps these rumblings of a plot against Elizabeth in the form of the Northern Rising and then the Ridolfi Plot, had encouraged the Pope to issue it at this point and encourage the plotters. The bull of excommunication absolved the English people of their loyalty to Elizabeth, which meant that Elizabeth's subjects were not just absolved of their loyalty to her but were being actively encouraged to act against her and overthrow her. Anyone who had wanted to act against the queen now had the backing of the Pope and, by extension, the other Catholic powers. The timing of the bull suggests that the Pope was trying to take advantage of the discontent in northern England at the time, but it was a miscalculation; the Pope had hugely overestimated Catholic support in England. Many people weren't devoted enough to the old ways to risk reprisals from the queen. They had other things on their minds, like how to survive day to day. Quarrels over who sat on the throne must have seemed a long way away for the common people. Ridolfi had told the French ambassador before the rising that he had a commission from the Pope to work with sympathetic Catholic nobles in England to restore Catholicism and Papal obedience to the country. The people wanted to be left to worship as their consciences demanded, but they did not want the Pope having political power in England. This was the power that Henry VIII had removed from England in the 1530s. Many people were probably merely sick of the constant changes and not knowing where they stood, wanting some consistency, which it was believed Elizabeth could provide. Elizabeth was a direct product of the Break with Rome and she determined to continue her father's line in this regard.

Elizabeth's excommunication in 1570 influenced the emerging succession problem in England across the 1570s.[12] It had been rumoured that Elizabeth would marry Robert Dudley, 1st Earl of Leicester, almost since she succeeded to the throne in 1558. However, the mysterious death of Dudley's first wife, Amy Robsart, on 8 September 1560, put a spanner in the works of this plan. Elizabeth would have put her throne at risk and even her life had she married someone suspected of having a hand in the death of his wife. That is something that Elizabeth would never have risked. Amy Robsart had been discovered dead at the bottom of a flight of stairs at Cumnor Place in Oxfordshire with a broken neck. There had been rumours that she was ill, but the death was considered suspicious, and an inquest was ordered. The verdict was accidental death, but rumours continued to accuse Dudley of playing a role in it. With these rumours, Elizabeth would never have risked marrying Dudley as she was too shrewd a politician not to recognise potential problems from the match. Elizabeth had several other potential suitors over the years, including her half-sister, Mary I's, widower, Philip II of Spain, King Eric XIV of Sweden, Archduke Charles of Austria, and Francis, Duke of Anjou. But Elizabeth would live and die as the 'Virgin Queen', never having married, or produced an heir. This made the issue of the marriage of Mary Queen of Scots more important. Mary was the closest heir to the English crown, though by the will of Henry VIII her line was inferior to the line of Henry's younger sister, Mary, Duchess of Suffolk. Mary Queen of Scots was descended through the elder sister, Margaret, who had married James IV of Scotland. If Mary Queen of Scots married Thomas Howard, 4th Duke of Norfolk, as the rebels planned, it would strengthen her claim to the English throne and perhaps even make her a more attractive proposition as an alternative queen, not just as a successor.

In June 1570, Thomas Howard, 4th Duke of Norfolk, gave a solemn undertaking not to interfere any more in the marriage of Mary

Queen of Scots. As we saw in the previous chapter on the Northern Rising, there were rumours of a marriage between Norfolk and Mary as early as 1569 and Norfolk was arrested and questioned at that time. When Norfolk made this promise, Elizabeth believed it was safe to release him from the Tower of London, which happened in August 1570. He was confined to his London home in Charterhouse Square in the charge of Sir Henry Neville. It was at this point, with Norfolk's release, that Ridolfi resumed his plotting. It is likely that he hoped to resurrect the marriage between Mary and Norfolk, and perhaps Norfolk did too. It would give him more power and restore the Howard name. The power of the Howard family peaked under Henry VIII when two of its women became queen, but tailed off with the execution of Henry Howard, Earl of Surrey, and arrest of Thomas Howard, 3rd Duke of Norfolk, in 1546/7. Prior to signing the submission, Norfolk sent Mary a copy of it, explaining that he only signed it because it would allow him a measure of freedom, and Mary signified her agreement to his signing it. This implies that Norfolk had no intention of carrying through with his promise not to intervene, or perhaps he was hedging his bets, unsure of which side would ultimately be successful.

Ridolfi wrote to Mary Queen of Scots in January 1571, informing her that he was a Papal agent and offering to act as her representative at the courts of Rome, Madrid, and Brussels, in an attempt to stir them into action on Mary's behalf. This is the first real act of the Ridolfi Plot. Ridolfi did in fact travel to Rome and Spain to try and convince the Pope and Philip of Spain that an enterprise against England was desirable and achievable. Philip declared that he would not invade England before the Catholic nobles rebelled.[13] His Armada wouldn't sail until after Mary's execution in 1587 and would ultimately be defeated by the British weather and a couple of fire ships. The plan was for a concerted attack, so had it already failed with Philip's refusal? Quite possibly, although it did not have much chance of succeeding in the first place. Ridolfi had also been responsible for distributing copies of the *Regnans in Excelsis* excommunication bull against Elizabeth I in England, having smuggled them into the country, so he definitely seemed to be very anti-Elizabeth. Although Cecil and Walsingham seem to have exposed the plot and the plotters relatively easily, it could have ended very differently for Elizabeth and her government had Philip decided to launch his Armada in 1571 rather than waiting until after Mary's execution, in 1588. It was Mary's execution which finally pushed Philip to action, but he had lost his most viable alternative to Elizabeth with Mary's death.

It seems that the Duke of Norfolk had needed quite a lot of persuasion to get involved in another conspiracy, having been imprisoned once already. On 8 February 1571, Mary Queen of Scots wrote to Norfolk to tell him that Ridolfi was going to advise Philip of Spain that there were many English nobles who would raise arms for Mary if they had Philip's financial and military support. She also made it clear that Norfolk would need to convert to Catholicism if the Spanish were to support the proposed marriage between them and launch an invasion on their behalf. Norfolk was Church of England which was considered heretical by the Catholic powers. His grandfather, Thomas Howard, 3rd Duke of Norfolk, was a staunch Catholic though his father, Henry Howard, Earl of Surrey, was known to have reformist sympathies, despite being raised in a Catholic household. Historian Anne Somerset argues that Norfolk was 'too spineless' to resist the pressure applied from both Mary Queen of Scots and Roberto di Ridolfi and, as he had already forfeited Elizabeth's favour, he could not afford to lose Mary's as well.[14] Ridolfi then made a personal visit to see Norfolk on 10 March 1571. He asked Norfolk to sign letters to the Pope, Philip II of Spain, and the Duke of Alba in support of plans for rebellion, but Norfolk refused. Ridolfi went away and drew up the letters anyway, along with a detailed set of instructions, supposedly from Norfolk. Mary Queen of Scots also wrote to Norfolk, encouraging him to escape from house arrest so that they could marry.[15] After discussions between Ridolfi, the Bishop of Ross, and the Duke of

Norfolk's secretary, William Barker, it was agreed that Barker should visit the Spanish ambassador, de Spes, and explain that, although Norfolk dared not put his signature to the documents, he approved of their contents and endorsed the requests made within them. How far Norfolk knew of what was being said in his name is unknown, but he did seem to be genuinely reluctant to get involved in any more conspiracies. No doubt spending time in the Tower of London under threat of execution would do that to any sane and sensible man.

Ridolfi set off for Brussels on 24 March where he had an audience with the Duke of Alba and asked him to press Philip of Spain to send an army to England to unseat Elizabeth and replace her with Mary Queen of Scots. Alba questioned whether it was the right time to launch an invasion, but he did admit to the 'essential desirability of the project'.[16] Alba and Philip both wanted to unseat Elizabeth and replace her but there were questions over finance and support for the plans in England. Alba dismissed Ridolfi, not believing his assurances that rebel forces in England would simultaneously manage to free Mary from her captivity, take control of the Tower of London which housed the armoury and the Royal Mint, and seize Elizabeth. It does seem quite unachievable, especially as Ridolfi could not be sure of the numbers who would rise in support of a rebellion. The Northern Rising had proven that large numbers could be gathered, but that the circumstances needed to be right for success, and that it needed a common aim that all believed in. Alba thought that it would only be worthwhile to send troops to England once Elizabeth was captured or dead, otherwise it could be a colossal waste of time, money, and men. Could Elizabeth have been overthrown without additional support? It is possible, but not very likely. The Pope blessed the mission as a Catholic uprising led by the Duke of Norfolk and backed by Spanish troops aiming to put Mary Queen of Scots on the English throne. However, he refused to give more tangible and concrete assistance.

That very same day, 24 March 1571, Elizabeth sent a message to Mary Queen of Scots that James Douglas, 4th Earl of Morton, who would become regent for Mary's son, James VI of Scotland, the following year, had returned to Scotland from England. It was said that he intended to gain the agreement of the Scottish parliament that Mary could retake her throne, possibly ruling alongside her underage son as joint monarchs. Morton had actually been active in obtaining the consent of Mary to abdicate the Scottish throne in 1568 and defeated her forces at the Battle of Langside that year. Whether he actually intended to, or believed that he could, obtain agreement for Mary to return to her throne is unknown. In April 1571, Morton wrote to Elizabeth and Cecil warning them to be wary of Mary plotting to escape her captivity. When he became Regent of Scotland in 1572, his actions put to bed the idea that Mary could return to her throne as he soundly defeated her supporters in Scotland. This put an end to the idea that Mary could be restored to her throne with native Scottish support. Morton would be forced to resign as regent in March 1578 when James VI, aged 11, declared that he would take power himself. Morton was accused in 1580 of complicity in the murder of Mary Queen of Scots' second husband, Henry, Lord Darnley, and was arrested. This could help to explain why he did not want Mary returned to Scotland in 1571, as she might have suspected his involvement. Morton was executed on 2 June 1581. He was James VI of Scotland's final regent and ended the civil war in Scotland over the position of Mary Queen of Scots, who would remain imprisoned in England.

On 12 April 1571, Charles Bailly arrived from the Netherlands, was arrested at Dover, and sent under arrest to William Brooke, 10th Baron Cobham, in London. Bailly had mastered several languages so was a useful agent to travel abroad and carry out foreign plots on Mary Queen of Scots' behalf. Bailly was courier to the Bishop of Ross, one of Mary's staunch supporters. Bailly had in his possession a copy of *A Treatise Concerning the Defence of the Honour of … Mary Queen of Scotland* written by the Bishop of Ross. Ross initially published the treatise under a pseudonym, Morgan Phillips, in order to divert attention from himself at a time when he was heavily involved in plotting for Mary against Elizabeth. This treatise suggests that Ross felt he had a strong duty to protect Mary and her rights as both Queen of Scotland and heir to the Queen of England.[17] As time passed, the chance of Mary being restored to the Scottish throne lessened. Ross argued that Mary was still Queen of Scotland, in spite of the fact that she had abdicated in 1568 in favour of her son, as the abdication was forced, and that she was the right and lawful successor to the English crown. There was also a suggestion that Mary would make a better alternate Queen of England to Elizabeth, not just as her successor. This treatise encompassed the arguments that were made to promote and support the Ridolfi Plot, and the later Throckmorton (1583) and Babington (1586) Plots as well.

Lord Cobham would later be suspected of complicity in the plotting in spite of Charles Bailly being put into his custody. Perhaps the suspicion was that Bailly had corrupted him. Bailly was also carrying a packet of letters in cipher from Ridolfi to the Bishop of Ross, which confirmed his involvement with Mary Queen of Scots, as Ross was an ardent supporter of Mary. The letters were supposed to be passed to William Cecil on Bailly's arrest, but Ross managed to intercept them and replace them with a less incriminating packet of letters. Bailly was sent to the Marshalsea prison, where he was kept in a cell with William Herle, who was in fact a government informant. Cecil had a hunch something was being kept from him, hence the deception of putting Bailly in a cell with a government agent, hoping he would reveal something more incriminating. After a couple of weeks in prison, Bailly confessed to knowledge of Ridolfi's discussions with the Duke of Alba in the Netherlands about the possibility of a foreign invasion to overthrow Elizabeth. Cecil had Bailly removed to the Tower of London for further questioning, where he was racked. Under torture, he admitted that Ridolfi had left England on 25 March 1571 with appeals from Mary Queen of Scots to the Duke of Alba, Philip II of Spain, and the Pope, to fund and organise an invasion of England. This invasion was intended to overthrow Elizabeth, put Mary on the throne in her place, and return England to Catholicism and Papal obedience. Bailly then admitted that he was carrying a letter addressed only to '40' and that he understood this to be a codename for an English nobleman, but he did not know the identity of the gentleman. There was another nobleman as well, codename '30', but Bailly was also unaware of that gentleman's identity.

William Cecil, Sir Ralph Sadler, Sir Walter Mildmay, and Thomas Radcliffe, 3rd Earl of Sussex, visited John Leslie, Bishop of Ross, on 13 May to question him; they learned that Roberto di Ridolfi had letters from Mary Queen of Scots to the Duke of Alba, Philip II of Spain, and the Pope concerning plans for funds and troops to come to Mary's assistance. George Talbot, 6th Earl of Shrewsbury, Mary's gaoler, was instructed to try and get Mary to reveal more of what she knew about the Ridolfi Plot, and to stop her sending and receiving letters. Perhaps it was hoped that stopping Mary's letters would at least delay the plotters, who either would not act without Mary's consent, or would believe they had been discovered and might try to be more careful. Ross admitted that Norfolk had spoken with the Duke of Alba and had proposed Harwich as the ideal port to land foreign troops at the time of an invasion. He claimed that Alba was the nobleman known as '30' and John Lumley, 1st Baron Lumley, was the nobleman known as '40'.[18] Lumley was son-in-law to Henry Fitzalan, 12th Earl of Arundel, who was also suspected of involvement in the conspiracy. Another suggestion is that '40' was actually the Duke of Norfolk.[19] This seems to make more sense, as Norfolk was a key conspirator in the plot, even if he was not always aware of how much his name was being thrown around and linked to the plotting. The letter, regarding '30' and '40' contained a detailed account of Ridolfi's meeting in Brussels with the Duke of Alba, where Alba had said, subject to Philip's approval, that Ridolfi would have all the assistance he required in order to rescue Mary and overthrow Elizabeth.

Ridolfi arrived in Madrid to meet with Philip of Spain at the end of June 1571. Philip appeared to believe Ridolfi's assurances that the English, particularly the Catholic population, would rise in support of a Spanish army that aimed to capture Queen Elizabeth. This seems naïve, without any real evidence. There was a meeting of the Spanish council on 7 July 1571 at which there was a suggestion that Elizabeth should be assassinated by a Spanish agent, but this was overruled in favour of sending a military force under the Duke of Alba from the Netherlands to England with the aim of unseating Elizabeth and placing Mary Queen of Scots on the throne. This is a similar plan to that proposed in 1588 with the Spanish Armada, although at that point an alternative to Mary Queen of Scots would have to be found. Alba protested the plan, but Philip claimed that they needed to overthrow Elizabeth in order to recover control of the Netherlands. Elizabeth was debating involvement in the Dutch Revolt and would eventually send troops in 1585. This method of invasion would later be echoed in the plans for the Spanish Armada in 1588, the ships of which were supposed to escort ships carrying soldiers from the Netherlands to England to undertake an invasion, but the British weather along with the use of fire ships would ultimately scupper that plan.

The full extent of the plotting was finally revealed in summer 1571 when John Leslie, Bishop of Ross, was arrested and confessed to what he knew. William Cecil had intercepted some documentary evidence to support the confession. Initially, Ross was put under house arrest where he insisted that his letters only related to Mary's correspondence with her supporters in Scotland and on the continent about rescuing her from English captivity and restoring her to the Scottish throne. He insisted that they did not relate to a projected invasion of England in Mary's support or aiming to replace Elizabeth on the English throne. Ross' ambassadorial status as Mary Queen of Scots' representative in England prevented him from being tortured as Charles Bailly, the courier, had been. Cecil was convinced that, if Ross made a statement outlining what he knew, the case against the

Duke of Norfolk would be watertight and he could be executed. This is what Cecil wanted to achieve, along with implicating Mary Queen of Scots, revealing the extent of her involvement in the plotting, and the danger she posed to Elizabeth and to England more generally. Mary was not deeply enough involved in the plotting at this time to warrant any serious talk of her execution. That would come in the following years as she became more desperate.

Elizabeth, however, was convinced of Mary Queen of Scots' complicity in the plot, intriguing with Philip of Spain and Pope Pius V in planning an invasion of England, the deposition of Elizabeth, and the restoration of Catholicism and Papal obedience. Mary denied any wrongdoing and would continue to do so through further plots in which she was involved, as well as her treason trial, dying in the guise of a martyr in 1587. This was despite plenty of evidence of her involvement, as will be seen later, including letters and testimony from the twenty years of her incarceration in England. Elizabeth refused to execute Mary at this point but declared that her cousin would be kept in closer confinement from now on to prevent any further plotting on her part. Mary had been moved to Sheffield Castle in November 1570, where she would remain for fifteen years until after the uncovering of the Throckmorton Plot where she was moved into even closer confinement at Chartley. Obviously, this closer confinement was not entirely successful with further conspiracies uncovered in 1583 and 1586, though how far Mary was set up, especially during the Babington Plot in 1586, is still debated. Mary declared that there had been nothing wrong in her conduct, and that she had not plotted any rebellion against Elizabeth. However, Mary did claim that Elizabeth had encouraged rebellion in Scotland and deprived her of her throne, perhaps trying to account for her own actions. Mary would continue to pass the buck, blaming anyone but herself for the trouble she found herself in.

At the end of August 1571, Mary Queen of Scots requested that part of her pension from the French crown, as a former Queen of

France, be sent to her supporters in Scotland to assist her. The money had been sent to the French ambassador in London while Mary was imprisoned in England. He contacted the Duke of Norfolk to arrange the transport of the money north. On 29 August 1571, Norfolk's secretaries, Robert Higford, and William Barker, handed a bag to a draper in Shrewsbury called Thomas Browne, instructing it to be delivered to Laurence Bannister, steward of the Dacre estates in the north. The Dacres were known to be a Catholic family and had been involved in the Pilgrimage of Grace in 1536 and the Northern Rising in 1569. Browne opened the package to discover £500 in gold (around £120,000 today), along with several letters in cipher, which made him particularly suspicious and so he alerted William Cecil in London. This made Cecil aware of Norfolk's actions and gave him evidence to use against him. The gold could be linked not only to Norfolk, but also to the French ambassador. Norfolk's secretaries and his agent in Shrewsbury were arrested and threatened with the rack, which made them reveal everything that they knew. Norfolk was more than just a courier: his house in London was searched and several more letters written in cipher were found, one of which Mary had sent to Norfolk in February 1571 recommending Ridolfi to him. This linked Mary, Norfolk, and Ridolfi inexplicably together and thus they were all logically involved in the plotting. The key to a cipher used to communicate with Mary Queen of Scots was found hidden between the tiles on the roof of Howard House. Norfolk could not legitimately deny that he was more involved in the plotting than he had ever admitted before, given the evidence that emerged from the search of his London home.

On 4 September 1571, Thomas Howard, 4th Duke of Norfolk, was arrested and again sent to the Tower of London three days later. Elizabeth refused to listen to any more of his pleas for mercy after his previous arrest two years earlier and promises not to get involved again with Mary Queen of Scots. Elizabeth had visited Norfolk on her summer progress at Audley End, just four days before his arrest and she had accepted his promise of loyalty and allegiance then. Perhaps this was just so that he would not panic and flee before he could be arrested. Norfolk refused to sign a statement of his involvement and guilt prepared by Sir Ralph Sadler, hence he was sent to the Tower. He had already been arrested before during the Northern Rising in 1569 in relation to his rumoured marriage to Mary Queen of Scots. When Norfolk was again linked to plotting with Mary Queen of Scots, Elizabeth was unwilling to give him another chance. By 11 October Norfolk had admitted that he had broken his oath to have no further dealings with Mary, and he confessed to having received a secret visit from Ridolfi as well. Norfolk had broken his word which was pretty damning in itself. However, he was adamant that Ridolfi had made no suggestion of a foreign invasion of England, claiming that Ridolfi only wanted to raise money abroad which would then be used to assist Mary's supporters in Scotland. If this was true then Norfolk had been incredibly naïve, but it seems unlikely that Norfolk would not at least have heard rumours of what was planned. He had to at least have suspected.

Norfolk stated that he refused to have anything to do with the plotting and had declined to sign any letters addressed to the Duke of Alba, Philip II of Spain, or the Pope. He said that his secretary, William Barker, had visited the Spanish ambassador without his knowledge or his permission. Barker crumbled when threatened with the rack and said that many nobles favoured the marriage between Norfolk and Mary Queen of Scots and spoke of invasion plans with foreign assistance aiming to land at Dumbarton, Leith, and Harwich.[20] According to Barker, Norfolk was aware of all of these plans, meaning that he was not innocent in the slightest. Even had he not acted in the plotting, failing to reveal what he knew was still treason and could be prosecuted as such. The suggestion is that Norfolk was pulled into conspiracy by more forceful characters than himself and that he did not really want to be involved. Had he made it clear to the conspirators that he was loyal to Elizabeth, Ridolfi might not have been so free in using his name in Brussels, Rome, and Madrid. Norfolk was culpable in the plotting by not openly declaring his loyalties.

It was only due to Elizabeth's direct intervention that Mary and John Leslie, Bishop of Ross, avoided sharing Norfolk's fate. Both were high-profile figures with plenty of supporters in Scotland and abroad. Execution could quite easily have resulted in war which Elizabeth was keen to avoid. There were demands from Parliament and the clergy that Mary should be executed and demands from the Scottish government to hand Ross over to them as a rebel. William Cecil, when Elizabeth refused to execute Mary, was trying to persuade her to hand Mary over to the Scottish to be tried for the murder of her second husband, Henry Stuart, Lord Darnley. Elizabeth did not like this idea either, even to get rid of Mary. The English had already attempted to try Mary for Darnley's murder when she first arrived in England, but the results were inconclusive. The execution of the Duke of Norfolk was a compromise of sorts. Unmasking the premier, and only, English duke as a traitor 'struck a blow to the heart of the Elizabethan state'.[21] Norfolk was the last duke in England; the country would be without a duke for the remainder of Elizabeth's reign, and well into the reign of James I, until 1623 when George Villiers, a favourite of the king, was created 1st Duke of Buckingham. This can be seen as a way of curbing the power of the nobility and limiting their ability to act against the monarchy.

By mid-September 1571 there was a royal warrant granted for the torture of Norfolk's servants to gain more information about the conspiracy. A month later, Cecil was completely convinced of Norfolk's guilt and released a tract called *Salutem in Christo*, to explain the conspiracy to the public. '*Salutem in Christo*' translates literally as 'Greetings in Christ' but it can also be taken to mean 'Joy in Christ', perhaps highlighting the joy that people felt that a conspiracy against their queen had been discovered and the plotters punished. Lisa Hilton describes it as a private letter from 'RG' which 'accidentally' found its way into the public domain. The plot has since become known as the Ridolfi Plot, although Ridolfi himself was known only as 'the messenger'.[22] The fact that Ridolfi is not named in the tract supports the idea that he was in fact a government spy, working for Walsingham and Cecil all along to report on, and perhaps act as the catalyst for, revolt. The tract claimed that Mary was responsible for the Northern Rising, that she had conspired to marry the Duke of Norfolk and had planned to take London and receive troops from the Netherlands, as well as promote an invasion of Ireland to weaken Elizabeth's hold there, all of which had been enabled by the Bishop of Ross.[23] Mary Queen of Scots had declared her right to the English throne on the death of Mary I in 1558, effectively claiming said throne rather than Elizabeth. At the time, Mary was married to the French Dauphin, Francis, who would become Francis II the following year in 1559. This declaration was used in the tract as a way of supporting the argument that Mary intended to take the English throne in 1571, thirteen years after her first pronouncement of her claim to the throne. There is no record that Mary herself declared her right to the English throne after Francis's death in December 1560. The tract ends by praying that God will keep Elizabeth 'under his special protection' to reign over England in peace.[24] The peace would not last, and Mary would continue to be a thorn in Elizabeth's and Cecil's sides for another fifteen years.

Francis Walsingham sent a letter to William Cecil on 8 October 1571 regarding the relationship between Mary Queen of Scots and the Duke of Norfolk, the latter of whom was described as 'a most dangerous subject, and that he should be so earnest in seeking the Queen of Scots' liberty, who was to the Queen so dangerous an enemy'.[25] The key word here is 'dangerous': Norfolk and Mary Queen of Scots were considered to be dangerous to both Elizabeth and the English state as well as the Protestant religion. Norfolk seemed to be absolutely desperate to free Mary from her captivity. However, he was being watched after his initial arrest in 1569, so there was no way that he could get away with any further conspiracy as was proven by his arrest in 1571. In November 1571, Norfolk wrote to Cecil asking him to intercede with Elizabeth on his behalf but Elizabeth herself charged Norfolk with treason, drawn from his own confessions made in the Tower. She refused to grant him mercy.

William Cecil obtained a ruling on 17 October which said that any ambassador who sought to foment rebellion in the realm to which they were sent forfeited any right to diplomatic immunity. This was intended to stop foreign ambassadors trying to persuade their masters to send an army to England, aimed at both Scotland and Spain in this instance as ambassadors for both countries had been pushing for an invasion of England. This ruling would become very significant for Spain, who seemed to be the most involved in plots across Elizabeth's reign. Spain was the leading Catholic power and they saw Elizabeth as a heretic usurper and Mary Queen of Scots as the rightful Queen of England. As a result of this ruling, Mary's representative in England, John Leslie, Bishop of Ross was arrested and taken to the Tower on 24 October. He expected that he would be racked if he did not reveal what he knew, so he did just that. Ross confirmed that Norfolk was the nobleman known as '40' and explained that he had sent the letter from Ridolfi, which Bailly had carried to England, to the Duke of Norfolk.

Thomas Howard, 4th Duke of Norfolk, pleaded not guilty but was tried and sentenced to death for treason in Westminster Hall on 6 January 1572. Norfolk claimed that Ridolfi had only written to him as he had lent him some money and wanted to discuss its repayment. This would be an innocent communication, but there was other, more damning, evidence against him, found in the search of his house. The peers of the jury did not believe his innocent explanation. He could not deny having received the letter from Mary Queen of Scots, which was found in his house, but he claimed he was horrified when he read it. That does not explain why he kept it and did not burn it or hand it over to Walsingham or Cecil to deal with. Mary denied that it was in fact she who had written the letter. Elizabeth delayed in signing the death warrant, as she would later do with Mary Queen of Scots in 1586/7. Elizabeth was reluctant to execute England's premier noble and only duke, so his life was preserved for a couple of months. She actually signed the warrant four times, revoking it each time, once revoking it at 2 a.m. on the morning of the execution. Perhaps she was haunted by the thought of executing one of her Boleyn/Howard relatives.[26] Norfolk was Elizabeth's second cousin (the grandchild of her great-uncle). Elizabeth did not want to be seen as cruel or unmerciful. Norfolk was eventually executed on Tower Hill on 2 June 1571. Parliament was still pushing for the execution of Mary Queen of Scots who was heavily implicated in the Ridolfi Plot, but Elizabeth held out. She did not want to try and execute a sister monarch, one of God's anointed. This could undermine Elizabeth's own power and position and would become a key part of Elizabeth's hesitation in 1587 even when faced with incontrovertible proof of Mary's guilt. A compromise between Elizabeth and Parliament meant that Norfolk was executed, but Mary was spared, even though the plot would not have happened without Mary's involvement.

William Brooke, 10th Baron Cobham, was imprisoned for several months for his supposed involvement in the plot, although the evidence against him was not strong. His wife, Lady Frances Cobham, retired from the court for a while as a result. She was also suspected of involvement due to her friendship with the Duke of Norfolk. Cobham would recover his political standing and would become a Knight of the Garter in 1585 and a member of the Privy Council in 1586. These appointments suggest that he was not heavily involved, and may have just been on a periphery, perhaps as an error of judgement rather than a conscious slide into rebellion.

It was after the uncovering of the Ridolfi Plot in 1571 that William Cecil was created Baron Burghley and a Knight of the Garter in 1572. Perhaps this was at least in part due to his involvement in uncovering the Ridolfi Plot; at least the timing suggests this. No doubt his years of service to Elizabeth, even before she became queen, also played a large role in his elevation to the peerage. Cecil had administered Elizabeth's lands when both Edward VI and Mary I were on the throne, and he was greatly trusted by Elizabeth throughout her reign, only being banished temporarily from her presence for his involvement in the execution of Mary Queen of Scots when the council enacted the warrant without the queen's direct command for them to do so.

Elizabeth came across very much as a 'political strategist' in the Ridolfi Plot.[27] She worked closely with both Cecil and Walsingham, drew up the charges against the Duke of Norfolk herself, met with Ridolfi, and authorised the use of torture on Norfolk's servants. These actions demonstrate that Elizabeth was personally at the heart of stamping out these conspiracies and, although some historians argue that Elizabeth was in a way manipulated by Cecil in particular across her reign, her involvement in this plot shows that she was fully informed and involved in strategising how to deal with it. She was advised and consulted on all actions taken. It was her personal intervention in this case that prevented the government proceeding against Mary Queen of Scots. Elizabeth managed to go about her normal business, going on progress and meeting ambassadors, while this conspiracy was coming together around her. She was willing to gamble with her own safety to bring down those who would wish her harm, being more concerned with keeping the power to hand out the succession as she saw fit in her own hands, rather than guarding against the crown falling into the wrong hands. In a sense, Elizabeth's actions were to protect her own power rather than considering what was best for England. She believed she had a divine right to rule so was determined to do what she needed to do to protect herself and England. Perhaps she also believed that Mary was unworthy to be queen, given her involvement in plotting and her poor judgement in her marriages.

Guerau de Spes, the Spanish ambassador, was expelled from England in the aftermath of the Ridolfi Plot for his involvement in it. Mary Queen of Scots was held in closer confinement at Sheffield Castle as a result of her involvement in the plot, still under the guardianship of George Talbot, 6th Earl of Shrewsbury. She was not allowed to ride or hunt in the adjoining parks initially, though these restrictions were eventually eased for her health. Her household was reduced to sixteen servants in 1571, but by 1580 this had increased to over forty servants. When the French learned that Mary had asked Ridolfi to obtain aid from the Spanish to assist in her release, it lessened French sympathy for their former queen, which the English government tried to exploit by sending to France copies of letters which Mary had written to the Duke of Alba. They aimed to alienate the French from Mary's cause. Elizabeth and Cecil were taking advantage of a situation which could have resulted in the assassination of the queen to turn foreign support away from Mary.

A new Treasons Act was introduced in 1571 which made it illegal to deny Elizabeth's right to the throne, or call her heretic, tyrant, or usurper. It was also treason to intend harm to the Queen, to levy war against her, incite others to levy war against her, question the succession to the throne, assert that someone else had the right of succession to the throne, or to say that Parliament could not govern the succession to the throne. This was intended to make any future conspiracies treason and to clarify exactly what treason was. This act effectively reinstated the Treasons Act of 1534, which was brought in by Elizabeth's father, Henry VIII, but was repealed by her brother, Edward VI, in 1547. This Act under Henry VIII was the first time that treason could be committed in speech or thought and not just actions. When the Act was introduced in 1534, it resulted in the executions of John Fisher, Bishop of Rochester, and Sir Thomas More. Another Act was passed in 1571 alongside the Treasons Act, the Act Against Fugitives Over the Sea that focused on Catholics who chose exile rather than remaining in England, naming them rebels and traitors, which would have meant that they could be tried for treason if they returned to England. These new parliamentary measures were intended to further protect Elizabeth and the English throne from those who would wish harm. They meant that rebels and conspirators in the future would suffer the harshest punishment without question for their actions. It would entrap those who claimed that Mary Queen of Scots had a better claim to the throne than Elizabeth and make it difficult not to demand execution for their crimes.

Roberto di Ridolfi would eventually die in February 1612 in Florence as a respected senator, without having suffered any punishment for his plotting against Elizabeth and the English government. He had left England after the plot unravelled to serve the Medici dukes. He managed to get away, unlike many conspirators against Elizabeth. Because Ridolfi was in Paris when the plot was exposed, there was not much chance of Cecil, Walsingham, and Elizabeth getting hold of him. Directly after the plot he went into the service of the Pope before entering politics in Florence. Perhaps it was an error of judgement to leave Ridolfi at liberty in November 1569 to continue plotting against the queen and state. There are definite indications that Ridolfi was a double agent and playing a dangerous game. How did he manage to get away without any punishment if he really was conspiring against the crown? Ridolfi left England only after a personal interview with Elizabeth and was given a passport to do so. He was also lax about security, writing to Mary Queen of Scots in plain English rather than any form of cipher.[28] The downfall of the Duke of Norfolk could have suited both Cecil and Mary Queen of Scots, so perhaps this was the plan all along, although it does seem like a very long game with a by no means certain outcome. The circumstances of his leaving England suggest that Ridolfi was in fact a government agent, and perhaps acted as a catalyst to bring out those who really would revolt against their queen.

The Ridolfi Plot opened the eyes of Elizabeth's government that there was some underground plotting going on, not just to affect the succession, but actually to overthrow the queen in favour of a replacement with a very different religious bent. This was over more than just the succession. It was in a sense a battle between Protestant and Catholic, the new and the old ways. In many ways this plot can be explained by the publication in February 1570 of the bull of excommunication against Elizabeth, which absolved her subjects of their loyalty and allegiance towards her. It opened the door for plotting and conspiracies for many years to come. As a result of this plot, Elizabeth would also stop working to restore Mary to the Scottish throne. She came to believe that Mary was not worthy of a crown and country, and that Scotland would be better off under James VI and a regency than allowing Mary to retake the throne. The Ridolfi Plot made Cecil and Walsingham focus more on possible revolts and conspirators in the future. Perhaps it was this plot that encouraged Walsingham to grow the intelligence network which would ultimately bring Mary Queen of Scots to her execution in Fotheringhay Castle in February 1587.

It was not just that senses were opened to plots and conspirators lurking, but the eyes of the people were also opened to Mary Queen of Scots. To many she was a romantic figure, trapped in the wilds of England, who had lost her liberty and her son, but with the Ridolfi Plot and her involvement in it, these opinions began to change. Mary began to be seen as a foreign-born Catholic trying to depose the rightful English Protestant queen.[29] The Ridolfi Plot marked a clear turning point in how the English people saw Mary. Prior to 1571, there had not really been any definite proof against her and so it was easy to believe her innocent. There was evidence of Mary's involvement with Ridolfi, however, and Cecil made sure that this became common knowledge. If the people knew that Mary was willing to act against Elizabeth, and with foreign assistance, it would raise English xenophobia and national pride, which would peak with the Spanish Armada in 1588 and Elizabeth's speech at Tilbury: 'I know I have the body but of a weak and feeble woman, but I have the heart and stomach of a King, and of a King of England, too.' This sense of national pride awoke in the English people when their beloved Protestant queen was threatened by a foreign Catholic one. For many of the English people, it was the fact that they loved their queen, that she was the daughter of Henry VIII, and that she seemed determined to protect England, that made them come out for her and turn against Mary.

The Ridolfi Plot, along with those engineered by Throckmorton (1583) and Babington (1586), set off a chain of events assisted by a darkening international scene, and bitter Catholic vs. Protestant conflict, which would lead in 1587 to the execution of Mary Queen of Scots. The plotting in 1571 changed the minds of many about Mary Queen of Scots. Norfolk was seen as a sacrifice so that Cecil could bring Mary's plotting out into the open. Mary was cast as a serpent who wished to kill Elizabeth.[30] It is quite possible that the plot was a complete fabrication by Francis Walsingham to bring Mary Queen of Scots' perfidy out into the open and try and stem any future plots with her at the centre before they got started. There was also a crackdown on those practising the Catholic faith, as plots against Elizabeth seemed to swirl around those who favoured the old religion. If this was the plan, it certainly seemed to work for a while. There would be no more major plots against Elizabeth until that in 1583 which took its name from Sir Francis Throckmorton.

Chapter 4

Throckmorton Plot 1583

'To remove her Majesty from her Crowne and state'[1]

Probably one of the most complex of the myriad conspiracies against Elizabeth I, the Throckmorton Plot of 1583, involved England, France, and Spain, the latter of whom were heavily implicated in supposed military involvement and support. The French harboured those rebels who had fled England but continued to plot in support of Mary Queen of Scots. While there were plenty of conspirators, there was only a single execution as a result of this conspiracy. Like the Ridolfi Plot before it, the Throckmorton Plot would also result in a Spanish ambassador being banished from England. It built on what the Ridolfi Plot had started, hoping to replace Elizabeth I on the English throne with Mary Queen of Scots once she had been broken out of her captivity at Sheffield Castle. Part of the plan included a foreign invasion, as possible landing points were scouted along the Sussex coast by the conspirators.

The Throckmorton Plot was much more than just a plan to usurp and replace a woman seen as an illegitimate and heretic ruler. It was a result of the French succession crisis, rather than the English succession crisis, and Throckmorton himself was no more than a cog in a bigger international machine.[2] Francis Throckmorton played only a small, but very significant, part in the plotting. The French kings repeatedly seemed to die without issue; it was hoped that, if Mary Queen of Scots was on the English throne and could marry once more into the French royal family (she had previously been married to Francis II of France who died in 1560) and produce an heir, it would secure the succession to both the English and French thrones in one fell swoop. France would be a great power in the world, in combination with England, to rival Spain and the Empire. Throckmorton likely did not understand these wider international implications and did not see past the immediate future of overthrowing Elizabeth, whom he saw as a Protestant heretic, and replacing her with the Catholic Mary Queen of Scots. The Catholic vs. Protestant divide would be at the heart of rebellions in support of Mary, with Catholics generally on Mary's side.

The key figure in the plot was Francis Throckmorton (also sometimes written Throgmorton). He was the seventh of eight sons of a well-known West Midlands Catholic family and was educated at Oxford in the 1570s, where he was hugely influenced by Catholics and may have first developed some of the ideas which later led to his involvement in rebellion. He then entered the Inner Temple in London in 1576 to train for a career in law. The family seat was at Coughton Court in Warwickshire. This is where the wives of the conspirators involved in the Gunpowder Plot in 1605 had waited for news of the success or failure of the plot, giving Coughton Court a further Catholic connection. Throckmorton had been seen in the company of idealistic young Catholics, and by the late 1570s his family were attending household Masses celebrated by a missionary priest. Sir Nicholas Throckmorton, the prominent English diplomat was Francis's uncle, and Francis's cousin, Bess Throckmorton, would become the wife of Sir Walter Raleigh. He was thus well connected and seemed to have had a bright future ahead of him by 1579 in spite of his religious leanings. There does not really seem to be any witnesses as to his character. We can only infer from the scant surviving evidence. The historian John Cooper states that Throckmorton had seemed like an 'unlikely revolutionary' who 'rejected the quiet loyalism of the Catholic mainstream'.[3] Perhaps he had a determination to see Catholics worshipping in public and not being forced to do it behind closed doors and it was this that pushed him to act in a revolutionary way. Elizabeth had appeared to promote acceptance of differences in religion, but her line hardened as the years passed and plots built up against her. Throckmorton's story has to be reconstructed from trial records and other government papers, which may not necessarily be entirely true as the story could have been adapted for propaganda purposes.

In 1580, Throckmorton travelled abroad in France and Spain. It was in Paris that he met both Thomas Morgan and Charles Paget, who would become important in both the Throckmorton and Babington Plots. They were Catholic agents of Mary Queen of Scots and, as result of this meeting, Throckmorton agreed to act as a courier for Mary when he returned to England. In 1581, Francis Throckmorton entered the household of the French ambassador, Michel de Castelnau, at Salisbury Court in London. By Christmas of that year, an embassy official, Claude de Courcelles, had recruited him to handle Mary Queen of Scots' correspondence from her supporters in Scotland and on the continent. Mary's letters were probably smuggled from Throckmorton's house at St Paul's Wharf in London by boat along the Thames to Salisbury Court and then left England for the continent in the French diplomatic bag. A secretary of the French ambassador became a spy for the Tudor government in 1583 and passed correspondence to Walsingham, including packets of ciphered letters to and from Mary Queen of Scots.[4] It was thanks to this source that the government obtained fore-knowledge of the Throckmorton Plot and the involvement of the French and Spanish in it, as well as Throckmorton's role in facilitating communications between the players in the plot.

It has been argued that plots against Elizabeth I stepped up once it became clear that she would not marry and produce an heir.[5] This would leave Mary Queen of Scots as the heir presumptive. There was a gap of twelve years between this plot and the previous one, the Ridolfi Plot, of 1571. Although plotting did not stop during this time there were no concerted efforts to unseat Elizabeth I. By 1583, however, Elizabeth was too old to bear children and so the succession became an open question. Perhaps some people believed that, as Elizabeth would not have an heir of her body, they may as well replace her now with her successor, who naturally was assumed to be Mary Queen of Scots, Elizabeth's first cousin once removed. She also had an heir herself who was ruling in Scotland – James VI who, on Elizabeth's death in 1603, would become James I of England. However, by the terms of Henry VIII's will the rightful heir was Edward Seymour, Lord Beauchamp of Hache, son of Katherine Grey and nephew of the ill-fated Lady Jane Grey. Henry VIII had passed over the line of his elder sister, Margaret, from whom Mary Queen of Scots was descended, in favour of the line of his younger sister, Mary, from whom the Greys were descended. Both political and religious views were becoming more polarised in England by the early 1580s and reached a breaking point.[6] This polarisation of religious views along with the succession question combined to put Elizabeth in a vulnerable position and encouraged rebels to take advantage of the uncertainty and instability and act against her.

Sir Francis Walsingham, the queen's spymaster, knew that something was afoot early on in the plotting, but he was distracted by the troubles in Scotland, and only stumbled over the plot almost by accident. The Raid of Ruthven in August 1582 had led to the capture of James VI of Scotland, who only regained his freedom in June 1583. While James had been imprisoned talks had resumed to try and reach an agreement between Elizabeth I and Mary Queen of Scots, but when James gained his freedom, these talks once again broke down and were postponed indefinitely. Elizabeth received word that, even while these talks were ongoing, Mary was plotting against her. As a result of this, Elizabeth would stop fighting to restore Mary Queen of Scots to the Scottish throne. This is what Walsingham was preoccupied with while the Throckmorton Plot was unfolding under his nose.

*

In June 1583, Francis Throckmorton was contacted by Charles Paget, a member of the Guise household in Paris, whom he had met two years earlier while in France. So began the connections that would result in Throckmorton's execution after a failed plot that bore his name. Throckmorton would act as an intermediary between Mary Queen of Scots and the Spanish ambassador in England, Don Bernadino de Mendoza. Although the plot had Throckmorton's name, he really only had a supporting role as those pulling the strings were behind the scenes in Paris and Madrid.[7] Throckmorton acted as their representative in England. He took most of the punishment for the conspiracy; he was not the instigator nor even one of the main plotters, but he was the one that the English authorities could most easily get their hands on.

At the same time as Throckmorton was being contacted by Paget, a meeting was convened in Paris by Henry I, Duke of Guise, a cousin of Mary Queen of Scots, to discuss a possible invasion of England. Six other men aside from Guise attended the meeting: Guise's spiritual confessor, Claude Matthieu, Archbishop James Beaton of Glasgow, who was a great supporter of Mary Queen of Scots, the Pope's nuncio in Paris, Catelli, William Allen, who guided English Catholics in exile and founded the Catholic seminary at Rheims, and François de Roncherolles, the Governor of Paris, who gave a military briefing. Allen favoured an assault on England where the others instead preferred an attempted landing in Scotland then marching south into England. The potential problem with this plan was that the men would have to march all the way south through England to London, giving Elizabeth and her government more time to act, raise support, and fortify the city. The plot intended to bring about a Catholic invasion of England, led by the Duke of Guise, and financially backed by Philip II of Spain and Pope Gregory XIII (Pope Pius V had died in 1572). It seems that King Henry III of France was kept in ignorance of the plot, in spite of the fact that the Duke of Guise was to lead the invasion of England. The initial plan discussed in 1582 was to send an army to Scotland to capitalise on the friendship between James VI of Scotland and Esmé Stewart, 1st Earl of Lennox, but the Raid of Ruthven where James was captured put paid to this plan and the preferred invasion landing site moved to England.

By the end of June, the Duke of Guise had a solid plan in place. A force of 12,000 men under the command of the brother of William V, Duke of Bavaria, would sail from Spain to Flanders and then land in Lancashire, provoking a popular uprising of English Catholics to join their army and overthrow the queen. The Duke of Guise himself would then land with a smaller force on the Sussex coast where he would use the strongholds of the Earl of Northumberland at Petworth and the Earl of Arundel at Arundel Castle. Rumours suggested that Guise himself planned to marry Mary Queen of Scots and rule England himself. Guise had wanted to invade England for over a decade, but his plans always seemed to be frustrated by a lack of military or political will from Philip II of Spain.[8] There also appeared to be a lack of money to fund the enterprise. In July 1583, Guise travelled to Normandy to prepare for the invasion and sent a gentleman secretly to Petworth to negotiate with Henry Percy, 8th Earl of Northumberland, as well as making contact with the Spanish ambassador, Mendoza, through Charles Paget.

On 24 August 1583, John Halter, who owned a boat and shipped supplies back and forth across the English Channel, was approached in Dieppe and asked to take a gentleman over to England and then bring him back to Dieppe. He never knew the identity of the gentleman as a condition of the arrangement was his anonymity, but it was later discovered by Walsingham's agents to be Charles Paget who was the 'especiall messenger'.[9] Halter was working for a London merchant taking wooden boards to Dieppe and was due to return to England with cards and writing paper.[10] In the first week of September 1583, Paget travelled from Dieppe to the Sussex coast at Arundel with Halter, with the crossing taking fourteen hours, to survey the most likely points for forces of the Duke of Guise to safely land for an invasion. He first travelled to the home of William Davies at Patching. From there, Paget made contact with Henry Percy, 8th Earl of Northumberland, and Henry Fitzalan, 12th Earl of Arundel, who both had strongholds along the south coast of England, and he hoped for their support. It would be invaluable in allowing foreign troops to land safely along the coast. Alternatively, Arundel and Northumberland could make it very difficult for invading forces if they chose by leading the resistance against an invasion. Walsingham later investigated, questioned hundreds of witnesses, and found information that compromised Northumberland, implicating him in the plotting. On 25 September, Halter and Paget sailed back to Dieppe, arriving two days later. Halter was quite used to taking people across the English Channel. Many of those he smuggled across to France were members of the Earl of Northumberland's household, either Catholics themselves, or with Catholic connections. Paget stayed in Dieppe for a day before returning to Rouen.

Charles Paget was the most 'subtle' of the Paget family. He was from Beaudesert in Staffordshire and was raised as a Catholic along with his older brother, Thomas.[11] Paget had crossed to France without Elizabeth I's permission and had offered to spy for Walsingham. However, Elizabeth's ambassador in Paris, Sir Henry Cobham, said that Paget was a known supporter of Mary Queen of Scots and could not be trusted. Walsingham watched Paget closely using English agents in France, but Paget also had an alias he used when he needed to fly under the radar: Mope. This was the alias he had used on his trip across the Channel with Halter to scope out possible landing sites for foreign troops. In late October 1583, Lord Thomas Paget wrote to his brother, Charles, in Rouen to say that the English government were not impressed by his stay in Paris, his move to Rouen, and his mixing with English Catholic exiles. The letter likely never reached Paget as it was discovered filed away in Walsingham's papers after his death.

In October 1583, Francis Throckmorton's mother, Margery, was planning to try and get her son, Thomas, out of England. Another son,

George, had already attempted it but had been stopped at the port. Margery heard that the best way to leave England secretly was to make contact with Anne Howard, Countess of Arundel, at Arundel Castle. Anne Howard had converted to Catholicism in 1582. The countess could be approached through her physician, Dr Fryer. Margery Throckmorton wrote to Francis asking him to be at Lewisham the following day to meet Fryer.[12] Throckmorton had told his mother to command Thomas not to leave England. Francis needed to be careful not to provoke Elizabeth, Cecil, or Walsingham, as he was working secretly for the Catholic powers in Europe: he did not want to draw attention to that fact. Both Francis and Thomas Throckmorton had travelled in Europe as young men and had Catholic connections on the continent, including Sir Francis Englefield. Involved actively in plotting against Elizabeth I, Francis Throckmorton needed to avoid drawing attention to himself or those around him who could potentially betray him, either consciously or subconsciously.

Throckmorton had written to Mary Queen of Scots to inform her of the plot to mount an invasion on her behalf and rescue her from her captivity. Mary had been moving between Sheffield Castle and Sheffield Manor Lodge since November 1570. She would be moved in the aftermath of the Throckmorton Plot in 1584. She responded to say that she was already aware of the conspiracy, and had asked Throckmorton to try and sound out what support could be expected from English Catholics once the invasion got underway. Walsingham was convinced that England was the target for a 'Catholic-inspired invasion', but he remained ignorant of where the attack might actually come from.[13] He believed the French were behind it all and set a watch on the French embassy in London. This would be the break he needed. He learned that Francis Throckmorton would visit the embassy at night, so set spies onto him as well. After six months of surveillance on Throckmorton, Walsingham ordered his arrest. Throckmorton had written to several of the other conspirators to say that he would rather die than implicate anyone else in conspiring against Elizabeth.

He knew what the punishment would be. The standard sentence for treason was hanging, drawing, and quartering.

On 5 November 1583, Francis Throckmorton was arrested and questioned regarding what he knew about a plot to unseat Elizabeth and replace her on the English throne with Mary Queen of Scots, encompassing a foreign invasion. Lord Henry Howard was arrested the same day. When government agents had arrived to arrest him, Throckmorton ran upstairs to destroy a letter he had been writing to Mary Queen of Scots even then. The letter was destroyed but he did not manage to destroy a list of ports that might be used in an invasion or a list of Catholic nobles who, it was hoped, would support the plot, so these documents were left to testify against him. There was also a written pedigree which detailed Mary's claim to the English throne. This confirmed that the aim of the plot was to oust Elizabeth and replace her with Mary. A document published after the discovery of the plot described what was found in the house search as follows:

> twelue petidegrees of the discent of the Crowne of England, printed and published by the Bishop of Rosse, in the desence of the pretended title of the Scottish Queene his Mistresse, with certaine infamous libelles against her Maiestie printed & published beyond the seas … you wil iudge the purpose wherefore he kept them[14]

The inference was that someone would only keep those kinds of documents if they were planning something seditious or treasonous, in order to replace Elizabeth on the throne with Mary Queen of Scots. They were almost propaganda documents to persuade the people of Mary's right to the throne over Elizabeth. However, Throckmorton would claim that he was set up and that the incriminating papers 'were foisted in … among his papers by the gentlemen that searched his house'.[15] There was enough other evidence against Throckmorton to be fairly sure that this was not true.

Throckmorton had acted as a letter courier for Mary, recruited by Sir Francis Englefield while in Paris, and he implicated both Mary and the Spanish ambassador, Mendoza, in the plotting. Throckmorton also admitted to pressing Englefield to push Philip II of Spain to invade England. Lord Henry Howard, younger brother to the executed 4th Duke of Norfolk, was arrested at the same time and questioned, sent to the Fleet Prison, but was eventually released. He would survive the plot and would be created 1st Earl of Northampton under James I, as well as First Lord of the Treasury and Lord Privy Seal. Evidently there was not enough evidence against him in the plot. He did, however, undergo several periods of royal disfavour, and his reputation suffered as a result, but he would go on to successfully serve James I after Elizabeth's death. William Cecil, Lord Burghley, and Francis Walsingham had been keeping an eye on correspondence passing through the home of the French ambassador in London, which Throckmorton knew well, and he had been seen coming and going from the house several times which led to them suspecting him of involvement in the first place.

One vital piece of evidence was missed in the search of Throckmorton's house – a casket covered in green velvet which was spirited out of the house and given to a servant, John Meredith, who passed it onto the Spanish ambassador. Throckmorton later confessed that the casket contained letters for Mary Queen of Scots from Thomas Morgan in Paris. Quite possibly there were also other documents in there as well, though the exact contents are not known. When imprisoned in the Tower of London, Throckmorton was allowed to meet a lawyer who brought with him paper and books. Throckmorton wrote a note in one of the books wondering whether the casket was safe. The lawyer found the note and passed it on to one of Throckmorton's household servants. It was a huge risk for Throckmorton that appeared to pay off. Throckmorton also tried to get a message to his brother, George, hoping that he would back up Francis's assertion that the lists of Catholic nobles and invasion ports found when his house was searched were written by a servant called Edward Nutteby, and not him.[16] However, the note was intercepted, damning him further. On 13 November 1583, Walsingham made an entry in his notebook for George Throckmorton's arrest. Walsingham was determined to arrest all of those who were involved in the plot or implicated in it, and those who would act against the Queen. He would also have been very aware of the fact that his fate was tied up with that of Elizabeth. If she was overthrown, he would be one of the first to die, probably along with William Cecil, Lord Burghley.

Francis Throckmorton had been tracked from the French embassy by Laurent Feron, a London-born clerk, who worked for Walsingham and kept him supplied with the contents of the French diplomatic dispatches. He worked for Walsingham from within the French embassy itself. There was a raid on the French ambassador's residence which led to Feron being able to pass on months of incriminating correspondence to Walsingham's agent, Walter Williams. Walsingham had previously tried without success to infiltrate the French ambassador's residence, but this time it worked like a charm. Walsingham had believed that the chief threat to Elizabeth and to England was a pro-Catholic invasion from Scotland. The contents of the diplomatic dispatches proved that there was a far greater threat from France and Spain to worry about. It almost seemed like there were more threats than could possibly be dealt with.

Throckmorton was first taken to the house of the Master of the Royal Posts on St Peter's Hill in London where he remained for a couple of days before being transferred to the Tower of London. He was racked in the Tower on 16 November but failed to reveal anything of import in this initial session. Torture was never legal in England but was occasionally used in cases of treason or heresy, notably with Anne Askew who was burned for heresy in 1546 under Henry VIII. Throckmorton managed to smuggle a note out of the Tower written on the back of a playing card to the Spanish ambassador, Mendoza, saying that he would rather die a thousand deaths than betray his friends. Throckmorton was threatened with torture once again on 19 November and with the fear of this he made a full confession and betrayed all of those involved. He admitted that there was an international conspiracy to invade England, capture Elizabeth, and put Mary Queen of Scots on the throne in her place. He also disclosed that he had pressed foreign powers like France and Spain to invade England in support of the plot. Throckmorton said that he had been told by his contacts in France that the Duke of Guise was planning a naval assault and invasion of southern England which intended to deprive Elizabeth of her crown and replace her with Mary Queen of Scots, supported by the English Catholic nobility who would rise in concert. Guise was allegedly waiting to see whether Philip II of Spain or Pope Gregory XIII would provide him with any additional military or financial support as the plot was supposed to be bankrolled by Philip, though no money or aid had yet been seen from him. Throckmorton explained that Guise believed that this additional assistance would be forthcoming for the invasion as he was confident that they wanted Elizabeth overthrown as much as he did. Walsingham had feared a Catholic enterprise against England for years, but this was much larger than anything had had envisioned and made him more determined to get to the bottom of the plot, and more concerned for Elizabeth's safety both at the current time and in the future. Possibly this fear led to the manipulation of the Babington Plot to end the threat posed by Mary Queen of Scots forever.

Charles Paget's elder brother, Lord Thomas Paget, left London on 23 November 1583, ostensibly for his estates in Staffordshire, but in reality, he was heading for the Sussex coast in order to flee to France. He knew that Throckmorton had been arrested, that the conspiracy had been uncovered, and that he had only a very short window of time to escape before the government would be after him for his involvement. He would have feared arrest, torture, and the disgrace of his family. Paget reached the coast two days later at Ferring and set sail for France, along with Charles Arundel, another

Catholic plotter. The pair managed to escape Walsingham's clutches by leaving England without the queen's permission. They would never be able to return. Paget would become involved with the Babington Plot in 1586 while Arundel was suspected as the author of *Leicester's Commonwealth* (1584) which attacked Elizabeth's favourite, Robert Dudley, 1st Earl of Leicester.

Francis Walsingham knew that the Paget brothers, along with Charles Arundel, were in Paris, and wrote to the English ambassador there on 1 December 1583, Sir Edward Stafford, asking him to keep a close watch on them to try and avert any plotting, or at least have forewarning of any possible conspiracies or plots against Elizabeth and the English government. On 14 December, Lord Thomas Paget's solicitor and secretary, William Warde, was questioned by Walsingham's agents to try and gain any additional helpful information.[17] He was asked what he knew about Lord Paget's property and affairs, his departure for France, and the people he had been meeting at his house. The latter was important as it could suggest others who were possibly involved in the conspiracy or might know something about it. It led to others being questioned about what they knew, rather like a snowball or domino effect as more people became caught up in it.

Throckmorton was again interrogated in the Tower on 2 and 4 December 1583 to see if he would reveal anything more about the plotters. He admitted that his plan of the Sussex harbours for possible landing points was gleaned from maps. He had not scouted the coast himself as that had been left to others. This led to the discovery of the exact involvement of Charles Paget in the plot, and his secret trip to England months earlier. Throckmorton admitted to a conversation with the Spanish ambassador in Paris, and the plot laid with the Duke of Guise. He confessed that he gave the Spanish ambassador a list of potentially sympathetic Catholic nobles and safe ports for a possible foreign invasion, likely copies of those found in the search of his house. Philip II of Spain had promised to fund half of the expedition, and envoys had been sent to the Pope to see if he would fund the other half as Catholic crusade of sorts.

On 13 December, Throckmorton received a letter at the Tower from his wife, Anne. The letter was likely smuggled into the Tower by Francis's brother, George Throckmorton, with the assistance of Cecily Hopton, who was the daughter of the Lieutenant of the Tower, Owen Hopton. On 15 December 1583, one of Throckmorton's servants revealed the existence of the letter and that it focused on the green velvet casket. Francis seems to have befriended Cecily Hopton during his time in the Tower and she mistakenly agreed to help him. Cecily was questioned on 14 December regarding her conversations with George Throckmorton when the letter came to light about what she did as a result of their conversations.[18] There is no note on what became of Cecily after this interrogation, or the details of the interrogation itself, just a note to say that it happened in the State Papers. No doubt Cecily revealed what she knew and damned Throckmorton further. Her father remained Lieutenant of the Tower until 1590 despite Cecily's involvement.

On 15 December 1583, Henry Percy, 8th Earl of Northumberland, was arrested and questioned and, by 9 January 1584, he was imprisoned in the Tower of London. By this point Walsingham knew all about Charles Paget's secret trip to England months before to scout the south coast for possible landing sites for a foreign invasion. Northumberland seems to have met with Paget on his secret visit, as he had property on the coast and was known to be from a Catholic family as well as being a sympathiser of Mary Queen of Scots. His involvement with Paget now known, he was suspected of complicity in the plot against Elizabeth I. Lord Henry Howard managed to evade most of the questions put to him and would be let off. There was no real evidence against him, either.

There was a rupture in Anglo-Spanish diplomacy as a result of the Throckmorton Plot. A second Spanish ambassador was evicted from England during Elizabeth I's reign when, on 9 January 1584, Don

Bernadino de Mendoza, the Spanish ambassador, was called in front of the Privy Council. He was told that the council knew about his part in the plot against Elizabeth, and he was told to leave the country within a fortnight and not to return. Walsingham wrote a letter to the English ambassador in Paris, Sir Edward Stafford, the following day, detailing that Mendoza had been told to depart the country within fifteen days for having plotted to spirit Mary Queen of Scots away, and having had conversations with the traitor, Francis Throckmorton.[19] The letter also confirmed that the Spanish had been planning an invasion with the Duke of Guise set to lead it. An English official was sent to Spain to explain the whole plot and Mendoza's involvement in it, to Philip II, but he refused to see the official. Throckmorton, when questioned, had been open about Spanish involvement in the plotting. Perhaps Philip did not want to hear that Elizabeth's government had thwarted him, though how much he knew about his ambassador's actions is open to question. Elizabeth felt that she could not maintain diplomatic relations with Spain any longer after the treachery of two of her Spanish ambassadors in twelve years in plotting to overthrow and replace her. Mendoza would be the last Spanish ambassador to England until Elizabeth's death in 1603. No further action could be taken against the disgraced ambassador by the English government as Mendoza was protected by diplomatic immunity. Mendoza would serve in France for the next six years and would be a key player in the Babington Plot against Elizabeth I in 1586. He seems to have been determined to assist in the overthrow of Elizabeth even if he was not allowed in the country and his animosity was out in the open. Mendoza's expulsion from England brought war with Spain closer.

Francis Throckmorton was tried at the Guildhall in London on 21 May 1584, found guilty of treason, and sentenced to death. He was hung, drawn, and quartered at Tyburn on 10 July that year as a traitor. Throckmorton was the only one of the conspirators to be executed, although many were imprisoned or escaped abroad. Most, however, were based abroad, like Charles Paget, or had immunity, like Mendoza, so could not be punished. This seems a particularly lenient approach to punishing a conspiracy intended to take the queen's crown, and her life. It would not have just been Elizabeth who would have been killed either, but probably many of her most prominent advisors including William Cecil, Baron Burghley; Henry Carey, Baron Hunsdon; and Sir Francis Walsingham, to name but a few. These advisors were those of the Protestant persuasion who were active in trying to bring down Mary Queen of Scots. They did not want a Catholic on the English throne. This echoes later feelings in the following century about James II and the Englishmen who invited the Protestant William of Orange (a different William of Orange to the one assassinated in the Low Countries in 1584) to depose him and take the throne. He would become William III and rule jointly with his wife, and James II's daughter, Mary II, after the Glorious Revolution of 1688. In many ways Francis Throckmorton can be seen as a victim rather than a perpetrator of treason, as it does not seem as if he wanted to be involved in unseating the queen; he wanted to assist Mary Queen of Scots but did not mean to become involved in an international plot against England.[20] He was tortured to provide a confession, so may have just said what the officials questioning him wanted to hear from him, rather than the whole truth of what was intended and what had actually taken place.

The official English version of the Throckmorton Plot was described in a pamphlet, possibly authored either by Cecil or Walsingham, entitled *A Discovery of the Treasons Practised and Attempted Against the Queen's Majesty* where the stated intention of the rebellion was 'to remove her Majesty from her Crowne and state'.[21] This pamphlet outlined the government's arguments to substantiate their actions against Francis Throckmorton – that he was plotting to promote a foreign invasion of England, the assassination of Elizabeth I, her replacement with Mary Queen of Scots, and the return of England to Catholicism and the authority of the Pope. It could also be used to explain war with Spain if that came to pass. It also mentions the green velvet casket in which Throckmorton had all of his writings hidden, as previously explored, and his connection with Cecily Hopton, daughter of the Lieutenant of the Tower. It defends the use of torture as a necessary weapon against rebellion, and defended the fairness of Throckmorton's trial, which appears to have been questioned by a few people, especially as his confession was obtained under torture and later retracted. The pamphlet ends by saying that the main reason that the plot failed to succeed was that they could not find a way to release the Queen of Scots from her imprisonment and bring her to safety. Had the rebels managed to free Mary, could the plot have succeeded? It would certainly have had more chance to, but we will never know for sure. The pamphlet was also translated into Latin and Dutch to target European support for any future rebellions. The thought was not just for the current rebellion, but any which might be planned in the future. Walsingham and Cecil were taking their charge of Elizabeth's safety very seriously indeed.

*

One of the most important things to emerge from the Throckmorton Plot was the *Act for the Queen's Safety* which came from the so-called *Bond of Association*. This Act became law in October 1584 and bound all of its signatories in an oath to prosecute and kill anyone who claimed a title to the throne as a result of the queen's murder, regardless of whether or not the claimant was personally involved in the plotting. Mary Queen of Scots actually signed it, most likely under duress. It seems unlikely she would have signed it of her own free will, given how involved she had been and would become once more in plotting against Elizabeth I. If discovered plotting against the queen again, Mary would face the full force of the law. The act also prompted Burghley to make plans for an interregnum if Elizabeth died suddenly, but Elizabeth would have no part in these plans.[22] It was intended to stop civil war and ensure a smooth succession for whoever would come to the English throne after Elizabeth. As it was, the interregnum plans were not required and the throne passed smoothly to Elizabeth's successor, James I, on her death in 1603. The *Act for the Queen's Safety* would form the basis for Mary's trial and execution after the Babington Plot in 1586. She would effectively be condemned through her own signature on that document. Mary would protest her innocence to the end, but there was plenty of evidence against her as we will see in the next chapter. The threat from Mary Queen of Scots was ever-growing in the minds of the English and Elizabeth's advisors would not stop until Mary was dead and no longer a threat.

After the Throckmorton Plot had been uncovered, James VI of Scotland decided to use his knowledge of the foreign intrigues surrounding the plot as a bargaining counter with Elizabeth I. However, what this told the English was that the Scottish king had known more about the conspiracy than he had previously admitted to.[23] This could have led to a breakdown in Anglo-Scottish relations, though Elizabeth likely wanted to avoid war with Scotland as war with Spain and involvement in the Netherlands was looking increasingly likely. Avoiding a war on two fronts was the sensible course of action and meant she would not have to split her army. Perhaps Elizabeth also felt a little sorry for James, who had only been released in June 1583 after the Raid of Ruthven. His position was still precarious, and perhaps Elizabeth understood that. Mary's involvement in the Throckmorton Plot still did not end hopes that she would be able to share the Scottish throne with her son, James VI. The proposition became more attractive as the plot had highlighted the dangers of keeping Mary in England against her will. This plot demonstrated that Mary might be more dangerous imprisoned in England than free and in power in Scotland, which was contrary to an earlier opinion. The safest course of action regarding Mary was still under debate in both England and Scotland at this time.

A sad ending to this plot came on 21 June 1585 when Henry Percy, 8th Earl of Northumberland, who had been imprisoned in the Tower in December 1583 for his suspected involvement in the conspiracy, committed suicide. There was a suspicion that it was a political murder as his death looked like 'the convenient disposal of a traitor'.[24] He was found dead in his bed in his room in the Garden Tower at the Tower of London having shot himself through the heart. It was due to this event that the Garden Tower at the Tower of London is now known as the Bloody Tower. This is also said to be the location of the infamous deaths of the Princes in the Tower, Edward V and Richard, Duke of York in 1483. One of Northumberland's servants in the Tower gave him his supper as usual and saw him to bed. Northumberland got up and bolted the door, saying that he could not sleep without the door locked tight. This could suggest a fear of murder, in order for the government to get rid of a suspected traitor whom they actually had very little evidence against. Around midnight the servant was woken by a loud noise and got no answer from Northumberland when he knocked on the door. The Lieutenant of the Tower, Sir Owen Hopton, father of Cecily Hopton who had smuggled a letter into the Tower for Francis Throckmorton, was summoned and the door to Northumberland's chamber was broken down. Northumberland was found dead in his bed covered in blood with a wound in his breast seemingly caused by the pistol found lying on the floor beside the bed. The pistol had allegedly been hidden in the chimney of the chamber, though how Northumberland acquired the pistol is unknown. The government claimed that Northumberland's treason explained his self-destruction and suicide. To some, this sounds too convenient. However, it is very possible that Northumberland did not want to see his family shamed and face a possible public execution on Tower Hill, or even a lifetime in the Tower.

Many of the people involved in the Babington Plot of 1586 were in some way related to the conspirators of the Throckmorton Plot. Many Catholic families in England were interrelated so perhaps this is not such a shocking coincidence. Most people in England outwardly conformed to the Church of England and the Elizabethan Religious

Settlement of 1559. However, there were those who hid Catholic priests in priest holes in their homes so that they could continue to hear the Catholic Mass. There was a suggestion that the Throckmorton family in fact did this. Many of the conspirators of the Gunpowder Plot in 1605 were also related to Francis Throckmorton, like Robert Catesby and Francis Tresham. Protestants saw the discovery of the Throckmorton Plot as proof that England was of the elect, and that they would triumph over the Catholics. The same could be said of the Gunpowder Plot in 1605.

*

There was a footnote to the Throckmorton Plot, known as the Parry Plot. When the Parry Plot unfolded, the country was still reeling from the effects of the Throckmorton Plot and the assassination of William the Silent (popularly known as William of Orange) in the Low Countries in 1584. The difficult question was over intervention in the Low Countries. Intervening would mean war with Spain, but not intervening could mean Philip II seizing control and having the perfect point from which to launch troops against England. This was the background to the Parry Plot. William Parry would be executed on 2 March 1585 for treason and plotting against the life of Elizabeth I. The historian Lacey Baldwin Smith asks whether Parry was 'part of an elaborate confidence game and cover to win his way into Catholic circles' or had he 'experienced a religious conversion and became the willing instrument of militant Catholicism'.[25] Perhaps it was a mixture of both and it began as a confidence game to trick his way into the trust of the Catholics and, spending so much time with them, he actually started to believe in them so turned against his royal masters in the end. Maybe he began to confuse illusion with reality. All have been suggested as possibilities.

William Parry, born as William ap Harry, was the son of Harry ap David and his second wife, Margaret, who was the daughter of the Archdeacon of St Asaph's in Wales. According to Parry's own testimony, his father died in 1566 leaving fourteen children by his first wife and sixteen by his second. It is unknown when William was born, but he was educated at a grammar school in Chester, from where he escaped and ran away to London though he did manage to gain a law degree from the University of Paris in 1583. He married a widow, Mrs Powell, who had some wealth, and entered the service of William Herbert, 1st Earl of Pembroke, brother-in-law to Henry VIII's sixth wife, Katherine Parr. This placed him in the orbit of the royal court. Pembroke died in 1570 and Parry entered royal service. He was profligate and extravagant in his spending. After the death of his first wife, he married for a second time, to Catherine Heywood, who brought him manors in Kent and Lincolnshire, although this did involve him in some litigation issues in 1571 and he was threatened by his creditors.

Parry seemed to have an inflated sense of his own importance. This possibly enhanced his spending as he felt that his clothes and household needed to reflect his own status, which was not as great as he would have liked, or as he thought. He appears to have been vain, weak, and unwilling to accept his station in life. At one point, Parry demanded the mastership of St Catherine's hospital for providing information to the authorities but was refused. Perhaps this refusal and the more general failure to rise in the world was responsible for his descent into conspiracy and plotting. It is plausible that Parry was not entirely sane as he was completely unable to accept 'no' as an answer or to settle for what he had in life. He constantly seemed to want more recognition and a higher place in society. The sixteenth century was not really a time where social boundaries were pushed. You were expected to accept your station in life.

In financial difficulties, Parry applied to William Cecil, Baron Burghley, to be employed as a spy abroad. He may have requested a posting abroad to be able to escape his creditors. He tried to ingratiate himself with English Catholics on the continent including in places like Rome, the centre of the Roman Catholic Church, to extract secrets to send back to Burghley in England. He returned home in 1577 though still having financial troubles. He applied repeatedly to Burghley for financial aid but without much success. In 1579 Parry once again left England, though this time without permission, possibly again to escape his creditors, but he was back in England the following year. Parry assaulted one of his creditors, Hugh Hare, whom he owed £600 to (around £122,000 in today's money). He was convicted and sentenced to death, but Elizabeth intervened, and he was pardoned. Parry again asked licence to be allowed to travel abroad in 1582.

While spending time abroad, Parry had begun to take the Catholic side in religious matters, though he pretended that he was hunting out Catholic secrets to reveal to Cecil, Walsingham, and Elizabeth in England about plots against Elizabeth's life. He was received into the Catholic Church in Paris in 1582.[26] He urged a more lenient policy against Catholics in England, asking pardon for some of those exiled to the continent. Parry became involved with Charles Paget and Thomas Morgan in Paris, who were notable supporters of Mary Queen of Scots and championed the Catholic religion. Both Morgan and Paget were involved in plotting against Elizabeth I. Parry also began to read the writings of Cardinal William Allen, who ran the Catholic seminary in Rheims where he trained up Jesuit priests to promote the word of the Roman Catholic Church. On 10 May 1583, Parry wrote to Lord Burghley in England saying that he had 'shaken the foundation of the English seminary at Rheims'.[27] However, it appears that reading the works of William Allen prompted Parry to begin wondering if murdering princes or monarchs for the sake of religion was lawful. Elizabeth's name was mentioned as a possible target to restore Catholicism in England. On meeting with Thomas Morgan in Paris, Parry agreed to kill Elizabeth on the understanding that it would be sanctioned by Pope Gregory XIII who would absolve him of his sins.[28] However, Parry also continued to try and seek patronage from William Cecil, Lord Burghley, in England. Although he seems to have integrated himself quite well into the lives of English Catholic exiles on the continent, he also appears to have kept up links with the English government. This is why it is often difficult to decipher Parry's true beliefs and intentions. Parry was back in England by January 1584.

On his return to England, Parry had an interview with Elizabeth I and admitted that he had had dealings with the Pope, Charles Paget, and Thomas Morgan. They had been involved together in the Throckmorton Plot in 1583 and had planned to act against Elizabeth I in favour of Mary Queen of Scots and replace Elizabeth on the throne with Mary. Parry had conspired to act against Elizabeth while he was on the continent but claimed that he only did it in order to discover what was planned against the queen. In March 1584, Parry was pardoned for his treasonous actions and was given a seat in Parliament. Clearly, the queen still believed Parry was working for her. Within weeks of taking up his seat, Parry was in trouble for opposing an anti-Catholic bill ordering Jesuits and seminary priests to leave England within forty days on pain of high treason and death. Any attempt to conceal them would be considered a felony. He actually made a speech in defence of the Jesuits for which his parliamentary colleagues imprisoned him in the serjeant's ward. Parry was imprisoned for a few hours until the queen ordered his release after his own apologies were ignored.[29] Even at this point, Elizabeth did not seem to suspect that Parry's loyalties had changed or were suspect.

Parry turned to spying again and met with another double agent, Edmund Neville, to whom he proposed a plot to assassinate Elizabeth I, assisted by an invasion of between 20,000 and 30,000 Scots. The pair discussed the moral imperative of regicide and dreamt up ways to rescue Mary Queen of Scots from her imprisonment, raise the north in rebellion against Elizabeth, and seize Queenborough Castle on the Kentish coast as a base of operations for rebellion. Possibly Parry was attempting to get Neville to incriminate himself. Neville, however, revealed Parry's suggestion of assassination to a courtier who went to the queen with what he knew. Parry was arrested and accused of encompassing the queen's death. He made a full confession in January 1584 which was used against him in his trial. Initially when he was questioned by Walsingham, he protested that he had never mentioned the matter since his return from France and pardon from the queen. Walsingham did not believe him, and Parry remained in custody until the following morning when he said he had remembered mentioning to a kinsman a statement he read in a book about the potential lawfulness of killing princes for religion. Parry was confronted with Neville to try and make him confess, but he continued to deny all talk of murdering the queen. The third time of being questioned regarding the plotting, Parry made a full confession of everything he had said and done, which was confirmed in a personal letter he wrote to the queen afterwards. He said he had been sent by Catholic malcontents abroad to murder the queen and revealed what he knew. He also produced a letter from Cardinal Como, Papal Secretary of State, assuring him of Papal blessings in his assassination mission.

In his personal letter to the queen after his confession, Parry wrote that he was sorry he had ever become involved in the plotting against her, however commendable he had once thought the plan. He also spoke about Mary Queen of Scots, saying that she should be kept under guard but honourably treated.[30] The fact that he did not ask for Mary's release possibly means that he realised how wrong he was in promoting her claim, but perhaps he did not want to provide any more ammunition against himself, or others involved, by provoking the queen further. This kind of thinking would demonstrate that Parry had not lost all sense of reality and likely realised that he would die. Parry remains 'something of an enigma', possibly suffering from 'delusions of grandeur'.[31] We will likely never know for certain where his true loyalties lay.

Parry was arraigned on 25 February 1585 and pleaded guilty. He appeared to be cooperative and even offered to read his confession

Above: 1. A pencil drawing of Elizabeth I's grandparents, Henry VII and Elizabeth of York, her father, Henry VIII, and her stepmother, Jane Seymour, who provided Henry VIII with his only legitimate son who would become Edward VI.

Right: 2. Anne Boleyn, second wife of Henry VIII and mother to Elizabeth I. Elizabeth never really spoke about her mother but wore a ring with her mother's portrait in it until her death, suggesting a deep connection with her.

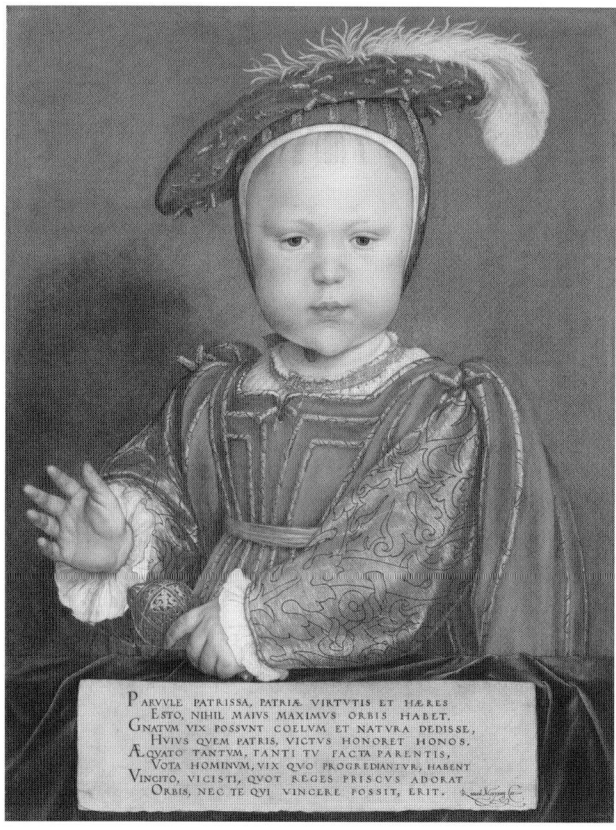

Above: 3. The Tudor succession showing, from left, Philip II of Spain and Mary I (1553–1558), Henry VIII (1509–1547), Edward VI (1547–1553), and Elizabeth I (1558–1603).

Left: 4. Henry VIII's only legitimate son, Edward VI, who came to the throne aged 9 in 1547 and died of what is thought to be tuberculosis, aged 15 in 1553.

5. Elizabeth's half-sister, and Henry VIII's eldest daughter, Mary I, who married Philip II of Spain and took England back to the Roman Catholic Church. She imprisoned Elizabeth I in the Tower for suspected involvement in rebellion.

6. Elizabeth I, also known as 'Gloriana' whose rivalry with Mary Queen of Scots would dominate her reign. She would invoke a sense of national pride in the defeat of the Spanish Armada.

7. Mary Queen of Scots, daughter of James V, and mother of James VI/I. She would spend nineteen years imprisoned in England before her execution in 1587 for plotting against Elizabeth I.

8. An engraving of Elizabeth I with her two advisors: William Cecil, 1st Baron Burghley on the left, and her spymaster, Sir Francis Walsingham, on the right.

9. William Cecil, 1st Baron Burghley, who had been with Elizabeth since her days at Hatfield before she became queen and would be one of her must trusted advisors until his death in 1598.

10. Sir Francis Walsingham, Elizabeth's spymaster, who would uncover several plots against his queen, and entrap Mary Queen of Scots through the Babington Plot in 1586.

11. Robert Dudley, 1st Earl of Leicester, was Elizabeth's favourite and her Master of Horse. There were rumours that the pair would marry but this never happened, and Elizabeth remained the 'Virgin Queen'.

Right: 12. Thomas Howard, 4th Duke of Norfolk, who nearly became the fourth husband of Mary Queen of Scots. He would be executed as a result of his involvement with Mary and the Ridolfi Plot in 1571.

Below: 13. A memorial to the executed, on Tower Hill, includes the name of Thomas Howard, 4th Duke of Norfolk, who was executed in 1572 after his involvement in the Ridolfi Plot against Elizabeth I the previous year.

Henry Courtenay, Earl of Devon	1538
Thomas Cromwell, Earl of Essex, K.G.	1540
Henry Howard, Earl of Surrey	1547
Edward Seymour, Duke of Somerset	1552
Sir Thomas Wyatt	1554
Thomas Howard, 4th Duke of Norfolk	1572
Thomas Wentworth, Earl of Strafford	1641

14. An engraving of Elizabeth I in Parliament. Parliament kept pushing for Elizabeth to act against Mary Queen of Scots, but she refused to give in until irrefutable evidence emerged of Mary's involvement in the Babington Plot in 1586.

15. The cipher used by Anthony Babington and Mary Queen of Scots to communicate during their fateful plotting in 1586. This is a copy signed by Babington after his arrest to verify its authenticity.

16. The White Tower at the Tower of London. Prisoners did not tend to be kept in the White Tower, but it is the symbol of the Tower. The Babington plotters were imprisoned and questioned in the Tower of London before their executions.

17. An engraving by one of the Babington plotters, John Ballard, in the Beauchamp Tower at the Tower of London. It reads, 'Honour all men. Love the brotherhood. Fear God. Honour the King. 1 Peter. John Ballard'.

made only for forstefeinst ye plots in case of need against the puritants of this realme: the principall workeof gebuig the chiefe forces of the same in the lowe Con= tries Laine (as you may lett the bruite goe) desperitual to ruine and overthrowe at their returne spine the whole Catholiques, and to usurpe the Crowne not only against mee and all other lawfull pretenders therv= vnto but against thir owne Quene that now is. of she will not altogether remitt her selfe to their only gouernament: The same pretextes may serve to forme and establish amongest you all an association and confederation generall as done only for your owne iust preservations and defence aswell in religion as libertis and goodes against the oppres= sion and attemptes of the said puritants, no doutt tourhning chiefly by writing and thing against that Queen, but rather promis yo selves vallues to mainteine her and her lawfull power after her comming heere. The affaires being thus prepared and forces in readines both without and within the realme, then shall yt bee time to sett the six gentle= men forwoork takinig order vpon the arcomp lisfing of their designement, I maie bee sodenly transported out of this place, and that all yo forces in the same time bee on the feilds to meete mee in tarying for the arriuall of the forraine aid wch then must bee haste= ned with all diligence. Now for that there can bee no certaine daie appointed of the arcom= plishing of the said gentlemens designement, to these that offert maie bee in readines to take mee from hence: I woute that ye said gentlemen

Above: 19. A magazine sketch, romanticised, of the execution of Mary Queen of Scots in 1588. Her ladies are pictured disrobing her ready for the axeman.

Left: 20. James I of England and VI of Scotland, the son of Mary Queen of Scots who would go on to rule England after Elizabeth I's death in 1603. He would have his mother reburied in Westminster Abbey on his accession.

21. Philip II of Spain, former husband of Mary I. His ambassadors were heavily involved in plotting against Elizabeth I and Philip would launch the Spanish Armada in 1588 to try and invade England.

22. An effigy of Elizabeth I on a medal made after the defeat of the Spanish Armada in 1588. The image of Elizabeth on the medal was to remind people that she was the mother of England and a symbol of her national identity.

23. Robert Cecil, later 1st Earl of Salisbury, was the son of William Cecil, 1st Baron Burghley, and would replace his father as Elizabeth I's chief minister.

24. Robert Devereux, 2nd Earl of Essex, rebelled against Elizabeth I in 1601 after a failed command in Ireland and a surprise visit to Elizabeth's bedchamber. He feared bankruptcy and a loss of favour.

aloud to the court. However, he did state that he had never intended to harm the queen, even though he pleaded guilty to treason. Technically, it could be argued that he was guilty of discussing the murder of the queen without any authority from a royal minister to attempt an entrapment, even if he was in the employ of the queen, which would still be treason. The Parry Plot was certainly directed against the queen herself, rather than any of her ministers, as had been alleged in earlier plots. Whether Parry actually intended to assassinate Elizabeth is another question, but it seems unlikely from what we know of his personality that he would have had the resolution to murder. Parry was sentenced to be hanged, drawn, and quartered, and was executed in Westminster Palace Yard on 2 March 1585. After just one swing of the rope, Parry was cut down alive and had his heart and bowels removed from his body while still conscious. Ordinarily traitors were allowed to lapse into unconsciousness before they were ripped open.[32] Parry was not: he would have seen the whole gruesome thing before he finally died and his limbs were cut off to be displayed above the gates of the city, and his head impaled on London Bridge.

There are a couple of possible theories about William Parry's execution. It could potentially be seen as a cover-up: the destruction of someone on the inside of the royal court who knew too much and had to be removed. It has also been seen by some as a plot by Walsingham and Burghley to keep Elizabeth and the realm believing that they were threatened by a religious conspiracy. Neither of these arguments is entirely convincing, and there are problems with both. Had Parry been on the inside and his execution was a cover-up to conceal what he knew, surely Walsingham and Burghley could have continued to make use of him? It seems inconceivable to rid yourself of an asset who might still be useful to you, unless they believed he had lost touch with reality, and it was more dangerous to keep him alive. It also seems unlikely that Walsingham and Burghley would have plotted to keep the queen and realm under the shadow of religious conspiracy without Elizabeth at least suspecting that something was wrong. She was a notably intelligent woman who was involved in all aspects of government. She would have noticed had a conspiracy like that been orchestrated by the people she was closest to, and who were assisting her to run the country. It's difficult to believe otherwise. This seems a similar argument to that about her father, Henry VIII, and how Cardinal Thomas Wolsey and then Thomas Cromwell ran the country with Henry VIII almost as a puppet. Henry was completely in control and pulled down Wolsey and Cromwell when they seemingly acted against him. Elizabeth no doubt would have been as firm as her father in dealing with Burghley and Walsingham. Another argument, which seems more plausible and possibly ties in with the first argument, above, is that Parry was in deep cover to maintain his links with Catholics and began to confuse illusion with reality. He began to believe in the Catholic cause because he was spending so much time pretending. Therefore, his execution could have been a cover-up because the government realised that Parry was unstable and therefore might reveal things that they did not want people knowing. Had Parry turned double agent and contemplated treason in thought if not yet quite in deed? If so, Elizabeth almost subconsciously helped him to achieve it.

Elizabeth seems to have been quite negligent about her own safety in many ways, making Walsingham and Burghley's job much harder than it needed to be. Despite several plots and assassination attempts, Elizabeth continued to keep an open court and did not seem to like being surrounded by guards when she was outside. Parry had intended to take advantage of this by proposing a plan to assassinate her as she walked in the gardens at Whitehall Palace and then fleeing over the palace walls to one of the landing sites nearby and escaping by barge. A plan was also discussed regarding attacking Elizabeth in her carriage as she travelled to St James's Palace with himself and Edmund Neville approaching from each side and plunging their daggers into her. Parry decided on the Whitehall plan and waited in the gardens for the queen to appear. When she did, Parry claimed that he was so awed by her majesty and seeing the image of her father, Henry VIII, that he could not carry it out.[33] This was just before Edmund Neville confessed all to the authorities. In this way of being lax about her own safety and security, Elizabeth allowed those who would act against her the means and opportunity to do so. It was only the actions of Walsingham and Burghley and the spy network they controlled that prevented Elizabeth I being assassinated. The Parry Plot is a prime example of this in action.

*

With the Parry Plot following so quickly on the heels of the Throckmorton Plot, the 'government was determined to extract from [it] every possible ounce of propaganda value'.[34] It was hoped that these plots against the queen would rally the English people to support her as she was much loved by her people and always had been. There were huge celebrations in November 1558 when Mary I died, and Elizabeth succeeded to the throne. Mary was unpopular by the end of her reign, in huge contrast to just five years earlier when she acceded to the throne, and it was hoped that Elizabeth would be different and more tolerant. However, the people would not begrudge some punishment for those who would act against her. Elizabeth I was their rightful queen and the Ridolfi, Throckmorton, and Parry Plots had shown the people how much danger their queen could be in and the lengths that foreign powers would go to in order to unseat Elizabeth and return England to the Roman Catholic faith. Foreign support for these plots enhanced English xenophobia which promoted a kind of national pride which reached its peak in Elizabeth's reign with the defeat of the Spanish Armada in 1588, and which is still evident today.

The swift discovery and putting down of the Throckmorton Plot in 1583 and the Parry Plot in 1585 demonstrated the efficiency of Walsingham's spy network, a coup for the government.[35] Elizabeth's safety depended on this network functioning and rooting out those who would act against her. It showed that the government could be trusted to protect their queen, and that any future rebellions would also be put down just as effectively and efficiently. It was, however, a close-run thing as forces had actually started to muster in Normandy and Mary Queen of Scots' supporters were thrown into complete confusion when the plot was uncovered. The implied message was that there was no point in plotting rebellion because it would be discovered and those involved would be punished severely for treason. The Babington Plot of 1586 would bear this out in a brutal way.

Chapter 5

Babington Plot 1586

'Devilish and wicked-minded subjects'[1]

The Babington Plot of 1586 is probably the best known of the Elizabethan rebellions, possibly because there was so much intrigue and conspiracy. It also led directly to the execution of Mary Queen of Scots the following year because of the *Bond of Association*, also known as the *Act for the Queen's Safety* which was enacted after the Throckmorton Plot of 1583. The Babington Plot was the most dangerous rebellion against Elizabeth I since the Northern Rising in 1569, seventeen years earlier.[2] It demonstrated that there was enough organisation and willpower to try and overthrow Elizabeth and replace her with Mary Queen of Scots, and that there was a very real possibility of a foreign invasion from Spain. Philip II of Spain was becoming more determined than ever to restore England to Catholicism. This plot would have been an excuse for him to invade England. Mary Queen of Scots was a secondary concern for him, as evidenced by his sending the Spanish Armada to England in 1588 after Mary's execution the year before. The Ridolfi, Throckmorton, and Parry Plots come across almost as a rehearsal for the Babington Plot. It can be argued that the Babington Plot led directly to both Mary's execution and the Spanish Armada crisis.

As long as Mary was in England she would attract radical Catholics, who would try and help her escape. She was quite a tragic figure. Letters proving Mary's complicity in the plot were shown at her trial, along with confessions from the plotters and others, including Mary's own secretaries, Claude Nau and Gilbert Curle. Mary began to entertain conspirators that she saw as 'foolhardy or sinful before'.³ In other words, she became desperate, and desperation led to recklessness. What makes this particular rebellion so interesting is that the government likely knew about it from the beginning and had their own agents involved with the plotters from the start, specifically to try and get Mary Queen of Scots to implicate herself and thus push Elizabeth into signing a death warrant which, after a lot of prevarication on Elizabeth's part, is exactly what she did. Cecil and Walsingham were determined to protect Elizabeth and England at any cost. Mary's death was that cost.

It has been debated between historians how early into the plot Sir Francis Walsingham, Elizabeth's spymaster, became aware of it and decided to use it, or even whether Walsingham had manipulated it from the very beginning. It is possible, but not very likely, that Walsingham invented the Babington Plot in order to implicate Mary and lead to her execution. It is difficult to imagine why Walsingham would need invent a conspiracy when there was already so much plotting surrounding Mary Queen of Scots. It made more sense to use a plot already underway. He must also have understood that an entirely forged plot might not have the outcome that he desired and could in fact end with his own destruction rather than Mary's. A fake plot would strengthen Mary's defence at trial. All Walsingham needed to do was wait for one he could use and manipulate. There is a suggestion that the Babington conspiracy was actually a 'Walsingham conspiracy' which Mary got tangled up in and which was used to frame her.⁴ Perhaps the plot was so easy to manipulate because it was very much in the early stages when Walsingham discovered it, so it was simple for him to insert his own agents and use them to entrap Mary. Some of the key figures involved in the plot were actually Walsingham's agents, and without Thomas Phelippes, Walsingham's codebreaker, Mary's letters might not have been decoded so speedily, and the evidence presented at her trial might not have been so compelling. Compelling enough to end in her conviction and execution. Walsingham's network of agents worked together through this plot to bring Mary Queen of Scots to the scaffold.

Thomas Phelippes is an interesting character. Often in the shadows, working for Francis Walsingham, he is best known as the one who decoded Mary Queen of Scots' ciphered letters during the Babington Plot. He drew a small image of a gallows on Mary's letter to Babington where she agreed to the execution of Elizabeth I. This letter is thus known as the 'Gallows letter'. Thomas Phelippes was the son of William Phelippes, a London customs officer. He lodged in Leadenhall Market, within easy reach of Walsingham's home on Seething Lane in London. He was notably fluent in French, Latin, and Italian, although less so in Spanish.[5] He had served in France temporarily in aiding French Huguenots and controlling English spies in France as part of the household of Sir Amyas Paulet when he was ambassador to Paris. He returned to England and to Walsingham's service before the Throckmorton Plot of 1583. After the death of Walsingham in 1590, Phelippes was in debtor's prison for a time, though he did assist in the apprehension of the Gunpowder plotters in 1605. It is believed he died around 1625, having only done sporadic intelligence work since Walsingham's death.

The timing of the Babington Plot was absolutely crucial to the rebels at least, as many of Elizabeth's key advisors and leading Protestants, including Robert Dudley, 1st Earl of Leicester, were in the Low Countries in 1586. This involvement in the Dutch Revolt would anger Spain and would be part of the reason for the launch of the Spanish Armada by Philip II in 1588. The plotters therefore thought that, as many key figures were out of the country along with the army, this was a good time to bring about a Catholic Counter-Reformation in England, as there would be fewer commanders to lead armies against them, and fewer men to form that army. Walsingham could have foiled the plot much earlier had he wanted to, but he needed to ensnare Mary Queen of Scots to ensure Elizabeth's safety, and that of England, in the longer term. He took the risk of allowing the plot to develop and it paid off.

The plot acquired its name from the figure of Anthony Babington, who was an English Catholic gentleman from Dethick in Derbyshire. G.R. Elton describes Babington as a 'young man of more devotion than sense'.[6] During the plot Babington seemed to be completely devoted to Mary Queen of Scots and restoring Catholicism, but he did not seem to understand the complexity of plotting and how to make the plan succeed. His family outwardly conformed to the state religion, though they were at heart Roman Catholics and had many Catholic connections. In 1579, Babington married Margery Draycott, but before his marriage he had served as a page in the household of George Talbot, 6th Earl of Shrewsbury, who was gaoler to Mary Queen of Scots between 1568, when she arrived in England, and 1585, when she was moved to Chartley under the custody of Sir Amyas Paulet. Rumours suggested that Shrewsbury asked to be replaced as Mary's custodian after the breakdown of his marriage to Bess of Hardwick. Whether Babington met Mary at this point is unknown and thought to be unlikely, but he did seem to kindle a great admiration for her which would endure and lead to rebellion in 1586. He believed that the people of England did not need to be loyal to Elizabeth as she had been excommunicated in 1570 by the *Regnans in Excelsis* bull issued by Pope Pius V. This bull absolved the English people of their loyalty towards Elizabeth, and it even said that it was imperative to overthrow her. Many of those young men who supported Mary Queen of Scots and became involved in Babington's plotting 'offered their lives as love tokens'.[7] Mary was seen as a romantic figure to many who were willing to martyr themselves for her and for Roman Catholicism. This religion was also what Mary Queen of Scots would profess to be dying for. This devotion to Mary was able to provoke conspiracies, the like of which had not been seen before in England.

Anthony Babington acted as a courier to Mary Queen of Scots while at Lincoln's Inn studying law in around 1580. He fell in love with the mythologised version of Mary as a captive Catholic queen and became determined to assist in her release and accession to the English throne.[8] Historian Jane Dunn describes Babington as someone who knew little of Mary's history but saw her as a poignant captive figure adhering to her faith against all of the odds.[9] Mary had been very clear that she would sacrifice her life for her faith. Had Babington known of Mary's history and suspected involvement in the murder of Darnley? If he had, how could he not fail to be coloured by it in his view of her? Unless he saw the rumours as propaganda to sully her name and position. Babington was recommended to Mary by Thomas Morgan and the Archbishop of Glasgow, both of whom were greater supporters of Mary. In his final confession, Babington admitted to getting five secret packets of letters to the Scots queen before she was moved to the stricter care of Sir Amyas Paulet at Chartley in 1585. Babington was no longer required as courier after this point, as Mary's correspondence had been greatly restricted. Mary's correspondence had previously gone through the French embassy in London via the French diplomatic bag, as had happened during the Throckmorton Plot three years earlier in 1583. Twice after this point Babington allegedly received packets to forward on to Mary, but he refused to assist. The reason why is unclear, although it is possible that he was concerned he would be caught and questioned, or worse.

    Babington gathered around him during this period other disaffected Catholic gentlemen like John Savage, who would spearhead the assassination plans against Elizabeth, and his close friend Chidiock Tichbourne. They were joined by the Catholic priest, John Ballard, and Robert Poley, who was an agent of Sir Francis Walsingham, along with Gilbert Gifford, who would traffic much of the correspondence between Mary at Chartley, and the conspirators in London. Poley had been a government agent for two decades by this point and the conspirators met in his lodgings. Babington and his friends would reveal in their eventual confessions how they had been radicalised by Catholic priests both abroad and in England.[10] The Jesuits were said to openly teach the legitimacy and merit of murder if it was to overthrow a heretic, as Elizabeth was said to be by the Catholic powers and the Roman Catholic Church. Babington told the court at his trial that the murder of Elizabeth I had been represented as a lawful act, endorsed by the Church.

*

Mary Queen of Scots received a letter from her son, James VI of Scotland, on 12 March 1585 rejecting any plan of an 'association', meaning the pair working and ruling together in Scotland.[11] This had been the subject of discussions between England and Scotland for a few years, but James's refusal made Mary desperate. With this rejection, Mary was willing to listen to and endorse any rash plan that would free her, especially if it would also put her on the English throne. Walsingham had hoped that this would be the result of the letter from James; he wanted to push her into acting rashly and without too much thought, as she was more likely to make a mistake. Walsingham expected to find evidence in Mary's correspondence that would condemn her under the parliamentary statute; the *Act for the Queen's Safety* of 1584. This Act meant that anyone who knew about or consented to a conspiracy against the queen's life or reign would be tried for treason by a special commission.

In December 1585, Mary Queen of Scots was moved to Chartley and put in the care of Sir Amyas Paulet. It had been decided that she needed to be kept in stricter confinement to keep her out of trouble. It was thought that her previous gaoler, George Talbot, 6th Earl of Shrewsbury, had been too lenient with her, and there were even rumours of a relationship developing between the pair. This is likely, in part at least, what led to the breakdown of Shrewsbury's marriage to Bess of Hardwick, and they were unreconciled when Shrewsbury died in 1590, just three years after Mary's execution, which he had witnessed. Shrewsbury had also sat in judgement on Mary at her trial in October 1586. Possibly witnessing the execution contributed to Shrewsbury's death, although he did suffer from increasingly poor health over the years. This stricter confinement of Mary was part of Walsingham's plan to make her feel more isolated and desperate as she had never been cut off so completely before as when her correspondence was halted. Paulet had even demanded that Mary's charitable endeavours be stopped as there were worries that she would bribe her servants or use these charitable donations to try and foment rebellion on her own behalf.[12] Mary tried to complain to Elizabeth about her treatment, but nothing changed as a result of her protests.

Thomas Morgan recruited Gilbert Gifford who travelled to England from Paris at the beginning of 1586. Morgan had been in the Tower of London for three years before being exiled to France. Gifford landed at Rye in East Sussex and was immediately taken in for questioning. It seems likely that he never intended to betray Mary Queen of Scots but was pushed into it by the persuasions of Walsingham and his agents. However, it has also been suggested that Gifford's arrest was rather too prompt, and that it may have in fact been orchestrated and his arrival expected.[13] This would imply that he was already Walsingham's man, and his arrest was staged, possibly to give Walsingham and Gifford a chance to speak in private. Gifford managed to persuade Mary that there was a safe way she could communicate with her supporters in England and abroad. If someone wanted to get a letter to Mary secretly then there was a brewer in Burton who delivered the beer to Chartley, where Mary was being kept, who would receive the letter from Gifford himself. The brewer had been bribed to put the letters in a waterproof packet and slip it through the bung into one of the barrels of beer. One of the cellarmen within Chartley would then remove the waterproof packet from the barrel and pass it on to Mary's secretary, who would give it to Mary herself. The same process worked in reverse for Mary to send replies. All letters were sent in cipher in case they were intercepted, which had been designed by Thomas Morgan. Mary became desperate when, in September 1585, she was told that her letters could no longer be forwarded by the French diplomatic bag.

What Mary and the Babington plotters did not know was that Gifford was a double agent and turncoat working for Francis Walsingham, and that every communication passed through his hands before reaching its final destination. Gifford was a crucial link leading to Mary Queen of Scots' traitorous last letters with Anthony Babington. Walsingham had been watching the English Catholic exiles in France, and this is probably how Gilbert Gifford came to his attention. The brewer in Burton had been bought by Walsingham to act for him rather than Mary. Walsingham's chief codebreaker, Thomas Phelippes, would make a copy of the letter and decode it before resealing it and sending it on to its destination. Arthur Gregory was said to be able to re-seal letters with such precision that it was impossible to tell that they had been tampered with.[14] This was essential to avoid alerting the plotters too early that they had been discovered. Walsingham certainly seems to have recruited very talented men to work for him. Gifford would have already ridden north towards Chartley, and the letter was then rushed to him by express messenger and passed to the brewer who put it in the barrel. There were elaborate safeguards in place to prevent the government agents at Chartley from knowing who the other agents were. This meant that, had one agent been discovered, he could not reveal who the others were because he did not know. Mary Queen of Scots' Achilles' heel was her desperation for news from the outside world. It is what led to her getting involved in conspiracies in the first place. There had been packets of letters building up at the French embassy in London for Mary since the Throckmorton Plot in 1583 with the restriction of communications. With the new method of getting letters in and out these packets could now all be sent on to her.

Gifford's true allegiance is unknown. After the uncovering of the Babington Plot Gifford fled to France, where he died, having been ordained as a Catholic priest in Rheims. It is known that he did pass information to Walsingham which helped to capture the Babington plotters. However, it seems that he did also have some sympathy with the Catholic cause, as demonstrated by his ordination as a Catholic priest before his death in 1590. Not everything that he passed onto Walsingham may have been entirely true, but obviously enough of it was that the plotters were apprehended and eventually executed. Gifford managed to get out of England without Walsingham's, or the queen's, permission, and spent the rest of his life in France. He was sentenced in August 1589 while in France to twenty years' imprisonment for acting against the Catholic Church. Possibly Gifford fled England once the plot was uncovered to avoid being detained and questioned, and his true allegiance discovered. Or perhaps he simply wanted to be able to live without having to deceive and play both sides, living with the constant fear of discovery. We will probably never know. His allegiance seems to have leaned towards Elizabeth and Walsingham rather than Mary Queen of Scots, as he seems to have continued to act against Catholicism and kept in contact with Walsingham, passing him information.

Thomas Morgan was a cog in the plot, and he designed the cipher that would be used by Mary Queen of Scots and the conspirators during the Babington Plot. The plot would be broken apart by the interception and interpretation of encrypted documents. The cipher had twenty-three symbols with a further thirty-five standing for prepositions and other common words. Some were Greek or Arabic numbers and others came from musical notation. There was also one character which told the reader to double the following letter. This made frequency analysis, which is often used in codebreaking, difficult as you could not rely on how frequently a letter was appearing in any given message. 'E' and 'A' are considered to be the most commonly used letters in the English language so you can get an idea of an encryption from which are the most commonly used symbols. This would not work with the Babington cipher as it is a hybrid of a cipher and a code, sent out to Mary's correspondents including the French ambassador. The historian John Cooper examines the cipher in detail in his book, looking at how it was designed, how it was used, and how Thomas Phelippes manipulated it to incriminate Mary in the plotting.[15] All letters which used the 'beer keg' method to reach Mary were in cipher using the same code and were intercepted and deciphered by Walsingham, Phelippes, and other agents. The key to the cipher was sent out using this method as well so it fell into Walsingham's lap, making it easy for Phelippes to decipher any correspondence that was intercepted.

On Walsingham's instructions, Gifford approached the French ambassador. The French embassy in London was where much correspondence intended for Mary was sent. Nothing had managed to penetrate the protective shield around Mary for many months as restrictions around her had tightened in the aftermath of the Throckmorton Plot, and rumours spread of further conspiracies with her name attached to them. In January 1586, the beer keg method was tested, and Mary Queen of Scots received her first unauthorised communication in more than a year, from a French envoy, Guillaume de L'Aubespine, Baron de Châteauneuf. This proved to her that the plan would work, as she and the ambassador were completely unaware that all communications sent through this method were being monitored by the English government. This new method of exchanging messages also proved to Mary that she could trust Gilbert Gifford, who had proposed it. This was important for Walsingham's plan to entrap Mary – she needed to trust Gifford. The communication method was devised especially and specifically by Walsingham and his agents to entrap Mary, and Gifford presented it to the plotters as his own idea. Had Walsingham immediately acted against the plotters and arrested them, he would not have had enough evidence against Mary to push for her execution.

A seminary priest named John Ballard travelled to Paris in May 1586 to see the Spanish ambassador to France, Don Bernadino de Mendoza. Ballard told Mendoza that there was a plot afoot to assassinate Elizabeth, and he wanted Spanish support including an invasion force. Mendoza had already been involved in a plot against Elizabeth, working in 1583 with Sir Francis Throckmorton. Mendoza had been expelled from England in the aftermath and had taken up residence in France. This could explain why Ballard approached Mendoza in the first place, as Mendoza already had a proven record of acting against Elizabeth, though not successfully. He also had communications directly with Philip II of Spain, so would know whether the English could expect Spanish support. He could also act as an intermediary between the plotters and the hoped-for assistance from Spain and, possibly, France. Ballard told Anthony Babington that a Spanish invasion was planned for that summer and that, to ensure its success, Elizabeth would have to die. Once Babington agreed to this, he was guilty of treason. One of Gilbert Gifford's tasks was to convince Ballard and Thomas Morgan that there was far greater English Catholic support for the plot than there actually was, so that they would push ahead with their plans. Gifford was also tasked with delaying Ballard's flight abroad once the plot fell apart and he realised that English Catholic support was not as strong as he had been led to believe.[16] This realisation would mean that the plan would not have much chance for success. John Ballard was a key figure in the Babington Plot as a Catholic priest and a rallying point for the other conspirators. Although Babington gave his name to the plot, Ballard appears to have been a more central figure.

Over the course of the next two months, Babington consulted with others and gathered support around him to figure out how to proceed with their plans, and what kind of assistance he could count on, both in England and abroad. The plan was for English Catholics to rise in support of Mary Queen of Scots, in concert with a foreign invasion. Six men were to assassinate Elizabeth while, at the same time, a group of around a hundred men, led by Babington himself, were to rescue Mary from her imprisonment at Chartley and put her on the throne in Elizabeth's place. John Savage had said that he would murder Elizabeth himself, but Ballard and Babington agreed that

Savage would have a better chance at success if he was assisted by five other men. Reports suggest that Babington was sceptical about whether the plot could be successful at first, but Ballard overcame his doubts. Ballard appears to have been quite a successful and persuasive speaker. It does not seem like the final method for the assassination of the queen was decided upon, but ideas had been floated including ambushing Elizabeth in her coach, or as she rose from bed, or walked in the park, or even in the Presence Chamber itself. The historian A.N. Wilson has reported that the plotters did not just aim to kill Elizabeth, but also assassinate some of her most important advisors including William Cecil, Lord Burghley; Sir Francis Walsingham; and Henry Carey, 1st Baron Hunsdon, who had assisted in putting down the Northern Rising in 1569 and was the queen's cousin on her mother's side.[17] Taking out these important figures would mean that it would be easier to get Mary Queen of Scots onto the throne and keep her there, as it would remove key opposition. These men wanted Mary executed for treason. Mary would never be safe on the throne if Elizabeth's key advisors remained alive and at large. They were Protestants and would never be accepted by the Catholic Mary. At the same time as the attack was planned on Elizabeth, Babington would be waiting near Chartley with a hundred supporters to free Mary and whisk her to safety.

By 6 July 1586 Babington, Ballard, and the other plotters decided that their plans were far enough advanced to include Mary in the conspiracy, so Babington wrote to her outlining their plans and asking for her approval of them. The letter was, as has been previously discussed, written in cipher, and sent via Gilbert Gifford to Chartley in a beer barrel. Before the letter reached Chartley, it passed through the hands of Thomas Phelippes, who decoded it for Walsingham. They hoped that Mary's response to the letter would implicate her directly in her own hand in the plotting, and so persuade Elizabeth to sanction putting Mary on trial, leading to her eventual execution. Mary was almost coaxed into the plot and entrapped into acting against Elizabeth. The intent to murder Elizabeth was real, but the plot was actually being manipulated by the government itself. Babington was said to be so confident of success in the scheme that he commissioned a portrait of the six main conspirators. This portrait was later used to identify the men when they were on the run after the plot was uncovered.

Mary had received the letter by 13 July when she sent a message to Babington saying that she was still thinking about his letter and would respond as soon as possible. Around this time, Mary also learned that her son, James VI of Scotland, had concluded a treaty with Elizabeth I, so she became even more desperate. This ended any chance of Mary being returned to Scotland. This treaty would also inform James's response to his mother's execution, so as not to jeopardise his place in the English succession. Mary sent her reply to Babington on 17 July 1586, responding positively to his plans and agreeing to her own rescue and Elizabeth's assassination. She even offered advice on her liberation, suggesting one way was perhaps to create a diversion by setting fire to the outbuildings at Chartley, drawing the guards away from her. She also suggested trying to get the support of a magnate like Henry Percy, 9th Earl of Northumberland, or Philip Howard, 13th Earl of Arundel, as a figurehead. Mary believed that this would garner more support for the rebels against Elizabeth and provide noble leadership. However, she also raised logistical concerns over foreign support and armed men. Even if she ended up in the Tower of London, she hoped Babington would continue with the plan.[18] This suggests that Mary believed the plan was bigger than just her. But she also knew that, if the plan succeeded, she would be released, so continuing was in her own best interests.

Mary's letter suggested that her agreement to the plan stemmed from her own religious feelings. She was concerned that Catholicism would be wiped out in England and that this could spread to other countries as it had in the Low Countries. Mary believed that Catholicism was the saviour of people, and that Protestantism would be the ruin of whole countries. She framed her agreement to the Babington Plot as almost a religious crusade to save the souls of the English rather than an attempt to take the English throne for her own sake. She was determined to frame her agreement to the rebellion as a wider political move to save England:

> For divers great considerations, which are too long to be deduced here, I cannot but greatly praise and commend your desire to prevent in time the designs of our enemies for the extirpation of our religion from this realm, with the ruin of us all.[19]

Historian Retha Warnicke has suggested that, although Mary definitely agreed to her own rescue, it was debatable whether she really agreed to regicide and the murder of the queen.[20] She argues that Mary would not have resorted to so dishonourable an act. Even discounting the postscript forged by Phelippes, Mary did sign her name to treason in that letter by consenting to the assassination and not disputing it. She did add some preconditions before the plan could advance, however. She wanted to know how much support the plan could expect from English Catholics, what assurances there were of foreign support, not to arm their followers until they had a guarantee of foreign aid, and a foolproof plan to free her from captivity. Before sending his deciphered copy of the letter on to Walsingham, Phelippes drew a small gallows at the bottom of the page to signal the letter's importance. Mary Queen of Scots had finally condemned herself.

Before sending the letter on to the conspirators, Francis Walsingham instructed Thomas Phelippes to add a postscript to the letter, asking for the names of the six gentlemen who would assassinate Elizabeth. Because Phelippes had the cipher used to encode the letter this was not difficult to do. They wanted to gain as much information as possible before arresting those involved. They also hoped to gain evidence of other people involved whom they may have been unaware of up to this point. Elizabeth, however, was pushing for immediate arrests. If any of those involved remained undetected there was the serious worry that one or more of them might act against her in the future, and this was the angle that Walsingham and Burghley were pushing to persuade Elizabeth to wait. Some accounts suggest that the postscript was 'poorly forged and sat oddly with the rest of the letter'.[21] Perhaps the conspirators guessed it was a forgery, though Babington did still respond to the letter, but not identifying the gentlemen whose names were requested. By forging this postscript, it later allowed Mary to argue at her trial that it was not just the postscript that was forged but the whole letter, and that she never wrote to Babington at all. The allegation Mary made was that all correspondence was falsified, and she could not be condemned on that alone. Efforts were taken to ensure that Mary did not know that the letter had been doctored when evidence was presented at her trial. Babington's confession was read out, but any mention of the postscript was omitted. However, once Mary realised that Walsingham had access to her correspondence all along, she played on this.

On 29 July 1586, Babington received Mary's reply to his letter. He did not give much information in his answering letter, which has given rise to speculation that the forged postscript aroused his suspicions that their plot had been discovered, or that there was a double agent in their midst. He could not have known that there was not just one double agent but several, and that Walsingham had known about the plot almost from the beginning. Perhaps Babington believed that Mary would never ask for that kind of information in a letter, knowing the possibility that letters could be intercepted and deciphered, even written in cipher or code. Mary had been very careful in her communications up to now, so maybe it was stretching credulity too far to believe that Mary would want that information committed to paper. But she had also thrown caution to the wind in responding positively to Babington's plans in writing, so perhaps she was just so desperate to have her freedom that it did not really matter to her anymore what happened. Either explanation could have been legitimate, but there was something that did not sit right with Babington about the postscript as he failed to respond to that particular request.

John Ballard was arrested on 4 August 1586 for being a covert Catholic priest. Robert Poley was arrested at the same time, presumably to preserve his cover rather than being outed as one of Walsingham's spies. Walsingham had Mary's letter (known to posterity as the 'Gallows letter') and did not want to delay any longer in arresting the conspirators in case they fled and managed to escape or burned any incriminating evidence. It was given out that Ballard was arrested just for being a priest rather than for involvement in a treasonous plot against the queen, but Babington felt, quite rightly as it turned out, that the net was closing in around him. On hearing of Ballard's arrest, Babington went straight to Savage to ask him to expedite his plans to kill Elizabeth. It was felt that if they did not act at that moment then they would not get another opportunity. Savage said he was willing but claimed that he would be refused admittance to the court as he was not correctly dressed. Babington gave him a ring and told him to sell it to buy what was required to get him into the court and close enough to Elizabeth to assassinate her. This seems like a desperate last-ditch attempt to get the plan to work as the conspirators must have known, with Ballard arrested, that all was lost. Ballard was tortured and confessed everything, implicating Babington, and the others.

Babington was dining with a fellow plotter, John Scudamore, at a London inn when a message arrived for his friend. Babington saw the message which told his 'friend' to arrest him. The penny dropped that their group had been infiltrated by double agents working for Walsingham, and that his dining companion was one of them. Babington left the table on the pretext of paying the bill and left the inn, leaving behind his cape and sword, and fleeing. He headed north out of London. It was impossible for Babington to remain at large for long with so many people looking for him. Ballard had named all of those involved in the conspiracy and a nationwide manhunt was underway for all the plotters. Authorities searched houses across London, many belonging to recusants who were thought to sympathise with the plotters and their cause and might hide them. Babington was eventually arrested on 14 August 1586 hiding in St John's Wood disguised as a peasant with green slime on his face from walnut shells. He was taken to London for his trial and execution alongside the other conspirators who had been caught, including John Savage, Chidiock Tichbourne, and John Ballard. He suspected his friend, Robert Poley, was a government agent who had handed him over to Walsingham. Babington's arrest, and that of his fellow plotters, was aided because Babington had commissioned portraits of himself and his six main accomplices (Ballard, Savage, Tichbourne, Robert Barnwell, Charles Tilney, and Edward Abingdon) and copies of these were posted across England. Babington's first confession after his arrest was taken by William Cecil, Baron Burghley, and Sir Christopher Hatton. He confessed what he knew and all of those who were involved, including Mary Queen of Scots and the Spanish. Babington claimed that he had been recruited by Cardinal Beaton and Thomas Morgan in 1580 while in Paris, and he returned to England a year later, converted to Mary's cause. Gilbert Gifford had already fled England by the time that the arrests were made, despite being in Walsingham's pay, fearful that he would be arrested and scapegoated.

There had been some ongoing discussions about the best way to arrest Mary Queen of Scots. On 11 August 1586, her gaoler, Sir Amyas Paulet, suggested that Mary could ride out on a hunt towards Tixall near Chartley. On 16 August the hunt set out. Mary's secretaries, Claude Nau and Gilbert Curle, rode out with her. Paulet lagged behind as a group of horsemen rode towards the group. For a moment it is possible Mary believed that these were her rescuers and that the plot had been successful. Sir Thomas Gorges was part of the group and he accused Mary of conspiracy during the arrest.

She was taken completely off guard and by surprise but protested her innocence. She seems to have attempted to resist the arrest, sitting down on the ground, and refusing to move, but eventually kneeling under a tree and praying before riding on.[22] She would rather have moved on her own and retained some dignity than be dragged away, which was what was allegedly threatened. Mary was separated from her servants and taken to Tixall while her chambers at Chartley were searched. Incriminating documents and letters were found along with keys to ciphers used for communication. She had not heard by this point that the Babington Plot had failed, and that the conspirators had been arrested and questioned. However, her own trial had already been ordered and preparations for it were underway, even before her chambers were searched. Mary had been kept isolated on purpose, possibly to try and make her feel friendless and alone so when the possibility of this plot arose, she would jump at the chance to get involved, free herself, and even take Elizabeth's throne. Some historians have suggested that Mary was not actually that concerned over the English throne, but just wanted her freedom. Perhaps she came to realise that the only way she could be free was if Elizabeth was dead. Mary's two secretaries, Claude Nau and Gilbert Curle, were also arrested and questioned as to what they had written on Mary's behalf. They had written Mary's letters and put them in cipher, so she could claim, if the plot was uncovered, that she had not been involved, and that Nau and Curle had acted without her authorisation. It would be their testimony which would convict Mary, along with the Babington letters.

The papers found at Chartley when Mary's chambers were searched named several prominent noblemen as Catholic sympathisers and so they had to work to prove their loyalty to Elizabeth, whether they had actually been involved in the plot or not. These were Edward Manners, 3rd Earl of Rutland; George Clifford, 3rd Earl of Cumberland; Anthony Browne, 1st Viscount Montague; and John Lumley, 1st Baron Lumley. There is no evidence to suggest that they knew of the plot in advance or were working with Mary and the conspirators, just that their names had been put down as people who might possibly support Mary and the overthrow of the Protestant Elizabeth. The Elizabethan government was coming down harder on those suspected of Catholic sympathies in light of the plots against the queen. Mary briefly returned to Chartley after a fortnight at Tixall once her chambers had been searched and anything incriminating had been taken away. Many of Mary's belongings were also removed, but Mary said that she had two things that could never be taken from her: her royal blood and her Catholic religion.[23] She would cling to these to the very end. She was then moved to Fotheringhay Castle for her trial. Fotheringhay was larger, more imposing, and easier to defend. The Privy Council had wanted Mary taken to the Tower of London, but Elizabeth had refused, possibly remembering her own experiences there.

In August 1586, Elizabeth I wrote to Mary's gaoler, Sir Amyas Paulet, to thank him for his 'wise orders and safe regards' when dealing with Mary 'so dangerous and crafty a charge'.[24] Mary posed a threat to Elizabeth and the Protestant religion in England. The Babington Plot had just come to light, and Paulet's time as Mary's gaoler was coming to an end, as she would be moved to Fotheringhay Castle for her trial. In her letter, Elizabeth promised Paulet a reward for his service. However, he would not have long to enjoy it, as he would die in September 1588, having been made Chancellor of the Order of the Garter. Elizabeth also asked Paulet to tell Mary that she had better ask for God's forgiveness for her 'treacherous dealing' with one who had saved her life (Elizabeth herself). Elizabeth seemed determined to paint herself as the good one and Mary as the sinner which, looking at the evidence, appears to be true. However, the evidence was meant to make Mary look bad, whereas Mary herself did not see it that way as she saw Elizabeth as a heretic usurper, so killing her would have been right, and endorsed by the Pope. Elizabeth would also have been thinking about how it would look to her people, whose love she had depended on since before she even became queen. Elizabeth had sent instructions to Paulet on how Mary was to be treated, hoping that she would die of natural causes if her life was made difficult, sparing her the agony of signing a death warrant for her cousin.

Elizabeth wrote an open letter to the citizens of London on 18 August 1586 which would have been proclaimed aloud to the crowds who would have gathered to hear it, explaining the plot and the arrests that had been made. There would likely also have been printed versions distributed for those who were able to read it. Babington and his accomplices were described as 'devilish and wicked-minded subjects' and the queen acknowledged how happy her people were that the plot was uncovered, and Elizabeth was saved, and she thanked them for their love and devotion.[25] This is almost a public declaration of what the letter to Paulet hinted at. Elizabeth loved her people and knew that they were the ones who would protect England in the event of an invasion. This open letter was a clever way of ensuring that her people supported her and heard the government line. Almost in the same sentence she takes the loyalty of the people as a given and expresses the 'inward love and dutiful affection'.[26] This includes even those who might have been sympathetic towards Mary and considered rebellion, but Elizabeth is pulling them back into the fold and letting them know that they are forgiven if they stay loyal to her now. It is a very clever piece of writing and would have assured the people that Elizabeth and her council were very much in control of the situation. The loyalty of the English people to their queen would manifest in the Spanish Armada crisis of 1588.

Babington's friend and accomplice in the plotting, Chidiock Tichbourne, wrote a poem in the Tower during his imprisonment called his 'Lament' or 'Elegy'.[27] It was likely written sometime between 17 and 20 September 1586 after his condemnation but before the execution. Every word used is a single syllable. This makes the poem run smoothly when you read it, and also emphasises the harsh reality that Tichbourne is coming to terms with. There is a sense of having no time to use long words. The first line 'my prime of youth is but a frost of cares' recalls that Tichbourne was in the prime of his life, only aged around 28 in 1586 and married, but that his life will end because he became entangled in a political conspiracy which condemned him. 'My youth is gone and yet I am but young' suggests that physically he is still relatively young, but that he has been involved in so much that he can no longer be considered young. Richard Hirsch describes the poem, as a sense of 'unrelieved hopelessness'.[28] Tichbourne could remember the joy in his life but knew that he would not experience it again. He had only days left to live when this was written and knew that he could not undo it. He would not be allowed to live having threatened the life of the queen and the security of the English crown. The same line closes each of the three stanzas of the poem 'and now I live, and now my life is done'. Hirsch explains that this is a sense of his life being over before it has really begun at all.[29] The repeat at the end of each stanza is almost a reinforcement of him trying to accept the fact that he is alive now, writing these words, but soon he will be dead. It is echoing the sense of helplessness that runs throughout the poem as a whole and makes it very sad to read.

On 20 September 1586, Anthony Babington and six of his accomplices – John Ballard, John Savage, Chidiock Tichbourne, Charles Tilney, Robert Barnwell, and Edward Abingdon – were hanged, drawn, and quartered at St Giles Fields near Holborn in London. Elizabeth had asked for the judges to leave sentencing to the council so the rebels could suffer more. Burghley convinced her this would be illegal and might provoke outrage in the population, so she decreed that the rebels should suffer the full penalty for treason: drawn on a hurdle to the place of execution, being hanged, cut down while still alive, and their insides pulled out while they watched. The night before his execution, Babington wrote to Elizabeth begging for mercy and forgiveness. He was heard to cry out, '*Parce mihi, domine Jesu*' ('Spare me, Lord Jesus') as he was killed. There are reports that the crowd were so disgusted by this that when more executions were carried out the following day, Elizabeth ordered that the prisoners be allowed to hang until they were dead before being disembowelled. Elizabeth wanted to keep the love of her people, so she bowed to public pressure in this instance. This second batch of prisoners led to their deaths were Edward Jones, Thomas Salisbury, John Charnock, Robert Gage, John Travers, Jerome Bellamy, and Henry Donne, the elder brother of the famous poet, John Donne. These men had just been involved largely on the periphery and there is little evidence of what their actual participation in the conspiracy was. They were not included in Babington's portrait of the conspirators. However, it is important to recognise that they, too, died for their involvement. Babington's head and body, as well as those of the other plotters, were displayed across London to deter others from rebellion against their rightful queen.

Elizabeth was convinced of Mary Queen of Scots' guilt and treachery, but she found it difficult to face the political consequences of her trial and execution, as well as the constitutional implications of such an act. The means of entrapping Mary made some people uncomfortable, as much as they wanted Mary to be executed and England freed from the threat she posed. Elizabeth knew that Mary's execution could give both France and Spain the excuse they needed to launch a Catholic crusade against Protestant England, as indeed Philip would attempt to do with the Spanish Armada in 1588. As Mary was a former Queen of France by her first husband, Francis II, this was a real concern for Elizabeth and her Privy Council as Mary had maintained her links with France and still received a pension from them as a former queen. The constitutional impact could be more wide-ranging as the execution of an anointed queen regnant, even one who had abdicated, would set a precedent and would allow others to believe that perhaps Elizabeth herself or one of her successors could be tried, found guilty of treason, and executed. This worry was played out during the English Civil War when Charles I was executed in 1649. Elizabeth allegedly said that, if Mary admitted her guilt and showed herself ready to make amends, she would forgive her. This chimes with Elizabeth's reluctance to execute her, but Mary would never admit her guilt, and keep asserting her innocence up to her death, dying in the guise of a Catholic martyr.

Just before the trial of Mary Queen of Scots, Elizabeth wrote to James VI of Scotland, Mary's son, thanking him for his good wishes to her and the 'joy' he took from her 'narrow escape from the chaws [jaws] of death'.[30] Elizabeth blamed the Jesuits for promoting Catholicism in her realm and implored James not to allow the same to happen in Scotland. She was attempting to bring herself and James together, united under Protestantism, in contrast to Mary's Catholicism. Perhaps she hoped that their shared religion and disgust at Mary's actions would stop James from acting against her if Mary was found guilty and executed. In the event, James would not act against Elizabeth and England, probably due to the fact that he knew that he was next in line to the English throne, and not wanting to jeopardise that possibility. By 1587 Elizabeth was aged 54 so it was known that she would not have any children. By Henry VIII's will, the next heir would have been Edward Seymour, Lord Beauchamp of Hache, son of Katherine Grey, who was Lady Jane Grey's sister, and great-grandson to Mary Tudor, Henry VIII's sister. However, his legitimacy was questioned, as Elizabeth never sanctioned the marriage of his parents, Katherine and Edward Seymour, 1st Earl of Hertford. James was unquestionably legitimate and was descended from the elder sister of Henry VIII rather than the younger, Margaret Tudor, Queen of Scotland. In constitutional terms, James's claim to the throne was the strongest. He would not have wanted to do anything to upset Elizabeth or her council, and so jeopardise the possibility of him becoming King of England as well as Scotland, as would happen on Elizabeth's death in March 1603.

On 21 September 1586, Mary Queen of Scots was moved from Chartley to Fotheringhay Castle for her trial. At this point she was not aware that her letters had been intercepted and decrypted throughout the plotting. She believed that the only evidence against her was the testimony of her accusers, as the information regarding the intercepted communication method through the beer barrels had been kept from her. Mary believed this communication method was still secret and unknown to the government. She did not know the strength of the case built against her, and that the result of the trial was effectively a foregone conclusion. She would be condemned for treason. She had initially refused to attend the trial until persuaded by Sir Christopher Hatton that this was her chance to defend herself. She was convinced that she could prove her innocence, but this was a delusion. Perhaps Mary thought that Elizabeth would never condemn a fellow queen and her own cousin. If this was her thinking, she was wrong. Elizabeth may have struggled with it, but in the end she did what she believed was right for England and herself. Even if she did attempt to put the blame on others, saying she never meant for the death warrant to be used.

At her trial in October 1586 at Fotheringhay Castle in Northamptonshire, far from both London and Scotland, Mary Queen of Scots repudiated any knowledge of the Babington Plot and denied having written any letters to Anthony Babington or to any of the other conspirators. She demanded to be shown the original with her signature. Of course, this was not possible as Babington had burnt them, and they had been written in her secretary's hand and not her own. Only the copies made by Phelippes existed. Phelippes had copied and deciphered Mary's letters to Babington, while the originals were then sent on to their intended destinations. What was produced at the trial was Phelippes' copy of the decoded letter, then he also produced a copy where he had re-encrypted it into the original cipher. This shocked Mary as it meant that Walsingham and Phelippes had known all about the plot right from the beginning, and that her 'secret' method of communication was never in fact secret at all. It demonstrated the extent to which she had been manipulated and entrapped. Mary also denied having received letters from Babington in the first place and that, if some had arrived at or been sent from Chartley then her secretaries must have acted without her knowledge or approval.

Mary's secretaries, Claude Nau and Gilbert Curle, had given full statements which were read out to the court saying that Mary had dictated the letters to them in French, which was her most comfortable language. They were then translated into English and put into cipher. Nau and Curle were not called to testify in person, as Walsingham was concerned that seeing Mary might persuade them to change their minds about what they had written in their statements which would be hugely damaging to the case against her. Nau and Curle were devoted to Mary, so this would have been a real concern for Walsingham and the rest of the council, who were determined to see her convicted and executed. Mary accused Walsingham of forgery in open court, which he refuted. She claimed that all of the letters were fraudulent, and that Walsingham had created them to entrap her and execute her. Despite her spirited defence, Mary was found guilty of treason and sentenced to death. She was executed in the great hall at Fotheringhay Castle, the same place where she was tried, on 8 February 1587. Mary's destruction in 1586 is often blamed solely on Walsingham and his spy network, as if Mary herself had done nothing wrong. Walsingham and his network would not have been able to act against Mary had she not been involved. There is little doubt that she was guilty of engagement in the Babington Plot and of conspiring against Elizabeth to take the English throne.

*

Anthony Babington's failed plot to replace Elizabeth I with Mary Queen of Scots led directly to Mary's execution the following year, in February 1587. Walsingham called Mary Queen of Scots a 'bosom serpent' and was convinced that Elizabeth could not be safe while Mary lived.[31] The serpent was a sign of corruption, slyness, and cunning, as evidenced by the story of Adam and Eve being thrown out of the Garden of Eden in the Book of Genesis. Mary was said to be sly and cunning in the way she acted against Elizabeth in the two decades of her captivity in England and how she corrupted others into acting on her behalf. The Babington Plot marked the end of a series of conspiracies against Elizabeth in Mary's favour. Mary's execution in 1587 meant that there was no longer a figurehead to justify revolt against the crown. It also marked the end of a series of plots throughout Elizabeth's reign which had involved Mary. The only rebellion to happen after Mary's death was fifteen years later in 1601, when the Earl of Essex had lost Elizabeth's favour. So, this was a very different kind of selfish revolt, rather than a conspiracy of plots which were attempting to put Mary Queen of Scots on the throne. Those surrounding Mary had a wider political agenda. Mary's death went unavenged by those in France and Spain who had the power to act. France was descending into civil war with conflicts over religion and the succession, and James VI had a lot to lose in breaking the alliance signed with Elizabeth I in 1586 including an English pension and the chance to succeed to the English throne.[32] The international situation was complex, and it meant that the timing of Mary's execution possibly saved Elizabeth and England from Scotland and France exacting revenge for it.

As a result of the plots against Elizabeth in favour of Mary Queen of Scots, culminating in the Babington Plot, Catholicism became more closely associated with treason and conspiracy. The Gunpowder Plot of 1605 would bear this out. Protestantism became connected with English national identity. It was during the reign of Elizabeth I, and partly as a result of plots against their 'Gloriana' that England really began to develop her national identity. This would solidify with the defeat of the Spanish Armada in 1588, where English Catholics and Protestants came together to protect their country and their queen. Perhaps this is why the reign of Elizabeth I is known as the Golden Age; England started to become England as we would recognise it today.

The uncovering of the Babington Plot and the execution of Mary Queen of Scots was the 'greatest triumph of Walsingham's career'.[33] It made the English crown safer because there was no longer such an obvious catalyst for revolt. It was a 'crude effort' at conspiracy by the Babington plotters and it was easily uncovered by the government.[34] But even if the plot was easily discovered, Walsingham had managed to use it to entrap an anointed queen into incriminating herself in treason and persuaded another queen, and her cousin, to sign her death warrant. The Babington Plot demonstrated how the art of deception and espionage could be used to overcome a situation which threatened the survival of an entire nation.[35] It was quite a new idea to make espionage part of the framework of English government, but it worked and protected a queen from being overthrown, taking a foreign queen to the block at the same time. Walsingham protected Elizabeth up to the end of his life, in spite of a long illness that sapped his strength. He refused to give up and let his queen down. He would die in 1590, having served Elizabeth faithfully for two decades, but leaving behind a pile of debts for his work in his country's service. It seems that Walsingham had paid for his network of informers and spies out of his own pocket, without financial recompense from the crown or government.

William Cecil, Lord Burghley, would die in 1598, before the final rebellion against Elizabeth, leaving his son, Robert Cecil, to fill his shoes. As these stalwarts of the Elizabethan regime died off, they left Elizabeth more vulnerable, devoid of some of her strongest supporters and greatest friends. She had already lost the person who many believed was the love of her life in 1588: Robert Dudley, 1st Earl of Leicester. Burghley had been with Elizabeth since the reign of her half-brother, Edward VI, and had stood by her through her imprisonment in the Tower of London under her half-sister, Mary I. In a way, the execution of Mary Queen of Scots was a watershed in English history, and certainly in Elizabeth's life. Elizabeth had broken what was a sacred link between monarch and people by executing Mary Queen of Scots.

Chapter 6

Essex Rebellion 1601

'What is allotted to us by destiny cannot be avoided'[1]

The Essex Rebellion of 1601 is singular among Tudor rebellions and among most rebellions in English history. This is because it happened essentially for selfish reasons and the Earl of Essex's overwhelming belief in his own importance. Rebellions more generally tend to have a political or economic aim. Robert Devereux, 2nd Earl of Essex, had lost the favour of Elizabeth I, having been her favourite since the death of Robert Dudley, 1st Earl of Leicester, in 1588. It had been suggested at the beginning of her reign that Elizabeth might marry Leicester, but it never happened. Perhaps Essex reminded her of this youthful dalliance. Essex was also a tenuous link to Leicester, as Leicester had married Essex's mother after the death of her first husband. Essex had lost sight of the fact that Elizabeth was a queen, ruler, and monarch first, and a woman second. He did not treat her with the respect due to her rank, but as an equal. This upset Elizabeth's equilibrium and her sense of her own majesty.

Essex's failure in Ireland in 1599 was the straw that broke the relationship completely. Essex had had ups and downs with the queen as he had been involved with several failed military and exploratory expeditions over the previous few years. He had also married in secret Frances Walsingham in 1590, the daughter of Elizabeth's spymaster, Sir Francis Walsingham, and the widow of Sir Philip Sidney. Essex was one of only two councillors in Elizabeth's reign to be executed. The other was Thomas Howard, 4th Duke of Norfolk, who was executed in 1572 after the failed Ridolfi Plot the previous year. Elizabeth's reluctance to execute is demonstrated in the fact that, of all rebellions, only two of her councillors were executed despite several being implicated. Possibly Elizabeth remembered her own time in the Tower under threat of execution, or the fate of her mother, Anne Boleyn. She seems to have avoided executing her nobility if she could help it, and Essex was no exception, but she did capitulate in the end when faced with incontrovertible proof.

Robert Devereux, 2nd Earl of Essex, was born in 1565, the son of Walter Devereux, 1st Earl of Essex, and Lettice Knollys. Lettice was the daughter of Catherine Knollys née Carey and the granddaughter of Mary Boleyn, sister to Henry VIII's second wife, Anne Boleyn. It has been rumoured that Catherine Carey was in fact the illegitimate daughter of Henry VIII from his affair with Mary Boleyn before his marriage to Anne. This would make Robert Devereux a descendent of Henry VIII, as was Elizabeth I, but through an illegitimate line. However, whether Catherine was really the daughter of Henry VIII is unknown. He never acknowledged her as he did his illegitimate son, Henry Fitzroy, 1st Duke of Somerset, by his mistress, Elizabeth 'Bessie' Blount. Even if Devereux was not descended from Henry VIII, he was still a cousin of Elizabeth's on her mother's side, as Mary Boleyn was the sister of Elizabeth's mother, Anne Boleyn. Perhaps this distant familial connection made Essex bolder in his dealings with Elizabeth than he might otherwise have been. Although, from what we know of his personality, perhaps that is just how he was – overfamiliar. Essex's mother, Lettice Knollys, incurred the wrath of Elizabeth I by marrying, as her second husband, the queen's favourite, Robert Dudley, 1st Earl of Leicester. Elizabeth could not stay mad at Leicester for long and forgave him, but she never forgave Lettice. Leicester was welcomed back to court, but Lettice was not.

The historian Alison Plowden notes that Essex was arrogant, impatient, and tried to bully Elizabeth, which resulted in several arguments between the pair.[2] Elizabeth did not like being gainsaid or her position and authority questioned or manipulated. She was still fond of Essex but would not allow him to build up too large a following as this would threaten her own position and make others jealous of his preferment and favour. As Essex became more reckless and comfortable in Elizabeth's favour, some courtiers began to question his loyalty to the queen. There were doubts among the Privy Council over whether to appoint Essex to suppress a rebellion in Ireland, but he was still England's foremost military commander by 1599 so he was appointed Lord Deputy. However, his command was a complete failure and he achieved very little of any note, which was a huge disappointment to Elizabeth and the Privy Council, who had hoped for more from him. The historian Carole Levin reports of a woman named Joan Notte who had dreams on two successive Saturdays at the beginning of 1601 warning of assassination plots against Elizabeth I and Robert Cecil.[3] This could be seen as a warning of Essex's upcoming revolt. With hindsight we could say this, but there was no way of knowing at the time what would happen. Today we might not pay much attention to dreams and prophecies, but these were very important in Medieval and Tudor England. People listened to them and believed in them. In the 1530s, the Holy Maid of Kent, Elizabeth Barton, had gained a huge following based on her prophecies about Henry VIII and Anne Boleyn and how Henry would not live for six months married to Anne. The prophecies did not come true, but people still listened to them and believed in her.

Francis Bacon wrote to Essex to warn him not to underestimate Elizabeth and not to overrate the importance of a military expedition. This was in 1596 after the capture of Cadiz, which saw Essex at his zenith. It was good advice which Essex failed to heed as he saw military expeditions and victories as the way to the queen's favour and further power. From this point he began to lose favour and thus became naked to his enemies, of which he had many. He was rash and hot-headed and had stopped a plot against Elizabeth in 1594 masterminded by Rodrigo Lopez, the queen's physician, who had been accused by Essex of plotting to poison the queen. Essex had him questioned but there was some question over whether Lopez was in fact guilty, though he was tried and found guilty. Essex felt he did not get the praise and reward he thought he deserved for his actions. Sir Francis Walsingham had stopped countless plots against Elizabeth and England but died in debt having funded his espionage networks largely out of his own pocket, so this was not unusual behaviour on Elizabeth's part. In 1598, the Privy Council were discussing a peace deal with Spain, but Essex was in favour of the continuation of the war instead. This put him at loggerheads with Sir Robert Cecil, the queen's key advisor after the withdrawal of his father, William Cecil, Lord Burghley, from public service in 1596. Burghley would die in August 1598. Robert Cecil would remain Elizabeth's most trusted servant until her death in 1603. He would then go on to serve James I and become 1st Earl of Salisbury as a reward for his service.

The last straw was Essex's command of the failed Irish expedition in 1599. Essex was sent to crush a rebellion, but he began with a minor campaign which wasted time, money, and men, before he made peace with Hugh O'Neill, 2nd Earl of Tyrone. The peace was made without Elizabeth's knowledge or approval. She was furious when she discovered his betrayal. The peace was 'murky' as Elizabeth did not know exactly what Essex had promised the Irish rebels in her name.[4] She had initially given Essex licence to put a deputy in his place in Ireland should he need to return to England to consult her. In light of Essex's talks with Tyrone, she revoked this permission. If Essex wanted to leave Ireland, he needed Elizabeth's explicit consent. Even before setting off for Ireland, Essex had quarrelled with Elizabeth's chief minister, Robert Cecil, about who the new Lord Lieutenant of Ireland should be. Elizabeth initially supported Cecil's choice and Essex turned his back on her, an insult to her royal status. Essex, however, was really the only credible choice to send to Ireland as a military commander. This disagreement with Cecil, along with his insult to Elizabeth, meant that, when Essex departed England for Ireland, he left behind an enemy with Elizabeth's ear, so when he failed to follow orders while in Ireland, he provided Cecil with ammunition to use against him when he was not there to defend himself.

The historian Anne Somerset has also suggested that Essex was upbraided for creating too many knights while in Ireland.[5] This could be seen as him creating his own private army, who owed their lives, advancement, and loyalty to him and not the queen. It was said that, while in Ireland, Essex ceded to most of the demands of the Earl of Tyrone in exchange for the latter's promise of help should Essex decide to invade England.[6] Francis Bacon wrote an account of the events of Essex's Rebellion with the assistance of the Privy Council and he concurred that Essex intended to 'pleasure and gratifie the Rebell with a dishonourable peace, and to contract with him for his owne greatnesse'.[7] However, we have to take this with a pinch of salt as Bacon was writing with the collusion of the council so this was in effect government propaganda and not everything stated within can necessarily be assumed to be true. It was suggested that Essex intended to impose his will on Elizabeth by force. This implies Essex was planning rebellion even before his upbraiding by Elizabeth on his return to England.

In a letter which Elizabeth wrote to the Earl of Essex on 14 September 1599 she wondered why, having 'possessed us with expectation that you would proceed as we directed you' Essex had not done so, and had in fact acted against her wishes, giving her no time to countermand him.[8] Elizabeth's comment implies that Essex had promised to do as directed while in Ireland. Elizabeth had instructed him to march north to Ulster and attack the Earl of Tyrone there, but this never happened. Essex essentially achieved nothing in Ireland and Elizabeth no doubt felt betrayed by someone she trusted and someone who had broken a promise. It was a waste of money and him going against her orders also in a sense diminished her power as queen, which would have been completely unacceptable to her. She saw her authority as God-given, a divine right, and would not have taken kindly to being disobeyed. She was noted to have her father's temper. She was always very focused on image and projected power, intended to make her seem very much in control, which generally she was. Elizabeth was furious and told Essex not to return to England or to court. Suddenly, on 24 September 1599, Essex abandoned his command in Ireland and returned to England, bursting in on the queen in her bedchamber at Nonsuch Palace. He wanted to explain his actions to her in person, and not let others influence her opinion of him in his absence. He worried that, if he did not return at this point, that he would lose everything with no chance to defend himself. He was convinced that Robert Cecil was working to undermine him and bring him down so that he would be the queen's undisputed right-hand man. Essex was convinced that being there in person would turn the tide in his favour, believing he could use his charms to win Elizabeth over. However, Elizabeth was becoming immune to his charms.

The Essex Rebellion was motived solely by 'one spoilt young man's ego and his immature reaction to losing his position as Elizabeth's favourite'.[9] He had no life skills and seemed to be emotionally immature as well as selfish and reckless. This was a volatile mix which became explosive when it seemed his world was falling down around his ears. Essex seems to have been able to depend on others his whole life and did not really know what to do when he had to fend for himself. He felt like he was losing everything and so turned to rebellion to try and regain it all, obviously not realising that it would instead seal his fate. He resented that Elizabeth had power over him and that she could spurn him if she wanted to, but he still also believed that he was untouchable because he had Elizabeth's favour, even if she occasionally tried to put him in his place. Essex obviously had not learnt from previous rebellions that revolt turns the monarch against you, not for you. Perhaps he was just too far gone to understand or realise what the fatal consequences would be.

*

When Essex burst in on Elizabeth in her bedchamber at Nonsuch Palace on 28 September 1599 on his return from Ireland, she is reported to have greeted him quite serenely and kindly, though she was not wigged or dressed. She seems to have been taken unawares and thus could explain her manner towards him, giving her time to collect her thoughts and figure out what to do next. Lord Grey had come across Essex at Lambeth in the early hours of the morning and ridden at speed to Nonsuch to warn Robert Cecil that Essex was en route to the palace. Grey arrived only fifteen minutes before Essex so there was no time to warn the Queen or increase the guards around her.[10] Elizabeth also did not know at this point whether Essex had returned with an army or what his intentions were. She needed to be careful and assess the situation rather than acting rashly. Her manner when Essex burst into her chamber was to put him on the back foot, as he was likely expecting rage and censure. It may have then shocked him when her famous Tudor temper came to the fore the following day because she had seemed very calm initially. Essex left with the promise that Elizabeth would speak with him later when she was ready. Elizabeth instead referred Essex's conduct to the Privy Council for investigation and he was questioned the following day for three hours by the council on charges of disobeying the queen's explicit orders, deserting his command in Ireland, creating too many new knights, and entering the queen's bedchamber on his return uninvited. The precise manner of his arrival may also have alienated the queen. Essex did not stop to change his clothes or wait until Elizabeth was ready to receive him.[11] This demonstrates his recklessness and desperation, but also his lack of understanding of Elizabeth. She liked her privacy and very few were allowed in her inner sanctum, especially seeing her deshabille without the trappings of queenship. Image was incredibly important to Elizabeth and this more than anything would have put her on the back foot when Essex burst in to her room.

On 1 October 1599, Essex was put under house arrest under the control of Lord Keeper Sir Thomas Egerton in York House.

His servants were afraid to meet in case they were accused of collaboration with Essex against the government. It was an atmosphere of fear and expectation. Robert Cecil seems to have promoted some kind of reconciliation between the queen and Essex over the next few months though it is not known exactly what form this took. Cecil does not seem to have wanted Essex's downfall, though Elizabeth was determined to teach him a lesson and put him in his place. Essex believed that Cecil and his friends were plotting his downfall but there is no evidence of this prior to the rebellion. Essex and Cecil had been at loggerheads since they were children when Essex had teased Cecil about his scoliosis (a curvature of the spine, a disability also suffered by Richard III). Their mutual dislike had continued into adulthood and helps to explain why Essex was so determined to believe that Cecil was acting against him, even though there is evidence to the contrary. It seems that Essex's personal relationships had a lot to do with why he revolted against the queen in 1601. He seems to have struggled to maintain normal friendships with people of his own class in particular, believing they were out to undermine him or bring him down without any evidence of the fact.

Around November or December 1599, Essex fell ill and Elizabeth sent her own physicians to attend him, but then became angry when her ministers used the excuse of his ill health to pray for him. By January 1600, however, Essex had recovered with no lasting physical effects. The following month he was moved to house arrest in his own house on the Strand, under the guardianship of Sir Richard Berkeley, with the only visitor allowed being his wife, Frances. It was announced that he would be judged by the Court of Star Chamber at Westminster, but in the end, this would not take place. There was a concern that, as Essex had a huge following in London and many supporters, that there would be violent demonstrations in his favour had he been tried in public. The council feared this and being unable to control any crowds. Regardless, rumours began to circulate that Essex was being condemned without a trial. It seems to have been Robert Cecil who had Essex's trial in front of Star Chamber abandoned. As previously intimated, Cecil did not appear to be seeking Essex's downfall, as Essex claimed, but he was concerned about the public reaction as Essex was a popular figure. However, Cecil came to realise, as Essex spun further out of control, that there was no reasoning with him. He would not listen to sense and needed to be neutralised.

On 5 June 1600, Essex was tried at York House on the Strand in London charged with neglect and misgovernance in Ireland. There were five charges against him in all: deserting his post when he left Ireland to return to England without permission, failure to subdue the rebels in Ireland, the appointment of the Earl of Southampton against the Queen's orders, his private interview with the Earl of Tyrone, and the tone of his letters which were imperious and overbearing. Essex was interrogated while on his knees in front of the council as a form of humiliation and a way of putting him in his place. He needed to know that he was answerable to the queen and Privy Council, and that the queen's favour did not make him exempt from retribution. He was cleared of disloyalty by eighteen commissioners, but his offices were all forfeit, except for Master of Horse, and he had to remain under house arrest. Had Essex been tried by the Court of Star Chamber at Westminster, he would likely have been more harshly treated: imprisoned and fined. By 26 August 1600, Essex was given his freedom but told to stay away from the royal court on pain of further imprisonment or other punishment. Essex could not afford complete withdrawal from court as many of his ventures required royal approval, so he became desperate and began to talk what effectively amounted to treason. His family tried to intercede for him with the queen and Privy Council but were unsuccessful. The general mood of the public was that Essex was being ill-treated and there were some adverse feelings towards the queen and Robert Cecil in particular as a result.

The last straw for Essex was when Elizabeth refused to renew his monopoly on sweet wines, leaving him on the brink of bankruptcy as this accounted for much of his income. It had done since he was first granted the monopoly in 1588 after the death of his stepfather, and Elizabeth's favourite, Robert Dudley, 1st Earl of Leicester. Monopolies were granted as a sign of royal favour and the loss of this monopoly indicated that Essex no longer enjoyed the queen's favour. It was a very public fall from grace. Essex was used to a luxurious lifestyle which he would no longer be able to finance without the monopoly. However, he did not believe that Elizabeth was wholly responsible for his position. He blamed Elizabeth's councillors, particularly Robert Cecil. Around Christmas 1600, Essex wrote to James VI of Scotland saying that he needed to deal with Elizabeth's councillors in the interests of the queen. James promised his backing to Essex's coup d'état. Essex claimed that the Privy Council wanted to arrest and kill him, which was not true. He seems to have become paranoid that people were out to get him, not realising that his own behaviour was making things worse. Another of his grievances was that Elizabeth did not trust his political judgement or with patronage. This did make a certain degree of sense given his previous failures.

Historian Susan Doran claims that Sir Robert Cecil, Charles Howard, 1st Earl of Nottingham, Thomas Sackville, Lord Buckhurst (later 1st Earl of Dorset), Henry Brooke, 11th Baron Cobham, and Sir Walter Raleigh wanted rid of Essex by finding evidence that would lead to a charge of treason.[12] This suggests a plot or conspiracy to get Essex to implicate himself. Until Elizabeth refused to renew his monopoly on sweet wines, the evidence seems to point to the fact that Essex still hoped to earn her forgiveness. Perhaps he hoped that her temper would cool as it had so many times before. However, the loss of the monopoly would lead to bankruptcy for Essex, at which point he likely would not be able to regain her favour, and this forced him to act. Perhaps it was the anti-Essex party at court that persuaded Elizabeth not to renew his monopoly, though Elizabeth herself would not act unless she wanted to do so. There does not appear to be any concrete evidence of a conspiracy which set out to oust Essex from

Elizabeth's favour or to have him executed, more that he made his bed from his own mistakes.

Essex also seemed to believe that Cecil intended to stop James VI of Scotland from being named as Elizabeth I's successor as he wanted, favouring instead the Spanish Infanta, Isabella Clara Eugenia, daughter of Philip II of Spain and Archduchess of Austria. Isabella was descended from John of Gaunt, whose daughter had married into the Portuguese royal house. Cecil promoting Isabella as Elizabeth's successor seems unlikely as Cecil was already corresponding with James about the possibility of him succeeding Elizabeth, and Cecil would remain Secretary of State and Lord Privy Seal under James when he took the English throne in 1603 on Elizabeth's death. This implies that James was rewarding Cecil for his support. On Elizabeth's death the succession passed smoothly to James VI with no contest from the Spanish, implying that this was never really considered. English xenophobia probably also played a part as there would have been revolts had there been any consideration of England becoming an outpost of Spain. This was likely just a delusion in Essex's imagination. Elizabeth knew of Essex's correspondence with James VI, and it turned her more firmly against him as the succession was a sore point with her. She refused consistently to name her successor. To speak of the succession could be to suggest that the queen would die, which was treason in itself.

On 3 February 1601, Essex met with Henry Wriothesley, 3rd Earl of Southampton, John Davies, Charles Danvers, Ferdinando Gorges, and John Lyttelton at Southampton's home, Drury House. Also in the inner circle, but not present at the meeting, were Gelly Meyrick, Sir Christopher Blount, who was Essex's stepfather (his mother had remarried after the death of his father in 1576), and Henry Cuffe. Essex House had been open to malcontents like Puritan preachers, Papists, and ex-soldiers. It seems odd to think of Puritans and Papists coming together to act but, if there's a larger goal, then politics and power can trump religion. These disparate groups joined together to act against the queen and her advisors. Essex had put it about that the men were there to hear sermons, but no one really believed it. That Essex persuaded people to follow him in his folly demonstrates his powerful, personal charisma. Others named as being involved in the plot were Francis Manners, 6th Earl of Rutland, Robert Radcliffe, 5th Earl of Sussex, and Edward Russell, 3rd Earl of Bedford, as well as William Parker, 4th Baron Monteagle, Edward Cromwell, 3rd Baron Cromwell, and Essex's sister Penelope Rich. Essex had also sent a message to his successor as Lieutenant of Ireland, Charles Blount, 8th Baron Mountjoy, asking him to send troops to support his proposed insurrection. He did attract some important people who resented Cecil influence and power. The plan was for Essex's supporters to deploy themselves throughout Whitehall, according to the confession of Ferdinando Gorges and, at a given signal, seize control and clear the way for Essex to reach the queen to plead his case directly with her. Sir John Davies wrote down which men would be positioned where in the palace: some at the gate, some in the hall, guard chamber, and Presence Chamber, and others to accompany Essex to the queen.[13] The men met again at Essex House to discuss the plan, but were interrupted by the Secretary of State, John Herbert, who told Essex to attend court and explain himself. Essex refused, fearing arrest and further repercussions. This summons urged Essex to precipitate action. He had not intended to start his revolt until the Scottish ambassador arrived, but this summons from the court threw him into impulsive action.

Robert Cecil knew of Essex's planned revolt but wanted to allow it to develop in order that Essex would incriminate himself and could be charged with treason, rather than the chance of him getting off and repeating it, as had happened with Mary Queen of Scots. Mary could not be adequately implicated in earlier rebellions for the council to proceed against her. Walsingham set a trap for her in the end which she walked into, as we have seen in the previous chapter. Robert Cecil did not need to do this for Essex. All he had to do was wait. Cecil had realised that Essex was beyond reason and could not be saved. Cecil had learnt from the past, and from his father, and planned to use the same tactics to capture Essex in treason. There was no real chance of the plot succeeding and Elizabeth was not in any real danger. It was a calculated risk, and one that paid off in the end, taking Essex out and saving Elizabeth once again.

William Shakespeare's play, *Richard II*, was used as a catalyst for Essex's planned revolt against the queen and her councillors. Essex's friends and comrades commissioned a performance from the Lord Chamberlain's Men of Shakespeare's *Richard II* on 7 February 1601, with the deposition scene included. This scene was left out of many productions due to its sensitivity. The players said that it was not a popular play and that no one would attend, but Essex's men paid forty shillings for them to perform the show, so it went ahead.[14] Many of Essex's friends and supporters attended the performance. This had dangerous overtones, especially given how unhappy and desperate the Earl of Essex was. The performance was taken by the Privy Council as a signal that a revolt was about to begin. They were not wrong, but how far did their actions the following day force Essex to act, perhaps precipitously? On the very same day as the performance, Essex was summoned before the Privy Council, but he refused to attend, pleading illness.

The play signalled the start of a coup, and it was hoped that, by staging the play, the plotters would gain support for Essex's cause, but this hoped-for support never materialised. The citizens of London remained loyal to their queen. They did not try to halt Essex, but nor did they join him. It is essential to understand Essex's revolt that the context of this catalyst is also explored. The importance and significance of the issue of deposition of a monarch cannot be overstated. It was the worry of Elizabeth I, William Cecil, Baron Burghley, and Francis Walsingham during the period of Mary Queen of Scots' imprisonment in England and it reared its head again in 1601. There were concerns over who would succeed Elizabeth when she died as she refused to name a successor, but the performance of *Richard II* brought the issue into the spotlight and made the government realise that, although Mary Queen of Scots was dead, there were others who might attempt to seize the crown for themselves or violently promote a successor or even replacement.

Richard II was considered controversial at the time as it depicts the overthrow and murder of an anointed monarch. The deposition scene was often left out when it was performed with this action taking place off stage. Richard II was overthrown in 1399 by Henry Bolingbroke, who became Henry IV. It is unknown exactly when Richard died, but it is thought that he was intentionally starved to death so that there were no signs of violence on the body, and he died around February 1400. Henry had initially agreed to let Richard live, but this changed with the Epiphany Rising when the Earls of Huntingdon, Kent and Salisbury, and Lord Despenser all agreed to depose the new king, Henry IV, and restore the imprisoned Richard II. To save himself and his throne Henry believed that he had no choice but to kill Richard. He would not be safe while Richard lived, in much the same way as William Cecil and Francis Walsingham believed that Elizabeth would not be safe while Mary Queen of Scots lived. In Richard II's final speech in Shakespeare's play, as he is dying, he declares:

> Thy fierce hand
> Hath with the king's blood stain'd the king's own land.
> Mount, mount, my soul! Thy seat is up on high,
> Whilst my gross flesh sinks downward, here to die.[15]

Richard knew he would die, who was responsible, and believed he would ascend to heaven. Richard jinxes the land with his last breath, claiming that by killing the king, one of God's anointed, appointed by divine right, the land will be cursed. Indeed, within half of a century of Richard's death, the country would slide into civil war, the Wars of the Roses, with cousins fighting cousins, and would not emerge from it until the Tudors were on the throne. Richard II's own deposition and murder by Henry IV laid the groundwork for Edward IV to seize the throne from Henry VI, Richard III to seize it from Edward V, and Henry VII to seize it from Richard III. The overture which applied to Elizabeth I was that the execution of Mary Queen of Scots had cursed England and Elizabeth's reign, and the country would once again fall into war. The English Civil War, which would result in the fall of the monarchy itself and creation of a republic, was less than fifty years away by this point. The symmetry is inexplicable, but the implication for Essex was that a monarch could be deposed and replaced by a subject. Essex never claimed the throne, but it was certainly an implied threat.

Bolingbroke's own response to the murder of Richard II in Shakespeare's play echoes that of Elizabeth I when she was told about the execution of Mary Queen of Scots. Both Elizabeth and Bolingbroke mourned the death of a rival that would make them stronger theoretically. Bolingbroke's final speech, and the end of the play, declares:

> Lords, I protest, my soul is full of woe,
> That blood should sprinkle me to make me grow:
> Come, mourn with me for that I do lament,
> And put on sullen black incontinent.
> I will make a voyage to the Holy Land,
> To wash this blood off from my guilty hand.[16]

Bolingbroke declared his guilt, but believed God would understand and forgive his actions, hence the visit to the Holy Land. He also acknowledged that spilling Richard's blood made him stronger but that he did not really want to do it and mourned for him. This mourning certainly echoes Elizabeth, who publicly mourned Mary Queen of Scots, and punished those who had played a part in the execution. Her secretary, William Davison, was imprisoned in the

Tower, and William Cecil, Lord Burghley, was banished from her presence for the first and only time as a result. There were a lot of parallels between *Richard II* and the situation with Elizabeth and Mary Queen of Scots. There was also an underlying suggestion that the same could happen to Elizabeth in revenge. This explains why *Richard II* was so controversial at this time and acted as a catalyst for Essex's Rebellion. It also prompted the strong government reaction to the revolt, as it sparked real fears for the queen's life and the future of the crown of England.

At 10 a.m. on 8 February 1601 four Privy Councillors, Thomas Egerton, 1st Viscount Brackley and Lord High Chancellor, Edward Somerset, 1st Earl of Worcester, William Knollys, and Chief Justice John Popham, arrived at Essex House on the Strand in London and demanded an explanation of rumours that Essex intended to force his way into the queen's presence at Whitehall and demand the removal of his enemies like Robert Cecil, Sir Walter Raleigh, and Henry Brooke, 11th Baron Cobham, from the court. He wanted his own supporters to be put in their place. Essex had spread a rumour in London, again hoping to gain support, that he refused to attend council meetings because an ambush was being planned against him and he worried for his life. He was told to return to the court to answer for himself. Essex refused to respond to the accusations made against him and locked the councillors in his library. Ferdinando Gorges, one of the conspirators, had got cold feet and revealed the plot to Sir Walter Raleigh, who had alerted the council.[17] No double agents were involved in this plot, just a man likely convinced that it could not succeed and feared the consequences, who revealed what he knew. The historian Peter Ackroyd claims that, if the chance to appeal directly to the queen was denied him, Essex intended to push for a recall of Parliament to give him justice.[18] Whether this would have worked is debateable as Parliament could still be hugely influenced by the monarch. Parliament only really started to wield influence during Henry VIII's Break with Rome in the 1530s, and by Elizabethan times it still did not represent the whole population, but it was becoming an essential part of the English political system. The role of Parliament and its relationship with the monarchy would come to a head during the English Civil War in the 1640s and the establishment of a republic on the execution of Charles I.

Essex let his paranoia take over once he was isolated from the court and what were probably steadying influences on him. Essex and his supporters left Essex House after locking the councillors in the library and marched down the Strand via Ludgate to St Paul's, expecting the citizens of London to rise up and join them to overthrow his own enemies at court. This expected support failed to materialise as the people were not really interested in a petty rivalry between the queen's councillors; it did not affect their daily lives. They did not want to get involved and risk the deadly consequences if, as seemed likely from the beginning, the revolt failed. A barricade had already been erected between Whitehall and Charing Cross thanks to the warning of Ferdinando Gorges, preventing access to the palace, and the guard had been increased within the palace walls as well. Troops under Sir John Leveson occupied Ludgate. Essex's chances of reaching the Queen were miniscule. Had he marched directly on Whitehall rather than marching up the Strand he would have had a better chance of reaching the queen, but success would still have been unlikely. The court was shocked and taken by surprise by Essex's actions, having not expected him to act so rashly, but quickly put measures in place to halt his advance to the queen.

The rebels, numbering around 300 men,[19] largely Essex's own retainers and those of the Earl of Southampton who was his chief supporter, reached as far as Fenchurch Street and the house of Sheriff Thomas Smythe. It has been suggested that Essex spent three hours in Smythe's home while Smythe went to get the Lord Mayor and Robert Cecil barred the exit from the city. This account only seems to appear in Penry Williams' book about Essex being at the home of Sheriff Smythe.[20] The truth of this story has not been validated and it likely would have appeared in other sources had it been true. It seems unlikely that Essex would have sat still for three hours, allowing time for the authorities to act against him and seal the city to stop him getting to the queen. Others report that Essex contacted Smythe, but not that he was in his house for three hours. The historian Anne Somerset reports that Essex had a message supposedly from Sheriff Smythe putting 1,000 men at Essex's service.[21] This would explain why Essex approached Smythe in the first place. The sheriff reneged on his promise to help, and few men came forward to support Essex. Smythe was nevertheless suspected of supporting Essex because he was known to have been in contact with him, even had he not provided troops. In the aftermath of the revolt, Smythe would be removed from his office of Sheriff and sent to the Tower. Some people abandoned Essex when they heard that he had been declared a traitor, not wanting to share his inevitable fate.

Henry Wriothesley, 3rd Earl of Southampton, wrote to his wife that 'God's will must be done and what is allotted to us by destiny cannot be avoided'.[22] It is likely that he was parroting Essex and trying to explain their rebellion. Perhaps Essex had said this to his followers to persuade them to follow him and perhaps he even believed it himself after a while, that their revolt was providence. Essex's destiny seems to have been to die for his own stupidity in believing that he could reach Whitehall and persuade the queen to do as he willed. He condemned others who, had they not met him, likely would not have died. Elizabeth was known to have the Tudor temper and she likely would not have reacted well to being threatened or blackmailed. Had he reached the palace he may well have been condemned for treason and executed anyway. Essex would claim at his trial that the source of the allegations against Robert Cecil was in fact the Earl of Southampton and not himself. Southampton claimed that his source was Sir William Knollys, who was called into the court and in fact exonerated Cecil. Possibly Essex making the accusation in the first place was just his attempt to save himself, even if it meant bringing Southampton and Knollys down.

The rebels reached as far as Queenhithe or Ludgate Hill, near St Paul's Cathedral, depending on which account you read, having also been up Fleet Street and Cheapside. Essex continued to claim that Robert Cecil and Sir Walter Raleigh wanted to kill him, and that his uprising was to prevent that happening. The rebels were confronted by Elizabeth's guards at the barricade held by the Lord Mayor, Sir John Gerrard, and heralds proclaimed the Earl of Essex a traitor. The rebels believed that resistance to their cause would be slight but, as much as the people sympathised with Essex's situation, they would not rebel against their queen for his cause. Elizabeth inspired much loyalty and devotion. Essex's page was killed but Essex himself escaped the skirmish with just a few bullet holes in his hat. His followers had fled at the first sign of a serious engagement, demonstrating how unprepared they were for resistance to their scheme. The historian G.R. Elton claims that Essex had lost control and spent fifteen minutes holding onto a horse's bridle while he poured out his woes to the official on the horse.[23] This possibly suggests a complete breakdown in his mental state given how unstable he appeared before, or the onset of cold fear when he realised his cause was lost. The rebels did not have much support, so returned to Essex House to find that the hostages had been released by Ferdinando Gorges, who knew that keeping hostages sent from the Privy Council would only make things worse for all of them. It has been suggested that Gorges was a spy who had betrayed the scheme to Robert Cecil.[24] Perhaps he simply hoped that his actions would promote leniency towards him. The house was then surrounded by royal troops.

At 9 p.m. that evening, the Earl of Essex and other conspirators surrendered to Charles Howard, 1st Earl of Nottingham, and were taken to Lambeth Palace for questioning. Before surrendering, Essex burned a bag, probably containing his correspondence with the Scottish king, James VI, although there is no way to know for sure as Essex never confessed what exactly the contents were. Elizabeth had refused to go to bed until Essex was arrested and she was sure of her own safety and that of her crown. The following morning, 9 February 1601, Essex, and his followers, were taken from Lambeth Palace to the Tower of London for further questioning and detainment. Elizabeth issued a proclamation thanking Londoners for their loyalty to her and proclaiming Essex's crimes, to try and limit any public outcry of support for him. She was well aware of how popular he was and wanted to limit any damage or protest which might result from his arrest by making it clear she had no choice as he had committed treason. This fear also explains why Francis Bacon wrote his account of the rebellion *A Declaration of the Practises & Treasons attempted and committed by Robert late Earle of Essex and his Complices, against her Maiestie and her Kingdoms, and of the proceedings as well at the Arraignments & Conuictions of the said late Earle, and his adherents* with the collusion of the Privy Council. They wanted to ensure that the official story was out there and accepted as far as possible by the people.

Essex had not attempted to raise any affinity from his own estates so only had around 300 supporters to take London.[25] Other estimates suggest only 200 supporters,[26] or even as low as 140.[27] He was reliant almost exclusively on the population of London rising in his support. Regardless of the exact number, Essex had overestimated his support, and he did not have enough men to make a difference. Perhaps had he tried to raise supporters from his estate, the government would have been more concerned and more willing to negotiate with the rebels. Even then, however, Essex's rebellion was doomed to failure. He had overestimated the support coming from the King of Scotland, James VI, who did not want to become openly involved in a scheme which could jeopardise his chances of succeeding Elizabeth to the English throne. This is why James had not intervened to stop the execution of his mother, Mary Queen of Scots, in 1587. If James would not step in to save his own mother, why would he support a rebellion of a man he did not know? It was well known that Elizabeth was getting old, and James would succeed to the English throne sooner rather than later.

Essex also underestimated the scope of Cecil's intelligence network which had uncovered the plot before it had a chance to gain traction. This was partly Essex's own fault as he could not keep his mouth shut about what he was planning and exactly what his grievances were. This allowed Cecil to pre-empt him.

There was further intrigue to come. On 12 February 1601, just four days after Essex's failed rebellion and arrest, Captain Thomas Lee, one of Essex's followers, was also arrested. He had complained that Essex was being unjustly treated and that he had planned to burst in on Elizabeth when she was having dinner and persuade her to release Essex from the Tower. However, he had been thwarted at the door to the Privy Chamber and the plan failed. Even had he gained entry he almost certainly would have been arrested and imprisoned. Lee was arrested and charged with planning to imprison the queen and release the earls of Essex and Southampton from the Tower. He was executed at Tyburn, as he needed to be made an example of so that others would not try and emulate him. His actions sealed Essex's own fate and Essex spent his final days in the Tower in prayer with his chaplain, Mr Ashton. Lee's mission almost seems suicidal as it could not have hoped to succeed but he embarked on it anyway.

According to the government's version of events, Essex intended to depose the queen and take the throne for himself. This message was spread through London by preachers on 14 February 1601. It does not ring true as Essex did not have a claim to the throne and did not have widespread or powerful support as much as he was a popular figure. The message was intended to completely discredit him. He could have learnt from the failed attempt to put Lady Jane Grey on the throne in 1553 that the people preferred the rightful heir regardless of other considerations. Essex swore that he only wanted to remove Elizabeth's bad counsel, like Robert Cecil. Today some accept Essex's version of events, but he did raise men, try to force his way into the palace, and intended to carry out a coup. It would have been difficult for this to happen without some bloodshed and violence, or even the deposition of Elizabeth. Sir Christopher Blount confessed that no violence was intended against the queen, but that he did not know whether their aims could have been accomplished without bloodshed. He had the right idea. Had someone tried to make Elizabeth change her councillors or force her into doing something she did not want to do, they would have been out of favour at the very least, if not imprisoned.

In the Tower Essex was said to have suffered a complete nervous collapse and he made a fuller confession to Lord Keeper Egerton, Lord Buckhurst, the Earl of Nottingham, and Sir Robert Cecil. Essex himself was alleged to have said that Elizabeth could not be safe while he lived. The council had wanted to give Essex time to reveal more about the conspiracy and who else was involved or sympathetic to their aims. The council had men stationed in London over the next few weeks, fearful that there would be an uprising to release Essex before his trial and execution could be carried out. Essex's popularity meant that some explanation had to be found as to why and how he gave in to treasonous impulses. The prevailing opinion was to discover those who had led Essex astray, the 'evil and selfish leeches' who had inveigled him to commit treason.[28] This meant that Essex could be portrayed to the public as a tragic but essentially innocent victim, yet still be executed for treason. Elizabeth had no choice but to execute him as he was technically guilty, but others were to blame for it. Like with Mary Queen of Scots, the blame for the execution was shifted from Elizabeth even though she signed the death warrants.

Essex, along with the Earl of Southampton, was tried in Westminster Hall for treason and found guilty by a commission of twenty-five peers on 19 February 1601. Nine judges were also appointed, but Essex wanted to challenge three of the judges on the grounds of personal enmity with him which may have caused them to be biased. His request was denied. Verbal testimony had been obtained in the Tower from Charles Danvers, Sir Christopher Blount, the earls of Bedford and Rutland, and lords Sandys and Mountjoy, who had all been involved in the rebellion. Sir Francis Bacon also turned against Essex after earlier giving him a warning and claimed that he wanted to be king. The trial turned into a verbal dual between Essex and Cecil with both trying to get the upper hand over the other. This old childhood rivalry became a struggle for life, supremacy, and death. At his trial, Essex refused to plead for mercy and seemed to remain jaunty and upbeat throughout. Perhaps he believed that Elizabeth would never have him executed because of their previous closeness and friendship, as well as her previous relationship with his stepfather, Robert Dudley, 1st Earl of Leicester. Elizabeth signed Essex's death warrant the following day. It only seems to have been when the Dean of Norwich visited Essex in the Tower and warned him of the danger to his soul that he realised Elizabeth was serious about having him executed and that he would die. Perhaps Essex's conscience took over as the Earl of Southampton was reprieved when Essex appealed for mercy for his friend. Southampton was not executed but sentenced instead to life imprisonment for his role in the rebellion. Southampton remained in the Tower until the accession of James I in 1603, at which time he returned to court. Essex stated that he might legally be a traitor, but that he was innocent in his conscience.

On 21 February 1601, two days after his trial, Essex was visited by several members of the council who declared that he was a traitor, and that Elizabeth would never be safe while he lived. Essex, however, would claim to the end that he never intended any harm to the queen, that he only wanted to be able to state his grievances to her in person and he hoped that she would see his side of the argument. His pride was his downfall.[29] He thought too much of himself and it led him to do things that would lead himself and others to their deaths. Responsibility for Essex's execution fell on the shoulders of Robert Cecil, but the promptness of the actions taken against him suggest that Elizabeth was responsible for the final decision. Had she wavered, as in the case of Mary Queen of Scots fourteen years earlier, it could have been months before a death warrant was signed or it could have been signed and revoked several times. This did not happen. Elizabeth stood firm against Essex's treason. The historian Lacey Baldwin Smith claims that society saw him as 'a proud, ambitious, self-deluded traitor who had cast away salvation for a fantasy spawned by Satan himself'.[30] Possibly too much by today's standards to say that Satan spawned his ideas, but it did allow the idea to flourish that Essex had been corrupted and was in fact a victim. The idea of Satan corrupting people would really take off in the seventeenth century with the witch craze that was just beginning at this point. Essex paid the ultimate price for his errors.

Robert Devereux, 2nd Earl of Essex, was executed on 25 February 1601 on Tower Green within the Tower of London. Elizabeth granted him the private execution he had requested. He was the last person to be given such an honour. It seems to have been the Tudors who granted the privacy of executions on Tower Green rather than public on Tower Hill. It was a botched beheading and took three strokes to separate his head from his body. Essex had left his room at 8 a.m. that morning, accompanied by three servants, and wearing black with a scarlet waistcoat. He removed his ruff and gown then prayed and died whilst reciting the 51st psalm, the same psalm that Lady Jane Grey had recited before her own execution in 1554. He knew how to make a performance out of his death and developed a reputation for heroism and bravery. Some reputations of those executed were exonerated slightly by their deaths; notably that of Elizabeth I's mother, Anne Boleyn. After her death in 1536 some citizens were heard to doubt the official story of why she had died, and her reputation has generally improved as time has gone on. Perhaps Essex hoped to achieve the same for himself. His remains were buried in the Chapel of St Peter ad Vincula within the Tower complex, near the remains of Anne Boleyn, Katherine Howard, and Lady Jane Grey.

Some of Essex's key supporters were also executed: Charles Danvers, Sir Christopher Blount, Gelly Meyrick, and Henry Cuffe.

Historian Lisa Hilton claims that Elizabeth had to execute Essex, as she could not spare him without looking weak; his actions struck at the core of her 'personal power'.[31] If Elizabeth was seen as weak, others could try and take advantage. In the end she did not waver because she knew it was a necessary act to protect herself and England, regardless of any personal connection or affection. Francis Manners, 6th Earl of Rutland, was imprisoned briefly for his involvement in the rebellion. He later became prominent at the court of James I after Elizabeth's death. Robert Radcliffe, 5th Earl of Sussex, was rumoured to have been involved but was appointed to sit on the commission which tried the Earl of Essex, so it seems that there was no real evidence of his collusion. Edward Russell, 3rd Earl of Bedford, was fined £10,000 for his participation in the revolt but he was not imprisoned. The uprising was punished relatively leniently compared to other rebellions, possibly because Essex had incited the others to unrest, or the fact that comparatively there were relatively few people involved at all, and it was not a serious threat to Elizabeth or her throne.

Elizabeth later confided to the French ambassador that she would have spared Essex if she could without compromising the security of the realm. But she knew that Essex's execution was necessary. She also admitted that she had hidden the extent of Essex's disobedience and his collusion with the enemy from the council. Even with Elizabeth having hidden some of Essex's behaviour, there was more than enough to worry her Privy Council and for them to insist on his trial and execution. Her nobles had to understand that she was the power in England, and that she would not be manipulated or cajoled into things she did not want to do, or into getting rid of councillors who helped her and provided crucial support without good reason. Elizabeth also declared to the French ambassador that, had Essex made it to Whitehall Palace, she would have gone out to meet him to decide which of them ruled. This demonstrates Elizabeth's own sense of her personal power and how secure she felt in the love of her people. Blame for Essex's death fell chiefly on Robert Cecil because of Elizabeth's almost magical power over the English people.

*

Essex's failed rebellion had demonstrated that no subject was greater than the monarch and that no one could force a monarch to do something they did not want to do. The rebellion put an end to the idea that an over-mighty subject could challenge state authority. Essex's Rebellion was the last real aristocratic rising in England. After this point the power of the monarch increased until the Civil War of the 1640s, the abolishment of the monarchy due to a too-powerful king, and the establishment of a temporary republic in England. Then it was a case of the monarch working with the people and parliament as they understood that they could be overthrown if they failed to consult and take advice. It was rumoured that Elizabeth's depression over Essex's death hastened her own end just two years later. People at court after Essex's execution described how Elizabeth seemed to age more quickly and she seemed to grieve deeply for him. She would not have another close favourite as Robert Dudley, Earl of Leicester, and Robert Devereux, Earl of Essex, had been to her.

The Essex Rebellion was not really a serious threat in the way that other rebellions and conspiracies against Elizabeth I were. It was not cohesive and was essentially selfish in its aims. Plots raised in the name of Mary Queen of Scots were more dangerous than this revolt as they had the possibility of foreign support behind them, and a woman at the centre with an excellent claim to the English throne. Essex did not have either of these things to benefit his uprising. He was more like a child throwing his toys out of the pram when he could not have his own way.

Essex had disappointed Elizabeth and embarrassed her, and she could not forgive that. He had taken Elizabeth's favour and good grace for granted and in the end, it was his undoing. It has been suggested that Essex was trapped into treason, 'a victim of society and the paranoia it spawned'.[32] This is an interesting idea, that it was the precise set-up of society, and the royal court in particular, which drove Essex to rebellion, because he was so much in need of the queen's favour. Essex was Elizabeth's last favourite, and she would not have that close relationship with anyone else for the remaining two years of her life. First, she had lost Robert Dudley, Earl of Leicester, her childhood friend and quite possibly her true love, and now she had executed his stepson, her second favourite, Robert Devereux, Earl of Essex. Elizabeth earned reproach for Essex's execution even after her own death in 1603, and some people today cannot understand why she had to kill him. Elizabeth understood threats to her throne, and she acted to make sure her throne and her power were safe. She acted more swiftly in dealing with the Earl of Essex than she did with Mary Queen of Scots, because Mary's execution actually made her own position more unstable. Essex's execution would strengthen Elizabeth's own position and prove to other nobles that she was willing to do what it took to stabilise England. Elizabeth had demonstrated her power, and this was the final rebellion of her reign, and of the Tudor dynasty.

Chapter 7

Elizabeth and Rebellion

'Deprive the same Elizabeth of her pretended title to the crown'[1]

Elizabeth I had to deal with several rebellions during her -year reign. It was the longest reign of any Tudor monarch and is often considered a 'Golden Age' in spite of the religious and political upheaval which occurred during this period. The majority of these rebellions under Elizabeth involved Mary Queen of Scots in some way, who had fled to England from Scotland in 1568. The first rebellion against Elizabeth occurred in 1569 just a year later. The last rebellion against Elizabeth was in 1601, just two years before Elizabeth's death, though this was the first rebellion in fifteen years since the Babington Plot in 1586 and the execution of Mary Queen of Scots the following year. This implies that Mary was by and large the catalyst for revolt in Elizabeth's reign. However, religion also played a role as Catholics were the primary rebels, likely precisely because of their support for Mary Queen of Scots.

Even before her reign began, Elizabeth had experience with rebellions. Her father, Henry VIII, dealt with what was the largest rebellion of the Tudor dynasty, the Pilgrimage of Grace, just three years after Elizabeth's birth. This was as a result of his religious reforms which had enabled him to marry Elizabeth's mother, Anne Boleyn. Elizabeth would not remember this, but she would later have heard talk about the sheer number of rebels who acted against the king and how they could have won through numbers alone if it had come to battle. Luckily, the king's representatives opened up negotiations, so it never got that far, even if Henry did not honour any of the promises made in his name. Negotiating and making promises was used as a delaying tactic but they were never intended to be kept. Elizabeth would also have known about the Kett and Western Rebellions under her half-brother, Edward VI, in 1549 which happened when she was 16 years old. She was not involved in them but would have been aware of the numbers of rebels and the reprisals that were enacted on those who revolted against her half-brother and the Protector, both in the Western Rebellion and Kett's Rebellion in Norfolk, which took place almost simultaneously.

As we have seen in Chapter 1, the rebellion that Elizabeth was most closely associated with prior to acceding to the throne in 1558 was the Wyatt Rebellion under her half-sister, Mary I, in 1554. She was imprisoned in the Tower of London because of her suspected involvement with the rebels, although no concrete evidence against her could be found or made to stick. This must have been terrifying for her at age 21 as she was lodged in the same place where her mother, Anne Boleyn, had resided before her execution eighteen years earlier. Elizabeth must have feared that she would meet the same fate. There were few who went into the Tower of London who came out alive. Elizabeth was luckily in this minority. There is not really any evidence to suggest that Elizabeth was involved in the rebellion at all and Wyatt himself protested her innocence on the scaffold before his own execution. It was a cruel trick played by Mary I to send soldiers to Elizabeth's cell in the Tower on 19 May 1554, the very anniversary of her mother's execution eighteen years before. However, rather than the expected summons to her own execution, Elizabeth was told that she could leave the Tower for house arrest at Woodstock. A strange kind of symmetry, but no doubt a scary experience for Elizabeth.

The key lesson that Elizabeth learnt from these early experiences of rebellion was that the heir to the throne could be used to foment rebellion, even if they were not directly involved in said revolt. Their name could be used to rally support, as Elizabeth's was during the Wyatt Rebellion. Elizabeth probably hoped that this was the case with Mary Queen of Scots during the Ridolfi (1571), Throckmorton

(1583), and Babington (1586) Plots, but she had to accept in the end that Mary was herself involved and others were not simply using her name. A difficult thing to accept and helps to explain why Elizabeth deliberated so long in signing Mary's death warrant after her trial. There was irrefutable evidence of Mary's involvement so it could not be denied and in the end, Elizabeth had no choice. That was difficult for her to come to terms with. Mary was an anointed queen, and executing a person chosen by God in this way was anathema to Elizabeth and carrying out that execution weakened her own position. If one queen could be forced to abdicate and then executed on a charge of treason, what was to stop others doing the same to Elizabeth?

*

It is interesting to consider whether the five different rebellions examined in this book can really be considered rebellions. There were only two where there were people marching through the streets causing chaos and shouting their demands for all to hear, more like a popular movement than a conspiracy. This is really what is traditionally thought of as a 'rebellion', like the Pilgrimage of Grace in 1536 or the Wyatt Rebellion of 1554. The first Elizabethan rebellion, the Northern Rising of 1569, was without a doubt the largest-scale revolt under Elizabeth I with thousands of rebels involved. The Essex Rebellion of 1601 was on a much smaller scale but no one in London at least could fail to hear about what was happening with Essex and his supporters marching through the streets and shots being fired. The other three were plots, treasonous conspiracies, and intrigues whispered behind closed doors rather than out in the open. All resulted in executions as they were without doubt plotting against the queen and her government.

'Rebellion' is sometimes a controversial term with historians and scholars not being able to agree on what exactly constitutes a rebellion. The *Oxford English Dictionary* describes 'rebellion' as 'an organised armed resistance to an established ruler or government; an uprising, a revolt'.[2] The Northern Rising of 1569 and the Essex Rebellion of 1601 would seem to fall into this category as both involved armed followers, organised to a degree, and resisting Elizabeth and her government or, more specifically, Elizabeth's advisors like the Cecils. The Northern Rising was acting against William Cecil, Lord Burghley, and others considered to be of low birth whom Elizabeth trusted, and the Essex Rebellion was acting against Robert Cecil, son of William Cecil who had replaced his father as Elizabeth's right-hand man. Both sets of rebels believed that the monarch should be advised by her nobility rather than those she promoted from lower ranks to serve her even though they demonstrated their abilities and usefulness. Choosing power and wealth over ability can still be a problem today. Many of the nobility under Elizabeth's father, Henry VIII, felt the same way, as Henry was advised by the son of a butcher, Cardinal Thomas Wolsey, and the son of a blacksmith, Thomas Cromwell, who would later become the 1st Earl of Essex. This provoked much hostility towards these men and would be used in their downfall. Elizabeth would not turn on her closest and most trusted advisors in the way that her father did.

On the other hand, 'conspiracy' is something murkier, altogether darker, and often harder to uncover. It often seems to surround those closest to the throne rather than the 'common people'. The *Oxford English Dictionary* defines 'conspiracy' as 'a combination of persons for an evil or unlawful purpose; an agreement between two or more persons to do something criminal, illegal, or reprehensible (especially in relation to treason, sedition, or murder); a plot'.[3] The Ridolfi, Throckmorton and Babington Plots would fall into this category rather than a 'rebellion'. They are generally described as plots rather than rebellions, as there was not any armed rising or more general revolt. They were plots by a small number of people usually to force change or, if that was not possible, and particularly with the later plots, to replace Elizabeth I with Mary Queen of Scots and thus change the queen and succession. This was unquestionably treason and would have encompassed both murder and regicide had the plotting succeeded. The aims of these plots were more nefarious and potentially far more dangerous to the established order. They would have had more far-reaching consequences had they been successful. These are the more interesting of the rebellions and plots examined here as there is so much more to consider than just an armed revolt. They are also more complex as there is often less surviving evidence. Fewer people were involved but the stakes were much higher.

It is worth examining briefly the similarities between the Elizabethan rebellions and the Gunpowder Plot of 1605. The Gunpowder Plot took place just two years after Elizabeth's death when James I was on the throne. A group of Catholic conspirators including Guy Fawkes, Robert Catesby, Francis Tresham, John Wright, and Thomas Winter planned to blow up the Houses of Parliament with a store of gunpowder underneath the Painted Chamber at Westminster. They were all staunch Catholics who had been drawn into the plot by its instigator, Robert Catesby. Tresham had already been involved in the Essex Rebellion against Elizabeth I in 1601 and was imprisoned as a result at that time. The explosion would take out the royal family, Parliament, and many of the peers of the realm and the plotters then planned to install James's daughter, Elizabeth, on the throne as a puppet queen. It is unknown exactly how the plot was discovered and foiled in time, but there have been suggestions of a mole in the group of plotters, rather like Sir Francis Walsingham used with Robert Poley and Gilbert Gifford in the Babington Plot of 1586. This would have offered an insider view of the plot and could enable the government to know who was involved without having to resort to torture or other underhand methods to make that discovery. The idea of a mole in the group could also help to explain why it was foiled in time, discovering Guy Fawkes sitting on the barrels of gunpowder waiting for his moment. The discovery of such an audacious Catholic plot just two years into James I's reign in England demonstrates that

Catholic plotting had not stopped with the execution of Mary Queen of Scots, but it gives a sense that it had gone underground until a suitable alternative monarch was found. The young Princess Elizabeth was only aged 9 at the time, so could not have exercised power herself and could have been moulded into a Catholic queen. The Gunpower Plot ultimately failed and resulted in plenty of executions for treason as did rebellions against Elizabeth I when the Catholic plotters failed to unseat her. The Gunpowder Plot seems to have taken lessons from the plots under Elizabeth I to put Mary Queen of Scots on the throne. The plots against Elizabeth were not bold enough. The Gunpowder Plot was more audacious than the likes of the Ridolfi, Throckmorton, Parry, and Babington Plots because it needed to be to have a better chance of success as the government improved its own responses to plotting and the security around the monarch and parliament.

Plotting and rebellion offered people a chance to express themselves and to have a say of some sort in the running of the country before an established parliament and elections offered a legal way to do so. A rebellion defied the status quo and all of the revolts in this book do just that. They aimed for big changes in England but failed in their aims and resulted in multiple executions. Plots were discovered again and again against Elizabeth I and her Protestant government. Plotting seemed to be inevitable at a time where religion was so unstable in many countries. They were Catholic plots against a Protestant government, and religion seems to have been, and continues to be today, the most divisive issue of all.

*

The main consequence of the Elizabethan rebellions was the execution of Mary Queen of Scots in 1587, less than a year after discovery of the Babington Plot. Mary's name had been linked to plots and rebellions going as far back as 1569, the year after she fled to England from Scotland. There were rumours of a planned marriage between Mary and Thomas Howard, 4th Duke of Norfolk, which Elizabeth I was staunchly against. Norfolk was eventually executed in 1572 after the failed Ridolfi Plot. Elizabeth I was reluctant to prosecute Mary for her involvement and managed to hold off for nearly twenty years, while being pushed into it by her people, her Privy Councillors, and Parliament. Even after Mary was tried and found guilty, Elizabeth signed and destroyed the death warrant several times before signing it for the final time on 1 February 1587 and handing it to her secretary, William Davison. It has been suggested that William Cecil, Lord Burghley, had told Elizabeth that a Spanish Armada had landed in Wales in order to pressure her into signing the warrant.[4] This was underhand, but made Elizabeth panic. Walsingham and Burghley believed that Elizabeth and England would not be safe while Mary lived. On 3 February, the Privy Council met in secret without the queen's knowledge and decided to execute the warrant immediately, without involving Elizabeth any further. There were concerns that Elizabeth would rethink it and revoke the warrant yet again before it could be carried out. The council took matters into their own hands and would suffer for it, but many believed, as did Sir Ralph Sadler, that while Mary lived there was 'no safety for our most gracious sovereign'.[5] The council's determination to protect Elizabeth, and themselves, who would surely fall if Mary succeeded in overthrowing her, pushed them into action.

The executioner, Mr Bull, travelled to Fotheringhay Castle, where Mary was imprisoned under the auspices of Sir Amyas Paulet and where she had been tried in the Great Hall. On his journey, Bull dressed as a servant and hid his axe in his trunk. Mary was only told the day before that she was to be executed. She spent her final night in prayer and arranging for her things to be given away to those who were important to her and those who had served her. She was initially told that none of her ladies could accompany her to the scaffold, but that would have meant she had to be undressed by the executioner which was considered to be unacceptable for a lady and a queen.

There were concerns that her ladies would create relics from her possessions, or rags dipped in her blood. Eventually she was allowed to have a couple of ladies accompany her, in order that it could not be said she was denied anything owed to her rank and position. She had to promise that her ladies would not cry or create a scene or attempt to produce relics. Mary readily made the promise so that they could witness her death and spread the word of her as a Catholic martyr.

Mary was executed in the Great Hall at Fotheringhay Castle in Northamptonshire on 8 February 1587. When her ladies helped her to remove her outer garments for the executioner, she was wearing a scarlet petticoat, the colour of Catholic martyrdom. Mary believed that she was dying as a martyr for the Roman Catholic faith she had held her entire life. She was determined to present it that way, in any case, although really, she was dying condemned for treason against Elizabeth I. Mary's last request, to be buried in France either beside her mother, Mary of Guise, or her first husband, Francis II of France, was refused. She was interred instead in Peterborough Cathedral nearly five months after her death, close to the remains of Henry VIII's first wife, Katherine of Aragon. For five months after her death her body remained at Fotheringhay. Mary's servants were finally allowed to return home after the interment, having been kept imprisoned at Fotheringhay since her death. When Mary's son, James, succeeded Elizabeth on the English throne, he had her body removed from Peterborough and reinterred in Westminster Abbey, near the remains of Elizabeth and her half-sister, Mary I. This was considered a more proper burial place for the king's mother. These two mortal enemies, Elizabeth I and Mary Queen of Scots, are now closer in death than they ever were in life.

Almost everything that had surrounded Mary at her execution was burned, including the block itself. There was to be nothing left behind to become a relic to a martyred queen. The executioner was allowed to keep his axe, but the clothes and jewels which usually the executioner was allowed to keep as part of his payment, were scoured or burnt. When Mary's body was removed after the execution, her dog, a Skye terrier, was found cowering in her skirts. It had sneaked into the hall unnoticed to be with its mistress at the end. The dog was covered in blood and would not long outlast Mary, pining for her to the end. A set of rosary beads said to have been carried by Mary at her execution survived in the possession of one of her ladies but were stolen in a raid on Arundel Castle in 2021. These are one of the only surviving items said to have been with Mary at her end and are priceless and irreplaceable due to the historical significance attached to them. Mary's heart and entrails were removed when her body was embalmed and buried somewhere within the castle. The exact location remains unknown. Fotheringhay Castle itself no longer survives, only a mound of earth and some masonry.

After the execution, Elizabeth wrote to Mary's son, James VI of Scotland, on 14 February 1587 describing the 'extreme dolor that overwhelms [her] mind for that miserable accident which far contrary to [her] meaning hath befallen'.[6] Elizabeth refused to take responsibility for Mary's execution, even though she had signed the death warrant. She persistently said that she never intended for it to be used and only meant for it to be a form of security. In the letter Elizabeth goes on to say that 'if [she] had meant it [she] would never lay it on others' shoulders'.[7] If she had never meant for the death warrant to be used, then why did she sign it? It seems implausible somehow to sign it just for security. She could sign it at any time she wanted to. Unless she truly did fear for her life and intended for it to be used in the event of her assassination. Elizabeth wanted plausible deniability so did not command directly for the warrant to be used. The letter apologised to James for the death of his mother, which he did not really take any action to stop before it happened anyway, and he never took any action against Elizabeth or England afterwards. James knew he was the most likely candidate to take the throne after Elizabeth's death and he likely did not want to jeopardise that. James never really knew his mother as she had been taken from him when he was a child; he had heard of her plotting against the English queen, so perhaps he felt little love or filial obedience towards her. His life would, in a sense, be easier once Mary was dead, but he would move his mother's body to a more royal resting place.

The queen's secretary, William Davison, was used as a scapegoat in Mary Queen of Scots' execution. Elizabeth had given him the death warrant for safekeeping after she had signed it to get the Great Seal attached. Davison had taken it to Burghley and the Privy Council who had decided to execute it without consulting the queen further in case she changed her mind again. Davison had no real say in this decision, but it was he who was imprisoned, fined, and under threat of execution for a time in the Tower of London. In the end, he was sentenced to forfeit his office, imprisonment during the queen's pleasure, and to pay a fine of 10,000 marks.[8] Davison was eventually released from imprisonment in December 1588 after the Armada crisis; he kept his office but could not exercise the power of it or obtain any of the wealth from it. He would die in December 1608 in Stepney, not accepted back at court, even after Elizabeth's death. Perhaps James blamed Davison in part for his mother's death and did not want to see him around to be reminded of it. This would be understandable, even though Davison had no real role in the execution of the warrant. Burghley and Walsingham were already dead so could not be censured or punished for their role.

The execution of Mary Queen of Scots also led directly to the attempted invasion of England by Philip II of Spain using the Spanish Armada in 1588. Philip used Mary's execution as an excuse to invade England with the support of the Pope as a Catholic crusade, though he had been plotting against Elizabeth for many years prior to this. As we have seen, he was involved in plots against Elizabeth through his ambassadors in England, two of whom were expelled from the country as a result. There had been rumours of earlier armadas gathering but no moves were actually made. It took the execution of an anointed queen for Philip to actually act. He had been preoccupied with the Dutch Revolt and quelling rebellion there. The benefits of executing Mary Queen of Scots far outweighed the potential negative consequences of the decision for England as it 'physically removed the symbol of Catholic resistance'.[9] Without a physical symbol of resistance there was less for any potential future rebels to fight for. This was proved true with a quiet period without revolt in England after Mary's execution in 1587. The people actually celebrated Mary's death in London. The English navy managed to successfully see off the Spanish Armada in 1588 with the help of the British weather as the Spanish vessels scattered before the English fire ships, and were then wrecked in the strong winds off the coasts of Scotland and Ireland.

The execution of Mary Queen of Scots was probably the most important and consequential event that happened as a result of Elizabethan rebellion. The trial and execution of a former anointed regnant queen had never happened before in England. It could be argued that Lady Jane Grey was the forerunner, but as she only ruled for fourteen days and was never crowned, she does not seem to be recognised by most historians as a lawful Queen of England. Mary I declared herself queen at the same time as Jane. Of course, both Anne Boleyn and Katherine Howard, the second and fifth wives of Henry VIII, were executed, but they were not regnant queens: they were queen consorts. The execution of Mary Queen of Scots broke the belief that anointed sovereigns were sacrosanct, appointed by God and ruling by divine right, and that their bodies were sacred. The idea of the divine right of kings had been the cornerstone of monarchy for as long as anyone could remember. But, clearly, if one queen could judicially murder another one, what was setting them apart from the ordinary people? This would lead indirectly to the judicial murder of Charles I in the seventeenth century at Whitehall Palace, and the abolition of the monarchy completely for eleven years when England became a republic. In the end, however, the English people decided they wanted their monarchy back, so Charles I's son,

Charles II, reclaimed the English throne in 1660. English monarchy has remained unbroken from then until the present day.

*

A key part of Elizabeth I's response to rebellion came from the idea of divine right. Monarchs were chosen by God to rule over a country and ordained at their coronation with the holy oil, placing them outside of the rules applying to mere mortals. This is one of the things that made it so difficult for Elizabeth to sign the death warrant for Mary Queen of Scots. She had been ordained by God to rule in Scotland and was also dowager Queen of France. Mary was a queen twice over and Elizabeth was reluctant to demonstrate so publicly that the bond between a monarch and God could be broken so easily. If Elizabeth could execute Mary Queen of Scots, what was to stop someone doing the same to Elizabeth herself?

Antonia Fraser, whose biography of Mary Queen of Scots is considered a cornerstone by many, discusses the idea that it cannot have been legal for Mary, the monarch of a sovereign country, to be tried for treason in England when she was in no sense one of Elizabeth I's subjects.[10] This is a very interesting concept. In England, it was a cornerstone of justice that an accused person had the right to be tried by a jury of their peers. Who were Mary's peers? She had no peer in England except Elizabeth herself, as no one else was anointed with the divine right of ruling and directly under the auspices of God. Mary was tried by Elizabeth's peerage and her Privy Council. These men, no matter how qualified and no matter how many there were, could not be said to be Mary's equal. Therefore, was the trial even legal in that sense? Surely the correct course of action at the time, even had Mary engaged in activities against Elizabeth I which could be considered treason, was to expel her from the country? This had been considered over the nineteen years that Mary was imprisoned in England, but it was considered by the likes of Elizabeth, Burghley, and Walsingham, among others, that Mary would have been more of a risk free and abroad than imprisoned in England. She would have more chance of foreign support and of raising an army to attack England.

The real nail in Mary's coffin was the *Act for the Queen's Safety*, also known as the *Bond of Association*. This was used as a justification for Mary's trial and subsequent execution, in spite of the issue of divine right and being God's anointed. The Act declared that anyone who acted against Elizabeth I would be guilty of treason and subjected to the penalties of that conviction. It did not differentiate between the general populace, peers, and monarchs.[11] The Act was put into force precisely to try and catch Mary out and indict her on charges of treason to stop her being such a danger to Elizabeth. She promoted rebellion just by being alive and in England, so close at hand. Removing the figure of Mary would be the easiest and most conclusive way to stop these plots and revolts from manifesting. This would prove true with no further rebellions in England for fourteen years after Mary's death.

*

Two of the key figures in the reign of Elizabeth I were her spymaster Sir Francis Walsingham, and Secretary of State and Lord High Treasurer, William Cecil, 1st Baron Burghley. They worked closely together to uncover plots and conspiracies against their queen. They would have been the first to suffer had any of the plots been successful in unseating Elizabeth and replacing her with the Catholic Mary Queen of Scots. They were known to support the Protestant reforms and to be pushing for action to be taken against Mary to protect Elizabeth, Protestantism, and England. They would not have been able to reconcile themselves to a government headed by Mary Queen of Scots and returning to Papal obedience, though Cecil had managed to survive under Mary I. Walsingham and Cecil recognised the 'heightened sense of urgency' gripping England and the Privy Council to act against Mary as the 1570s and then the 1580s progressed.[12] There was an increased sense of pressure from the Pope and Catholic Europe, exacerbated by the *Regnans in Excelsis* excommunication bull issued against Elizabeth I in 1570. This bull will be examined, and its wider significance explored, later in the chapter. It did, however, give a sense of legality for the plotters against Elizabeth as the bull meant that they would have the Pope's backing to unseat her.

The pair were 'unequivocally dedicated to the protection of their queen, country, and religion'.[13] Walsingham and Cecil would have given their lives had they believed that it was necessary for the protection of Elizabeth and England. Luckily, it did not come to that, and they managed to protect England and preserve Elizabeth's queenship without having to sacrifice themselves. The ones who lost their lives in pursuit of safety and security were the likes of Francis Throckmorton, Anthony Babington and, of course, Mary Queen of Scots; those who rebelled against Elizabeth and were a threat to her rule. England seemed like a more dangerous place when these two men had passed on and handed the baton to others to carry on their work, others who would not be quite as zealous as Cecil and Walsingham or have quite such a productive working relationship with each other. England was definitely poorer with their deaths in the 1590s.

Moving on from the developing working relationship between Walsingham and Cecil, one of the most significant things to come out of the Elizabethan period was the building of a network of spies and informers, and the use of espionage, codes, and ciphers. This came about largely as a result of plots on behalf of Mary Queen of Scots, against Elizabeth I and the work of Sir Francis Walsingham. Things like this had been used before but not in any organised and efficient way by the English government. The intelligence network would become 'a silent offensive weapon eroding from within the very foundation of future Catholic conspiratorial activities'.[14]

Walsingham's intelligence network was at the forefront of halting Catholic conspiracies in their tracks. Without the intelligence network, the idea to use the Babington Plot to entrap Mary Queen of Scots could not have worked. Walsingham's agents like Gilbert Gifford and Robert Poley were absolutely key to the success or failure of the plan.

*

There are several interesting documents that are linked to Elizabethan rebellions that can offer a lot of insight into the feelings at the time from the perspective of different people. These include several documents meant as propaganda, both official and unofficial from both sides: government and rebels. Several have already been discussed in previous chapters including *Salutem in Christo*, *A discouerie of the treasons practised and attempted against the Queenes Maiestie and the Realme, by Francis Throckmorton*, and Francis Bacon's *A Declaration of the Practises & Treasons attempted and committed by Robert late Earle of Essex*. *Salutem in Christo* and the pamphlet regarding the treasons of Francis Throckmorton were both published anonymously, although there is some suggestion that the Throckmorton one was actually a government pamphlet written in part by Lord Burghley. The Francis Bacon one was written with the collusion of the Privy Council so was very definitely a type of government propaganda.

One of the most important documents to come out of the Elizabethan age was *Regnans in Excelsis*. This was the bull that excommunicated Elizabeth I, issued by Pope Pius V in 1570 after the Northern Rising. It gave those plots that followed, like those by Roberto di Ridolfi, Francis Throckmorton, Dr William Parry, and Anthony Babington, an almost legal basis as the Pope implied it was imperative to overthrow Elizabeth as a 'pretended queen' and 'servant of crime' who led England to a 'miserable ruin'.[15] Ironically, it would be Elizabeth who was lauded as 'Gloriana' reigning over England's

'Golden Age' though this can be seen as a gilded view, given the undercurrents explored throughout the Elizabethan rebellions. There had been pressure in the first decade of Elizabeth's reign from some of the Catholic community in Europe to excommunicate Elizabeth immediately on her accession, but this was not carried out in the hope that she could still be converted back to Catholicism. However, when Pope Pius IV died in 1565, a harder line Papal policy began to emerge with the accession of Pope Pius V.[16] He did not really want to ease Mary Queen of Scots' path to the English throne, but when it became obvious that Elizabeth I would not relent and convert to Catholicism, it was felt that there was little choice but to proceed with the excommunication. The first paragraph of the bull describes the Papal obedience and how God appointed the Pope:

> Made ruler over all peoples and kingdoms, to pull up, destroy, scatter, disperse, plant and build, so that he may preserve His faithful people … in the unit of the Spirit and present them safe and spotless to their Saviour.[17]

What this implies in a roundabout way is that the Pope has dominion over *all* kingdoms in order that the people of those kingdoms might ascend to heaven in the true faith, and not be dragged down to hell for involvement in heresy and schism. The key part is that the Pope was 'made ruler over all peoples and kingdoms', which suggests that it is not a choice made by individual countries or monarchs, but something which just is and cannot be undone, no matter how hard monarchs might try to usurp the power. Pope Pius V is very uncompromising in his wording of the document, which perhaps got Elizabeth's back up and made the English people more determined to resist Papal authority in general.

Pope Pius V had drafted the document while the Northern Rising was still in progress, when it was believed in Rome that Mary Queen of Scots was already married to Thomas Howard, 4th Duke of Norfolk.

It was intended to inspire the rebels in their revolt and lend them an air of legality as well as encouragement from one in power. The bull also hinted at the fact that Elizabeth had automatically become excommunicate by assuming the headship of the Church of England, so the bull was 'more of a formality than a necessity'.[18] Elizabeth's illegitimate and heretical status was not dependent on the bull, but actually already established in the eyes of the Roman Catholic Church. The *Regnans in Excelsis* bull merely put it into writing and proclaimed it across Europe. The key section of the bull as applies to rebellions under Elizabeth reads as follows:

> And also (declare) the nobles, subjects and people of the said realm and all others who have in any way sworn oaths to her, to be forever absolved from such an oath and from any duty arising from lordship. fealty and obedience; and we do, by authority of these presents, so absolve them and so deprive the same Elizabeth of her pretended title to the crown.[19]

This is the section of the bull that absolves the English people of their oath of loyalty to Elizabeth, and almost commands them to seek Elizabeth's overthrow and replace her with a loyal Catholic queen who would return England to Papal obedience. Mary Queen of Scots is not named in the bull, but she is the obvious alternative queen to Elizabeth, and a Catholic to boot. Other potential claimants were Lady Arbella Stuart and Edward Seymour, Lord Beauchamp of Hache, son of Katherine Grey. Arbella would actually marry into the Seymour family and unite the two claims. As a result, she would die in the Tower of London in 1615, having been imprisoned there by James I.

By the time that copies of the bull reached England, the only signs remaining of rebellion were the gallows and hanging rebel corpses across the countryside. The Papacy had acted quite speedily, with the whole process of issuing the *Regnans in Excelsis* bull taking just three weeks. Philip II of Spain wrote to his ambassador, Guerau de Spes, that he was concerned that issuing the bull would lead Elizabeth and her advisors to persecute Catholics in England more harshly and could lead to further reprisals against the rebels.[20] John Felton, a Catholic living in Southwark, on 15 May 1570 nailed a copy of *Regnans in Excelsis* to the Bishop of London's door. This is how the people of England found out that their queen had been excommunicated and the people came out in support of Elizabeth, publishing patriotic ballads and pamphlets.[21] Insults were aimed at the Papacy, and the people really did seem to support Elizabeth, not liking the idea that Rome once again wanted dominion over England, which had been banished by Elizabeth's father, Henry VIII. England was for the English and no one else should have dominion over them. This had been demonstrated in Wyatt's Rebellion in 1554 against the proposed marriage of Mary I to Philip II of Spain, and it would again be revealed in the reaction to the attempted invasion by the Spanish Armada in 1588. Englishmen had their national pride and would not allow a foreign power any authority in their country. The English people might have stretched themselves to accept the accession of Mary Queen of Scots to the English throne, in spite of her religion, but they would never have accepted Philip II of Spain. Not only was he a Catholic, but he was also a foreigner. The excommunication bull also raised the hackles of xenophobia in England and a fierce national pride.

Anyone who continued to obey Elizabeth would send their soul to eternal damnation according to the Pope. The bull made no real distinction between religious laws and civic laws, leaving a large scope for rebels to take advantage of, which was probably the whole idea. This provided the rebels under Ridolfi, Throckmorton, and Babington with a basis for their revolt, and a clear aim from where they could hope to gain support and assistance from the Papacy, the French, and the Spanish, all of whom were Roman Catholics. *Regnans in Excelsis* can help to explain why the plots against Elizabeth in the 1570s and

1580s extended beyond the borders of England, because there was a legal basis for her overthrow and English Catholic rebels expected the assistance of other Catholics across Europe.

*

Would Elizabeth I have had to contend with so much insurrection during her reign had Mary Queen of Scots not fled to England in 1568? We will never know the answer to this question, but it is an interesting issue to consider. There were no rebellions against Elizabeth prior to 1569, and only one after Mary's execution in 1587. Without the influence of Mary Queen of Scots in England, it is possible that there might only have been one, or possibly two, rebellions in Elizabeth's reign, removing the Ridolfi, Throckmorton, Parry, and Babington Plots. The Northern Rising would likely still have taken place, as this was as much to do with noble disaffection as with Mary Queen of Scots, and the Essex Rebellion as this was not anything to do with Mary at all as she was already dead. Mary Queen of Scots seems to have encouraged people to think that there was an alternative to Elizabeth, and that she was accessible to them. However, if people really wanted to oust Elizabeth, they likely would have found another excuse, and another claimant to fight for.

The main appeal to rebels who wanted to replace Elizabeth I with Mary Queen of Scots was that Mary was a Catholic. Those who supported rebellions with her at the core tended to have Catholic leanings, and the potential involvement of the Spanish as the most Catholic country in Europe also backs up this view, along with the support of the Pope, particularly with the publication of the bull of *Regnans in Excelsis* in 1570. Without Mary Queen of Scots in England there may have been less revolt because there was no Catholic alternative to Elizabeth close at hand. Mary's presence in England encouraged the Catholics to act on her behalf, persuaded as well by the circumstances of her imprisonment and how, to many, she had been forced to abdicate and unlawfully replaced on the Scottish throne by her son who was raised as a Protestant. Religion played nearly as much a part in these rebellions as the figure of Mary herself did as the two were inexplicably linked. Religion was key throughout the Tudor period as Edward VI had attempted to stop his Catholic half-sister, Mary I, coming to the throne after his death, nominating instead his cousin, Lady Jane Grey, to succeed him. But his Device for the Succession was overcome and ultimately Mary I succeeded to the throne, paving the way for Elizabeth. The Device had also barred Elizabeth from the succession, as both sisters were illegitimate in law.

Historian Lacey Baldwin Smith wrote that treason was the 'invention of the devil, in whose clever brain were first conceived those seductive but rational enticements that drew weak and susceptible subjects into rebellion'.[22] Mary Queen of Scots provided the 'enticements' that drew Elizabeth's subjects into rebellion. She was an alternative Catholic queen, an imprisoned, romanticised figure that men seemed to want to rescue and help in any way they could. This was the seductive element. Rationality came with the belief that Mary and Papal obedience would be better for England. The rebels who fought for Mary genuinely believed that this was true, and that England would rise as a greater power with Mary Queen of Scots at the helm. They believed that they could succeed because God was on their side. This belief in God was rational thought in Tudor England and God's hand was seen in everything including the weather, plague, and poor harvests. The rebels reasoned that they would be successful because of God's support and that what they were doing was good and right. Similarly with the Earl of Essex and his supporters, they believed that Essex deserved the power and wealth that he believed was rightly his, and Essex drew 'weak and susceptible subjects' into his rebellion with him. Though it could be argued that Essex himself was weak and susceptible, pulled all too easily towards rebellion when things did not go his way. Baldwin Smith offers an interesting view on rebellion, and the idea of the devil was certainly prevalent in Tudor England as a tool of blame for wrongdoing. Logically for the people, if God and heaven existed, so did the Devil and hell. The English people believed that the good would go to heaven and the bad to hell, although there is a much longer explanation for this with the differing Catholic and Protestant views on predestination, but that is not for discussion here. The essential argument is that rebellion was bad and that you would go to hell for revolting against your rightful queen.

*

Elizabeth I and Mary Queen of Scots never met in person, but letters survive between the pair. They were both stuck in a similar situation, being queens regnant where there was not really a precedent for it in their respective countries. The notorious work by John Knox, *The First Blast of the Trumpet Against the Monstrous Regiment of Women*, made clear the prevailing views of the sixteenth century on what the position of women should be, and it was not in ruling a country. 'Regiment' in this sense means 'rule' rather than an army regiment, so he was writing against the rule of women who, by rights, should be subservient to men. Knox would likely have blamed rebellion in England at this time on the fact that the two primary candidates for the throne were both women. An argument no doubt would have been made for the fact that it would not have happened had a man been on the throne. Today, we see this as sexist and discriminatory, but at the time it was a generally accepted view. Right at the beginning of his work, Knox states the following:

> To promote a Woman to bear rule, superiority, dominion or empire above any realm, nation or city is
> A. Repugnant to nature.
> B. Contumely to GOD.
> C. The subversion of good order, of all equity and justice.[23]

Women were always supposed to be inferior to men. Men were made to rule, whether over a country or a home, and women were to raise children and obey their menfolk, whether it was a father, husband, or brother who had dominion over her. Thus, women who wielded power were considered to be unnatural and subverting the natural order of things.

Knox's work was published in 1558, not aimed at Elizabeth I and Mary Queen of Scots, but at Mary I who was ruling in England, and Mary of Guise, who was ruling on behalf of Mary Queen of Scots in Scotland while Mary was in France. Both were Catholic queens, where Knox was a staunch Protestant. Knox's work seems to be more generally applied to Elizabeth and Mary Queen of Scots in the present day, and many of his reflections on gender and power could easily be applied to one or both of these women. When Elizabeth succeeded to the English throne in November 1558, Knox wrote to William Cecil and to the queen herself to defend his work. In writing to the queen, he explained that 'Nothyng in my booke conceaued Is, or can be preiudiciall to your graces iust regiment prouided that ye be not found vngrate unto GOD'.[24] Knox seems more willing to accept Elizabeth I as Queen of England because she was considered to be a Protestant queen who would not return England to Papal obedience, in contrast to Mary I, Mary of Guise, and Mary Queen of Scots. Knox appeared willing to temper his political views on the idea of women in power in order to promote what he saw as the true and proper religion and avoid a regression or counter-Reformation in England. He argued that women were responsible for the breakdown of order in both England and Scotland, and it could be claimed that, had the two claimants for the English throne in the 1570s and 1580s not been women, there would not have been so much contention and rebellion.

*

However, as we have seen, there were plenty of major rebellions under kings as well; the Lambert Simnel and Perkin Warbeck revolts under Henry VII, the Pilgrimage of Grace under Henry VIII, and the Kett and Western Rebellions under Edward VI. The situation between Elizabeth I and Mary Queen of Scots could be seen to echo that of Lady Jane Grey and Mary I in 1553, though that situation took much less time to resolve. Both resulted in the execution of the alternate queen (Jane Grey and Mary Queen of Scots) though neither Elizabeth nor Mary I seemed to want to sign the death warrant, but only felt that they had no choice. Mary I accepted the execution as her own action, but Elizabeth I tried to foist the blame onto someone else. Both were blamed and have been censured for their actions ever since.

It is interesting to examine the similarities between the situation with Mary Queen of Scots under Elizabeth I, and the Lambert Simnel and Perkin Warbeck rebellions under Henry VII. They took place nearly 100 years apart, under the first and last of the Tudor monarchs, but retained many similar qualities. The main difference between them, however, was that Mary Queen of Scots was undoubtedly a legitimate heir to the throne. In contrast, the status of both Lambert Simnel and Perkin Warbeck were questioned. Simnel claimed to be Edward Plantagenet, 17th Earl of Warwick, who was in fact imprisoned in the Tower of London at the time. Warbeck claimed to be Richard Plantagenet, Duke of York, the younger of the Princes in the Tower. Because the bodies of the princes were missing at the time and rumours spread that one, or both, of them had escaped from the Tower, Warbeck's identity was more likely to be real. However, historian Nathen Amin believes that, given all of the evidence, Warbeck was likely born in Tournai rather than being a Yorkist prince.[25] This seems to be the prevailing view, although there are still some who believe that Warbeck really was one of the Princes in the Tower come back to take the throne. Simnel and Warbeck were pretenders rather than true claimants to the English throne, so in this way differed massively from the situation of Mary Queen of Scots.

Simnel, Warbeck, and Mary all managed to gather foreign support for their claims. Simnel had the backing of the Irish. Warbeck managed to gain the backing of the Irish, Scottish, and even Margaret of Burgundy at various points during his long campaign for the throne. Mary Queen of Scots had the support of both the Spanish and French, though mainly the former. Spain was one of the greatest powers in the world at this point so their support would have been crucial to putting Mary on the throne. Elizabeth probably learnt from her grandfather, Henry VII's, experiences with rebellion on how to handle alternative claimants to the throne. Henry VII started off being lenient, sending Lambert Simnel to work in the royal kitchens when he was captured, but became harsher as the threat became more real, executing both Perkin Warbeck and the Earl of Warwick. Elizabeth too would learn this lesson, protecting Mary Queen of Scots in the beginning and preserving her life, but realising in the end that she was too dangerous to live and signing the death warrant.

Elizabeth needed to ensure that, when Mary died, it was known that she had died and there were witnesses to attest to it, otherwise she could have ended up in a similar position as that of Henry VII with the Princes in the Tower. Perkin Warbeck in particular was able to gain so much support for his rebellion in the 1490s precisely because it could not be conclusively proven that he was not Richard, Duke of York, the younger of the Princes in the Tower. The bodies of the princes had not been discovered; they just seemed to have vanished. It was not until renovations at the Tower under Charles II that two bodies were found buried under a staircase in the White Tower, but even now no DNA testing has been done to prove that these are in fact the Princes in the Tower, so there is still no closure to this story in that sense. Mary Queen of Scots was executed in view of members of the council and her own household so that there could be no doubt that she was dead and that there was no point in fighting for her anymore. This provided Elizabeth with some security in knowing that Mary was dead, in a way that Henry VII could not prove with the princes (whether he was involved in their death or not, the debate rages on, but it is not for discussion here). After Mary's execution in 1587 there was no further plotting in her favour, and in fact a period of relative calm began in England after a tumultuous twenty years, despite war with Spain.

Had Mary remained in Scotland, there would have been less temptation in England for people to conspire in her favour, but that is not to say that it would not have happened regardless. Catholics in Elizabeth's Protestant England would still no doubt have found an excuse to rebel, but they would not have had a figurehead or an alternative queen to replace Elizabeth with so close at hand. Mary would most likely have remained imprisoned in Lochleven Castle, at least until her son came of age and could make his own decisions regarding her residence and care. It does not seem like it would have been that different an existence to what she underwent in England, though it is difficult to imagine that James would have signed his own mother's death warrant, so she may have lived longer. Mary's son, James VI of Scotland, did succeed Elizabeth on the English throne after all as James I of England so Mary's line would triumph in the end.

Rebellion under Elizabeth I was certainly complex and murky, enhanced by the development of a spy network controlled by Sir Francis Walsingham, and conspirators who communicated in codes and ciphers, plotting to unseat the queen herself. By reading letters to and from Elizabeth, and some surviving letters between conspirators we can get a sense of what the underworld of intrigue and plotting was like and how plots developed into fully fledged rebellions. Elizabethan rebellions did not always involve thousands or even hundreds of people marching and stating their aims like the Pilgrimage of Grace under Henry VIII or Kett's Rebellion under Edward VI. More often than not, they were underground, which in a way threatened the crown beyond what an upfront revolt could do, exacerbated by arguments over religion and the Catholic vs. Protestant doctrine. Elizabeth herself remarked, 'There is only one Christ Jesus and one faith: the rest is dispute about trifles.'[26] If only Mary Queen of Scots and the rebels who supported her could have accepted this, there might well have been fewer rebellions in England during the sixteenth century as whole, not only under Elizabeth I. With the Northern Rising, Ridolfi, Throckmorton, Parry, and Babington Plots and the Essex Rebellion, religion, succession, and power all played a huge role. Although it was a 'Golden Age' for the likes of literature, art, and the building of national pride, there was certainly much conspiracy, intrigue, and treason in Elizabethan England.

Epilogue

What this exploration of Elizabethan rebellions has demonstrated is that Mary Queen of Scots was the catalyst and primary focus of rebellion against Elizabeth I. The first rebellion against Elizabeth was just a year after Mary fled to England from Scotland after her forced abdication, in 1569. Once Mary was executed in February 1587, there was only one further rebellion, and that was a selfish attempt to regain power and influence rather than something with wider aims regarding religion, the economy and social conditions, or the succession. Had Mary Queen of Scots not fled to England in 1568, would Elizabeth have had to deal with so much insurrection during her reign? That is a question we will never know the answer to, but it is interesting to consider, as we did in the previous chapter.

By looking at the early Tudor rebellions, as we did in Chapter 1, we can begin to understand the history of rebellion under the Tudors and how this influenced Elizabeth's own opinions and later actions against rebels, as well as her attitude towards Mary Queen of Scots. Elizabeth understood Mary Queen of Scots' position as the heir presumptive as others never could, as she had been in the same position under her sister, Mary I. Elizabeth's name was used to gather support in a rebellion in 1554 under Sir Thomas Wyatt the Younger where she took no active role but was still imprisoned in the Tower of London. Her exact involvement is unknown, as Wyatt did write to her, but there is no surviving evidence to suggest that she approved of the plot. She responded to him to say that she would do as she saw fit, but that is as far as their communication is thought to have gone. Elizabeth would always maintain her innocence in the rebellion, as would Wyatt from the scaffold on the day of his execution in April 1554. Elizabeth's experiences in the Tower of London during this time had to have made her fear the place and possibly be loath to send others there without very good reason. She was released from the Tower eighteen years to the day since her mother, Anne Boleyn, was executed there on the orders of her father, Henry VIII. The effect of this experience on a young woman cannot be overestimated. Elizabeth would always stand firm on not having Mary Queen of Scots sent to the Tower, hence her trial and execution took place at Fotheringhay instead. Perhaps Elizabeth's own experiences, rather than just the idea that there might be a rising in Mary's favour in London, played a role in this decision, at least for Elizabeth, if not for her councillors.

Elizabeth knew from her father, Henry VIII, how important the succession was. Henry VII had drilled it into his children from his own experience in the Wars of the Roses that you need an heir and a spare to make a throne secure. Henry VIII had only succeeded to the throne because his older brother, Arthur, died. He was in fact the spare rather than the heir. Henry VIII had annulled his marriage to Katherine of Aragon and killed Elizabeth's own mother, Anne Boleyn, because both had failed to produce a living son. Katherine had delivered a son who survived just eleven weeks and Anne miscarried a son around three and a half months' gestation. Even when Henry had a son by his third wife, Jane Seymour, Edward VI did not make it to his sixteenth birthday before he was dead, having ruled for just six years. Henry VIII was determined that a woman could not rule, but both of his daughters did just that, with Elizabeth I arguably the most successful monarch up to that point, ruling over England's so-called 'Golden Age'. The only female monarch prior to this was Empress Matilda, who was not allowed into London by the citizens to be crowned. Perhaps because Elizabeth did not name a successor, and the fact that there were several contenders, can explain why there was so much controversy. Had she named a successor, whether it was Mary Queen of Scots, Katherine Grey, Arbella Stuart, or someone else entirely, and then had Parliament ratify that decision, it would

Epilogue

have dampened the hopes of other possible claimants. However, it might have inflamed the issue even more, especially had Mary Queen of Scots not been the named successor. There would always be someone willing to fight for her, especially as the Catholic heir. There is no way to know what might have happened; it is one of the great 'what ifs' of the Tudor period.

There was not really a way that Elizabeth could have won over the rebellions she had to contend with. She acted at the beginning of her reign according to her conscience regarding the fate of Mary Queen of Scots and kept her alive and safe, if imprisoned. Elizabeth knew that Mary was still a threat to her and her rule in England. However, Elizabeth would always try and protect the sanctity of royalty and their divine right to rule, more so than Mary's life. It was only when Elizabeth was presented with incontrovertible proof of Mary's complicity in a plot to assassinate her that she acted against her, and then only very reluctantly and after she changed her mind several times. The death warrant was signed and destroyed repeatedly before being signed for the final time on 1 February 1587 and put into effect a week later when Mary was executed on 8 February 1587. Elizabeth did not want to take responsibility for her own actions and would blame Mary's execution on others, like William Cecil and her secretary, William Davison, who would be fined and imprisoned for his role. Elizabeth was beloved by the people and wanted to stay that way, which she could not see happening if she executed Mary. But in the end, she had no choice.

In a strange way, the Essex Rebellion of 1601 was the most intriguing of the plots against Elizabeth because it was so different to any other rebellion or conspiracy, not just under Elizabeth, but under any of the Tudor monarchs. Other rebellions had a wider purpose like religion (Pilgrimage of Grace 1536); succession (Babington Plot 1586); or socio-economic conditions (Kett's Rebellion 1549), but this was purely selfish, and doomed to failure from the beginning as a result. Robert Devereux, 2nd Earl of Essex never managed to get the support that he craved, and lacked the leadership skills to make the rebellion cohesive. Whether it could really be considered a rebellion at all is also up for debate. Essex was certainly rebelling against the queen and her advisors, but was it a rebellion in the sense of an organised and armed resistance, as explored in Chapter 7? Not really because it was not organised in a true sense; it was more a march until it turned into a rout. It also was not a conspiracy like the Ridolfi, Throckmorton, and Babington Plots as there was no agreement to act. Rather, Essex took the initiative, and no real planning went into it.

*

Elizabeth died in her bed at Richmond Palace on 24 March 1603 between two and three o'clock in the morning. She had been in fairly good health until the previous year, although the deaths of Robert Dudley, 1st Earl of Leicester, in 1588; William Cecil, Lord Burghley, in 1598; and Robert Devereux, 2nd Earl of Essex, in 1601, hit her incredibly hard. She was losing all of those people she had come to rely on, those she had spent the most time with, and the people she loved. On her death she was 69 and had reigned for forty-four years, having seen off rebellions, attempted Spanish invasions, plotting nobles, and heartbreak. Her ministers immediately sent word to James VI of Scotland, son of Elizabeth's greatest rival, Mary Queen of Scots, inviting him to take the English throne. Thus, he became James I of England and began the Stuart dynasty which would end in 1714 with the death of Queen Anne, but would encompass the English Civil War, the judicial execution of a king, Charles I, and the creation of a United Kingdom by the Act of Union in 1707.

Queen Elizabeth I, arguably the greatest of the Tudor kings and queens, and one of England's most remembered monarchs, was buried in Westminster Abbey on 28 April 1603. Her coffin was drawn on a hearse hung with black velvet by four black horses from the Palace of Whitehall, where her body had been moved to from Richmond Palace after her death. She was buried with her half-sister, Mary I, in a tomb with the Latin inscription *Regno consortes & urna, hic obdormimus Elizabetha et Maria sorores, in spe resurrectionis* which translates to 'Consorts in realm and tomb, here we sleep, Elizabeth and Mary, sisters, in hope of resurrection.'

The two did not get on well in life but have been together in death already for over 400 years. Their tomb is grand and well worth a visit. Mary Queen of Scots' impressive tomb is also nearby in a side chapel, along with those of Margaret Beaufort (also in a side chapel), and Henry VII and Elizabeth of York, whose magnificent tomb dominates the Lady Chapel. Edward VI is also buried nearby, but does not have a tomb, his burial place instead marked with a simple plaque. The first and last of the Tudors buried so close together has a lovely symmetry, as does Elizabeth I buried closer to her greatest rival, Mary Queen of Scots, than they ever were in life.

Elizabeth had to deal with changing times in England in the latter half of the sixteenth century, and it can certainly be argued that she reigned over a country discovering its own power and carving its place in the world. She had grown up during the tumultuous times of the Break with Rome in the 1530s, under the cloud of her mother, Anne Boleyn's, execution when she was just 3 years old, and under the contrasting religions of her half-brother, Edward VI, and half-sister, Mary I, while trying to survive herself. She was caught up in rebellions in her youth and lived under the threat of execution for several months and that after a supposed controversial dalliance with her stepfather, which in modern times would likely be referred to as child abuse or grooming. All of that was before she even came to the throne. What she learnt from these earlier experiences informed her later style of ruling, and in particular dealing with uprisings against her rule informed by the idea of divine right. Her own experience of rebellion in her youth had a particular effect on the way she approached the Mary Queen of Scots problem which is quite unique in English history. Other monarchs have been imprisoned in England before, but never judicially executed. The likes of Richard II and Henry VI were murdered in secret, where Mary Queen of Scots went to her death very publicly as a Catholic martyr.

This helps to explain why you cannot look at the rebellions of Elizabeth's reign out of the context of the times in which she lived and grew up, because all people are affected by things experienced in our youth, whether it is bullying, overbearing parents, or being completely spoilt. With hindsight, we can see that Elizabeth's problems were larger and with wider national implications than most of us will ever have to deal with in our lives.

There is much to each of the Elizabethan rebellions discussed in this book: differing motivations, participants, and aims, and new methods of uncovering treason through spies, ciphers, and codes. Elizabethan rebellions were full of conspiracy, intrigue, and treason. No one can argue with that.

Endnotes

Introduction

1. David Starkey, *Elizabeth* (2001) p.69
2. Elizabeth I, *Collected Works* (2000) p.17
3. Elizabeth I, *Collected Works* (2000) p.23
4. Laura Brennan, *Elizabeth I: The Making of a Queen* (2020) p.59
5. Susan Doran, *Elizabeth I and Her Circle* (2015) p. 41

1. Earlier Tudor Rebellions

1. *Parliament Rolls of Medieval England* (2005) 'Henry VII, October 1495'
2. David Loades, *Tudors: History of a Dynasty* (2012) p.10
3. Polydore Vergil, *Anglica Historia* (2005) Chapter 26 'Henry VII'
4. Peter Ackroyd, *History of England Vol.1: Foundation* (2011) p.428
5. Polydore Vergil, *Anglica Historia* (2005) Chapter 26 'Henry VII'
6. Bertram Fields, *Royal Blood: Richard III and the Mystery of the Princes* (2000) p.202
7. *The Chronicles of London* (2005) pp.219–221
8. Polydore Vergil, *Anglica Historia* (2005) Chapter 26 'Henry VII'
9. *Parliament Rolls of Medieval England* (2005) 'Henry VII, October 1495'
10. *Parliament Rolls of Medieval England* (2005) 'Henry VII, October 1495'
11. Nathan Amin, *Henry VII and the Tudor Pretenders: Simnel, Warbeck and Warwick* (2020) p.58

12. Peter Ackroyd, *The History of England Vol.2: Tudors* (2012) p.109
13. Leanda de Lisle, *Tudor: The Family Story* (2013) p.213
14. Jasper Ridley, *A Brief History of the Tudor Age* (2002) p.233
15. *Letters and Papers, Foreign and Domestic, Henry VIII, Volume 11, July–December 1536*, Lord Darcy to the Duke of Norfolk on 11 November 1536
16. *Letters and Papers, Foreign and Domestic, Henry VIII, Volume 11, July–December 1536*, The meeting at Pomfret (Pontefract) on 4 December 1536
17. Leanda de Lisle, *Tudor: The Family Story* (2013) p.214
18. 'Edward VI – Volume 8: July 1549', in *Calendar of State Papers Domestic: Edward VI, Mary and Elizabeth, 1547–80*, Circular Letter Sent 1 July 1549
19. Derek Wilson, *The Uncrowned Kings of England: The Black Legend of the Dudleys* (2005) p.160
20. Ethan H. Shagan, *Protector Somerset and the 1549 Rebellions: New Sources and New Perspectives* (1999) p.45
21. Peter Ackroyd, *The History of England Vol.2: Tudors* (2012) p.216
22. Chris Skidmore, *Edward VI: The Lost King of England* (2008) p.120
23. Ethan H. Shagan, *Protector Somerset and the 1549 Rebellions: New Sources and New Perspectives* (1999) p.34
24. Jane Dunn, *Elizabeth and Mary: Cousins, Rivals, Queens* (2003) p.134
25. Alison Plowden, *The House of Tudor* (2012) p.220
26. Peter Ackroyd, *The History of England Vol.2: Tudors* (2012) p.253
27. Elizabeth I, *Collected Works* (2000) p.41
28. Elizabeth I, *Collected Works* (2000) p.42

2. Northern Rising 1569

1. *Cecil Papers in Hatfield House, Volume 1, 1306–1571*, Queen Elizabeth I to the Earl of Sussex on 18 November 1569

2. K.J. Kesselring, *The Northern Rebellion of 1569: Faith, Politics, and Protest in Elizabethan England* (2007) p.11
3. K.J. Kesselring, 'Mercy and Liberality: The Aftermath of the 1569 Northern Rebellion', *History* (2005) p.214
4. Susan Doran, *Elizabeth I and Her Circle* (2015) p.79
5. Anne Somerset, *Elizabeth I* (1997) p.296
6. G.R. Elton, *England Under the Tudors* (2006) p.297
7. John Cooper, *The Queen's Agent: Francis Walsingham at the Court of Elizabeth I* (2012) p.53
8. *Cecil Papers in Hatfield House, Volume 1, 1306–1571*, Queen Elizabeth I to the Earl of Sussex on 10 November 1569
9. Anne Somerset, *Elizabeth I* (1997) p.295
10. Lisa Hilton, *Elizabeth: Renaissance Prince* (2015) p.192
11. Lisa Hilton, *Elizabeth: Renaissance Prince* (2015) p.193
12. A.N. Wilson, *The Elizabethans* (2011) p.95
13. A.N. Wilson, *The Elizabethans* (2011) p.100
14. G.R. Elton, *England Under the Tudors* (2006) p.298
15. *Cecil Papers in Hatfield House, Volume 1, 1306–1571*, Queen Elizabeth I to the Earl of Sussex on 18 November 1569
16. John Cooper, *The Queen's Agent: Francis Walsingham at the Court of Elizabeth I* (2012) p.54
17. Stow, John, *The Chronicles of England from Brute unto this present yeare of Christ 1580* (1580) p.1138
18. Anne Somerset, *Elizabeth I* (1997) p.300
19. J.B. Black, *The Reign of Elizabeth 1558–1603* (1959) p.140
20. Anne Somerset, *Elizabeth I* (1997) p.300
21. Susan Doran, *Queen Elizabeth I* (2003) p.89
22. Laura Brennan, *Elizabeth I: The Making of a Queen* (2020) p.112
23. M.E. James, 'The Concept of Order and the Northern Rising 1569', *Past & Present* (August 1973) p.79
24. Elizabeth I, *Collected Works* (2000) p.125
25. K.J. Kesselring, *The Northern Rebellion of 1569: Faith, Politics, and Protest in Elizabethan England* (2007) p.92

26. K.J. Kesselring, 'Mercy and Liberality: The Aftermath of the 1569 Northern Rebellion', *History* (2005) p.215
27. Susan Doran, *Elizabeth I and Her Circle* (2015) p.79
28. *Cecil Papers in Hatfield House, Volume 1, 1306–1571*, Queen Elizabeth I to the Earl of Shrewsbury on 26 November 1569
29. M.E. James, 'The Concept of Order and the Northern Rising 1569', *Past & Present* (August 1973) p.83
30. G.R. Elton, *England Under the Tudors* (2006) p.298
31. Pope Pius V, *Regnans in Excelsis* (1570)
32. Thomas Preston, *A Lamentation from Rome* (1570)
33. Thomas Bette, *Agaynst Rebellious and False Rumours* (1570)

3. Ridolfi Plot 1571

1. *Calendar of State Papers Foreign: Elizabeth, Volume 9, 1569–1571*, Francis Walsingham to William Cecil on 8 October 1571
2. G.R. Elton, *England Under the Tudors* (2006) p.300
3. R.G., *Salutem in Christo* (1571)
4. Susan Doran, *Elizabeth I and Her Circle* (2015) p.81
5. Antonia Fraser, *Mary Queen of Scots* (1994) p.424
6. Anne Somerset, *Elizabeth I* (1997) p.317
7. Antonia Fraser, *Mary Queen of Scots* (1994) p.425
8. Lisa Hilton, *Elizabeth: Renaissance Prince* (2015) p.196
9. John Cooper, *The Queen's Agent: Francis Walsingham at the Court of Elizabeth I* (2012) p.56
10. John Cooper, *The Queen's Agent: Francis Walsingham at the Court of Elizabeth I* (2012) p.58
11. Pope Pius V, *Regnans in Excelsis* (1570)
12. Aislinn Muller, *The Excommunication of Elizabeth I: Faith, Politics, and Religion in Post-Reformation England 1570–1603* (2020) p.123
13. Kate Williams, *Rival Queens: The Betrayal of Mary Queen of Scots* (2019) p.270

14. Anne Somerset, *Elizabeth I* (1997) p.319
15. Robert Hutchinson, *House of Treason: The Rise and Fall of a Tudor Dynasty* (2009) p.229
16. Anne Somerset, *Elizabeth I* (1997) p.320
17. John Leslie, *A Treatise Concerning the Defence of the Honour of ... Mary Queen of Scotland* (1571)
18. Lisa Hilton, *Elizabeth: Renaissance Prince* (2015) p.201
19. Anne Somerset, *Elizabeth I* (1997) p.325
20. Robert Hutchinson, *House of Treason: The Rise and Fall of a Tudor Dynasty* (2009) p.232
21. Stephen Alford, *The Watchers: A Secret History of the Reign of Elizabeth I* (2012) p.47
22. Lisa Hilton, *Elizabeth: Renaissance Prince* (2015) p.200
23. R.G., *Salutem in Christo* (1571)
24. R.G., *Salutem in Christo* (1571)
25. *Calendar of State Papers Foreign: Elizabeth, Volume 9, 1569–1571*, Francis Walsingham to William Cecil, Lord Burghley, on 8 October 1571
26. Laura Brennan, *Elizabeth I: The Making of a Queen* (2020) p.122
27. Lisa Hilton, *Elizabeth: Renaissance Prince* (2015) p.201
28. John Cooper, *The Queen's Agent: Francis Walsingham at the Court of Elizabeth I* (2012) p.59
29. Antonia Fraser, *Mary Queen of Scots* (1994) p.429
30. Kate Williams, *Rival Queens: The Betrayal of Mary Queen of Scots* (2019) p.274

4. Throckmorton Plot 1583

1. *A Discovery of the Treasons Practised and Attempted Against the Queen's Majesty* (1584)
2. Lisa Hilton, *Elizabeth: Renaissance Prince* (2015) p.234
3. John Cooper, *The Queen's Agent: Francis Walsingham at the Court of Elizabeth I* (2012) p.157

4. Susan Doran, *Elizabeth I and Her Circle* (2015) p.270
5. Kate Williams, *Rival Queens: The Betrayal of Mary Queen of Scots* (2019) p.290
6. R. Kent Tiernan, *Walsingham's Entrapment of Mary Stuart* (2017) p.151
7. John Cooper, *The Queen's Agent: Francis Walsingham at the Court of Elizabeth I* (2012) p.157
8. Stephen Alford, *The Watchers: A Secret History of the Reign of Elizabeth I* (2012) p.155
9. *A Discovery of the Treasons Practised and Attempted Against the Queen's Majesty* (1584)
10. Stephen Alford, *The Watchers: A Secret History of the Reign of Elizabeth I* (2012) p.152
11. Stephen Alford, *The Watchers: A Secret History of the Reign of Elizabeth I* (2012) p.156
12. Stephen Alford, *The Watchers: A Secret History of the Reign of Elizabeth I* (2012) p.158
13. Anne Somerset, *Elizabeth I* (1997) p.512
14. *A Discovery of the Treasons Practised and Attempted Against the Queen's Majesty* (1584)
15. *A Discovery of the Treasons Practised and Attempted Against the Queen's Majesty* (1584)
16. *A Discovery of the Treasons Practised and Attempted Against the Queen's Majesty* (1584)
17. *Calendar of State Papers Domestic: Elizabeth, 1581–90*, Record of interrogation of William Warde with regard to his dealings with Lord Thomas Paget on 14 December 1583
18. *Calendar of State Papers Domestic: Elizabeth, 1581–90*, Record of interrogation of Cecily Hopton with regard to her conversations with George Throckmorton on 14 December 1583
19. *Calendar of State Papers Foreign: Elizabeth*, Letter from Sir Francis Walsingham to Sir Edward Stafford on 10 January 1584
20. John Cooper, *The Queen's Agent: Francis Walsingham at the Court of Elizabeth I* (2012) p.189

21. *A Discovery of the Treasons Practised and Attempted Against the Queen's Majesty* (1584)
22. Alison Plowden, *Danger to Elizabeth: The Catholics Under Elizabeth I* (1974) p.217
23. Susan Doran, *Elizabeth I and Her Circle* (2015) p.100
24. Stephen Alford, *The Watchers: A Secret History of the Reign of Elizabeth I* (2012) p.175
25. Lacey Baldwin Smith, *Treason in Tudor England: Politics and Paranoia* (2006) p.17
26. Anna Whitelock, *Elizabeth's Bedfellows: An Intimate History of the Queen's Court* (2013) p.208
27. C.R.N. Routh, *Who's Who in British History: Tudor England 1485–1603* (2001) p.288
28. Anna Whitelock, *Elizabeth's Bedfellows: An Intimate History of the Queen's Court* (2013) p.208
29. Alison Plowden, *Danger to Elizabeth: The Catholics Under Elizabeth I* (1974) p.215
30. *Holinshed's Chronicles* (1587)
31. Alison Plowden, *Danger to Elizabeth: The Catholics Under Elizabeth I* (1974) p.216
32. John Guy, *Elizabeth: The Forgotten Years* (2016) p.42
33. Anna Whitelock, *Elizabeth's Bedfellows: An Intimate History of the Queen's Court* (2013) p.209
34. Lacey Baldwin Smith, *Treason in Tudor England: Politics and Paranoia* (2006) p.11
35. John Cooper, *The Queen's Agent: Francis Walsingham at the Court of Elizabeth I* (2012) p.160

5. Babington Plot 1586

1. Elizabeth I, *Collected Works* (2000) p.285
2. John Cooper, *The Queen's Agent: Francis Walsingham at the Court of Elizabeth I* (2012) p.211

3. Kate Williams, *Rival Queens: The Betrayal of Mary Queen of Scots* (2019) p.300
4. Stefan Zweig, quoted in R. Kent Tiernan, 'Walsingham's Entrapment of Mary Stuart', *American Intelligence Journal* (2017) p.154
5. Robert Hutchinson, *Elizabeth's Spy Master: Francis Walsingham and the Secret War That Saved England* (2007) p.99
6. G.R. Elton, *England Under the Tudors* (2006) p.368
7. Lisa Hilton, *Elizabeth: Renaissance Prince* (2015) p.251
8. Laura Brennan, *Elizabeth I: The Making of a Queen* (2020) p.131
9. Jane Dunn, *Elizabeth and Mary: Cousins, Rivals, Queens* (2003) p.467
10. A.N. Wilson, *The Elizabethans* (2011) p.234
11. Susan Doran, *Elizabeth I and Her Circle* (2015) p.87
12. Antonia Fraser, *Mary Queen of Scots* (1994) p.477
13. John Cooper, *The Queen's Agent: Francis Walsingham at the Court of Elizabeth I* (2012) p.209
14. Anne Somerset, *Elizabeth I* (1997) p.543
15. John Cooper, *The Queen's Agent: Francis Walsingham at the Court of Elizabeth I* (2012) p.207
16. R. Kent Tiernan, 'Walsingham's Entrapment of Mary Stuart', *American Intelligence Journal* (2017) p.154
17. A.N. Wilson, *The Elizabethans* (2011) p.231
18. Jane Dunn, *Elizabeth and Mary: Cousins, Rivals, Queens* (2003) p.470
19. *Calendar of State Papers, Scotland: Volume 8, 1585–6*, Letter from Mary Queen of Scots to Anthony Babington on 7 July 1586
20. Retha Warnicke, quoted in Susan Doran, *Elizabeth I and Her Circle* (2015) p.87
21. Kate Williams, *Rival Queens: The Betrayal of Mary Queen of Scots* (2019) p.302
22. Antonia Fraser, *Mary Queen of Scots* (1994) p.493
23. Antonia Fraser, *Mary Queen of Scots* (1994) p.496
24. Elizabeth I, *Collected Works* (2000) p.284

25. Elizabeth I, *Collected Works* (2000) p.285
26. Elizabeth I, *Collected Works* (2000) p.285
27. Chidiock Tichbourne, *Tichbourne's Elegy* (1586)
28. Richard Hirsch, *The Works of Chidiock Tichbourne* (1986) p.305
29. Richard Hirsch, *The Works of Chidiock Tichbourne* (1986) p.305
30. Elizabeth I, *Collected Works* (2000) p.286
31. Susan Doran, *Queen Elizabeth I* (2003) p.100
32. Susan Doran (ed.) *Elizabeth and Mary: Royal Cousins, Rival Queens* (2021) p.219
33. John Cooper, *The Queen's Agent: Francis Walsingham at the Court of Elizabeth I* (2012) p.209
34. J.B. Black, *The Reign of Elizabeth 1558–1603* (1959) p.381
35. R. Kent Tiernan, 'Walsingham's Entrapment of Mary Stuart', *American Intelligence Journal* (2017) p.147

6. Essex Rebellion 1601

1. *Cecil Papers in Hatfield House, Volume 11, 1601*, The Earl of Southampton to Lady Southampton on 8 February 1601
2. Alison Plowden, *Elizabethan England: Life in an Age of Adventure* (1982) p.272
3. Carole Levin, *The Heart and Stomach of a King: Elizabeth I and the Politics of Sex and Power* (1994) p.149
4. John Guy, *Elizabeth: The Forgotten Years* (2016) p.320
5. Anne Somerset, *Elizabeth I* (1997) p.681
6. David Cecil, *The Cecils of Hatfield House* (1973) p.111
7. Francis Bacon, *A Declaration of the Practises and Treasons attempted and committed by Robert late Earle of Essex* (1601)
8. Elizabeth I, *Collected Works* (2000) p.394
9. Laura Brennan, *Elizabeth I: The Making of a Queen* (2020) p.155
10. John Guy, *Elizabeth: The Forgotten Years* (2016) p.321
11. Anna Whitelock, *Elizabeth's Bedfellows: An Intimate History of the Queen's Court* (2013) p.315

12. Susan Doran, *Elizabeth I and Her Circle* (2015) p.189
13. Francis Bacon, *A Declaration of the Practises and Treasons attempted and committed by Robert late Earle of Essex* (1601)
14. Francis Bacon, *A Declaration of the Practises and Treasons attempted and committed by Robert late Earle of Essex* (1601)
15. William Shakespeare, *The Tragedy of Richard II*, in 'The Complete Works of William Shakespeare' (1998) p.440
16. William Shakespeare, *The Tragedy of Richard II*, in 'The Complete Works of William Shakespeare' (1998) p.441
17. J.B. Black, *The Reign of Elizabeth 1558–1603* (1959) p.439
18. Peter Ackroyd, *History of England Vol.2: Tudors* (2012) p.460
19. John Guy, *Elizabeth: The Forgotten Years* (2016) p.321
20. Penry Williams, *The Later Tudors: England 1547–1603* (1998) p.375
21. Anne Somerset, *Elizabeth I* (1997) p.690
22. *Cecil Papers in Hatfield House, Volume 11, 1601*, The Earl of Southampton to Lady Southampton on 8 February 1601
23. G.R. Elton, *England Under the Tudors* (2006) p.474
24. Peter Ackroyd, *History of England Vol.2: Tudors* (2012) p.460
25. David Loades, *Tudors: History of a Dynasty* (2012) p.89 and Susan Doran, *Elizabeth I and Her Circle* (2015) p.189
26. Richard Rex, *The Tudors* (2015) p.264, and Lisa Hilton, *Elizabeth: Renaissance Prince* (2015) p.312, and Alison Plowden, *Elizabethan England: Life in an Age of Adventure* (1982) p.275, and Judith John, *Dark History of the Tudors* (2017) p.209
27. Penry Williams, *The Later Tudors: England 1547–1603* (1998) p.374
28. Lacey Baldwin Smith, *Treason in Tudor England: Politics and Paranoia* (2006) p.249
29. G.R. Elton, *England Under the Tudors* (2006) p.470
30. Lacey Baldwin Smith, *Treason in Tudor England: Politics and Paranoia* (2006) p.272
31. Lisa Hilton, *Elizabeth: Renaissance Prince* (2015) p.313
32. Lacey Baldwin Smith, *Treason in Tudor England: Politics and Paranoia* (2006) p.239

7. Elizabeth and Rebellion

1. Pope Pius V, *Regnans in Excelsis* (1570)
2. 'rebellion, n.1'. *OED Online*. June 2021. Oxford University Press, www.oed.com/view/Entry/159201 (accessed 31 July 2021)
3. 'conspiracy, n.'. *OED Online*. June 2021. Oxford University Press, www.oed.com/view/Entry/39766 (accessed July 2021)
4. John Guy, *The Children of Henry VIII* (2013) p.197
5. G.R. Batho, 'The Execution of Mary Queen of Scots', *Scottish Historical Review* (1960) p.38
6. Elizabeth I, *Collected Works* (2000) p.296
7. Elizabeth I, *Collected Works* (2000) p.296
8. G.R. Batho, 'The Execution of Mary Queen of Scots', *Scottish Historical Review* (1960) p.40
9. R. Kent Tiernan, 'Walsingham's Entrapment of Mary Stuart', *American Intelligence Journal* (2017) p.155
10. Antonia Fraser, Mary Queen of Scots (1994) p.504
11. Antonia Fraser, Mary Queen of Scots (1994) p.505
12. R. Kent Tiernan, 'Walsingham's Entrapment of Mary Stuart', *American Intelligence Journal* (2017) p.147
13. R. Kent Tiernan, 'Walsingham's Entrapment of Mary Stuart', *American Intelligence Journal* (2017) p.148
14. R. Kent Tiernan, 'Walsingham's Entrapment of Mary Stuart', *American Intelligence Journal* (2017) p.152
15. Pope Pius V, *Regnans in Excelsis* (1570)
16. Alison Plowden, *Danger to Elizabeth: The Catholics Under Elizabeth I* (1974) p.92
17. Pope Pius V, *Regnans in Excelsis* (1570)
18. Aislinn Muller, *The Excommunication of Elizabeth I: Faith, Politics, and Religion in Post-Reformation England 1570–1603* (2020) p.30
19. Pope Pius V, *Regnans in Excelsis* (1570)
20. Alison Plowden, *Danger to Elizabeth: The Catholics Under Elizabeth I* (1974) p.94

21. Alison Plowden, *Danger to Elizabeth: The Catholics Under Elizabeth I* (1974) p.95
22. Lacey Baldwin Smith, *Treason in Tudor England: Politics and Paranoia* (2006) p.239
23. John Knox, *The First Blast of the Trumpet Against the Monstrous Regiment of Women* (1558)
24. John Knox, *The First Blast of the Trumpet Against the Monstrous Regiment of Women* (1558)
25. Nathen Amin, *Henry VII and the Tudor Pretenders: Simnel, Warbeck, and Warwick* (2020) p.273
26. Alison Plowden, *Danger to Elizabeth: The Catholics Under Elizabeth I* (1974) p.250

Bibliography

Primary Sources

State Papers

Calendar of the Cecil Papers in Hatfield House. Edited by R.A. Roberts. London: His Majesty's Stationery Office 1906. British History Online, accessed 26 June 2021, www.british-history.ac.uk/cal-cecil-papers/

Calendar of State Papers Domestic: Edward VI, Mary and Elizabeth, 1547–80. Edited by Robert Lemon. London: Her Majesty's Stationery Office. 1856. British History Online, accessed 3 May 2021, www.british-history.ac.uk/cal-state-papers/domestic/edw-eliz/1547-80

Calendar of State Papers Domestic: Elizabeth, 1581–90. Edited by Robert Lemon. London: Her Majesty's Stationery Office 1865. British History Online, accessed 23 May 2021, www.british-history.ac.uk/cal-state-papers/domestic/edw-eliz/1581-90

Calendar of State Papers Domestic: Elizabeth, 1598–1601. Edited by Mary Anne Everett Green. London: Her Majesty's Stationery Office 1869. *British History Online*, accessed 23 May 2021, www.british-history.ac.uk/cal-state-papers/domestic/edw-eliz/1598-1601

Calendar of State Papers Foreign: Elizabeth. Edited by Allan James Crosby. London: Her Majesty's Stationery Office 1874. British History Online, accessed 7 August 2021, www.british-history.ac.uk/cal-state-papers/foreign/

Calendar of State Papers: Scotland. Edited by William K. Boyd. London: Her Majesty's Stationery Office 1914. British History

Online, accessed 12 December 2021, www.british-history.ac.uk/search/series/cal-state-papers--scotland

Letters and Papers, Foreign and Domestic, Henry VIII. Edited by James Gairdner. London: Her Majesty's Stationery Office 1888. British History Online, accessed 31 July 2021, www.british-history.ac.uk/letters-papers-hen8/vol11

Online Sources

Anonymous, *A discouerie of the treasons practised and attempted against the Queenes Maiestie and the Realme, by Francis Throckmorton, who was for the same arraigned and condemned in Guyld Hall, in the Citie of London, the one and twentie day of May last past*. 1584. Oxford University Press Text Creation Partnership, accessed 8 August 2021, https://ota.bodleian.ox.ac.uk/repository/xmlui/bitstream/handle/20.500.12024/A13753/A13753.html

Bacon, Francis, *A Declaration of the Practises & Treasons attempted and committed by Robert late Earle of Essex and his Complices, against her Maiestie and her Kingdoms, and of the proceedings as well at the Arraignments & Conuictions of the said late Earle, and his adherents*. 1601. Oxford University Press Text Creation Partnership, accessed 18 December 2021, https://ota.bodleian.ox.ac.uk/repository/xmlui/bitstream/handle/20.500.12024/A01216/A01216.html

Bette, Thomas, *A Newe Ballade Intityled, Agaynst Rebellious and false Rumours*. 1570. Oxford University Press Text Creation Partnership, accessed 26 October 2021, https://ota.bodleian.ox.ac.uk/repository/xmlui/bitstream/handle/20.500.12024/A09509/A09509.html

Holinshed's Chronicles. 1587. The Holinshed Project, accessed 20 November 2021, http://english.nsms.ox.ac.uk/holinshed/index.php

Knox, John, *The First Blast of the Trumpet Against the Monstrous Regiment of Women*. 1558. Project Gutenberg, accessed 5 December 2021, www.gutenberg.org/files/9660/9660-h/9660-h.htm

Leslie, John, Bishop of Ross, *A treatise concerning the defence of the honour of the right high, mightie and noble Princesse, Marie Queene of Scotland, and Douager of France with a declaration, as wel of her right, title, and interest, to the succession of the croune of England: as that the regiment of women is conformable to the lawe of God and nature.* 1571. Oxford University Press Text Creation Partnership, accessed 8 August 2021, https://ota.bodleian.ox.ac.uk/repository/xmlui/bitstream/handle/20.500.12024/A05353/A05353.html

Parliament Rolls of Medieval England. Edited by Chris Given-Wilson, Paul Brand, Seymour Phillips, Mark Ormrod, Geoffrey Martin, Anne Curry & Rosemary Horrox. Woodbridge: Boydell 2005. British History Online, accessed 17 April 2021, www.british-history.ac.uk/no-series/parliament-rolls-medieval

Pope Pius V, *Regnans in Excelsis.* 1570. Papal Encyclicals Online, accessed 11 September 2021, www.papalencyclicals.net/Pius05/p5regnans.htm

Preston, Thomas, *A lamentation from Rome, how the Pope doth bewayle, that the rebelles in England can not preuayle.* 1570. Oxford University Press Text Creation Partnership, accessed 26 October 2021, https://ota.bodleian.ox.ac.uk/repository/xmlui/bitstream/handle/20.500.12024/A09509/A09509.html

R.G., *Salutem in Christo.* 1571. Oxford University Press Text Creation Partnership, accessed 7 August 2021, https://ota.bodleian.ox.ac.uk/repository/xmlui/bitstream/handle/20.500.12024/A01387/A01387.html

Stow, John, *The Chronicles of England from Brute unto this present yeare of Christ 1580.* London: Henrie Bynneman, 1580. Early English Books Online Text Creation Partnership, accessed 31 July 2021, http://name.umdl.umich.edu/A13043.0001.001

Tichbourne, Chidiock, *Tichbourne's Elegy.* Poetry Foundation, accessed 4 December 2021, www.poetryfoundation.org/poems/47443/my-prime-of-youth-is-but-a-frost-of-cares

Vergil, Polydore, *The Anglica Historia of Polydore Vergil A.D. 1485–1537*, ed. Dana J. Sutton, Library of Humanistic Texts at the Philological Museum of University of Birmingham's Shakespeare Institute, 2005, accessed 17 April 2021, www.philological.bham.ac.uk/polverg/

Printed Sources

The Chronicles of London. Edited by C.L. Kingsford. (Oxford: Clarendon Press, 2005)

Elizabeth I, *Collected Works*, 2nd Edition. Edited by L.S. Marcus, J. Mueller & M.B. Rose (London & Chicago: University of Chicago Press, 2000)

Leicester's Commonwealth: The Copy of a Letter Written by a Master of Art of Cambridge (1584) and Related Documents. Edited by D.C. Peck. (Athens, OH: Ohio University Press, 1985)

Shakespeare, William, *The Complete Works of William Shakespeare*. Edited by W.J. Craig (Cockfosters: Henry Pordes, 1998)

Secondary Sources

Books

ACKROYD, Peter, *The History of England Vol.1: Foundation* (London: Macmillan, 2011)

ACKROYD, Peter, *The History of England Vol.2: Tudors* (London: Macmillan, 2012)

ALFORD, Stephen, *The Watchers: A Secret History of the Reign of Elizabeth I* (London: Allen Lane, 2012)

AMIN, Nathen, *Henry VII and the Tudor Pretenders: Simnel, Warbeck and Warwick* (Stroud: Amberley Publishing, 2021)

BLACK, J.B., *The Reign of Elizabeth 1558–1603* (Oxford: Oxford University Press, 1991)

BRENNAN, Laura, *Elizabeth I: The Making of a Queen* (Barnsley: Pen & Sword History, 2020)
BREVERTON, Terry, *Everything You Ever Wanted to Know About the Tudors but Were Afraid to Ask* (Stroud: Amberley Publishing, 2014)
CASTOR, Helen, *Elizabeth I: A Study in Insecurity* (London: Penguin Books, 2019)
CECIL, David, *The Cecils of Hatfield House* (London: Constable & Robinson, 1973)
COOPER, John, *The Queen's Agent: Francis Walsingham at the Court of Elizabeth I* (London: Faber & Faber Limited, 2012)
DE LISLE, Leanda, *Tudor: The Family Story* (London: Chatto & Windus, 2013)
DORAN, Susan (ed.), *Elizabeth and Mary: Royal Cousins, Rival Queens* (London: British Library, 2021)
DORAN, Susan, *Elizabeth I and Her Circle* (Oxford: Oxford University Press, 2015)
DORAN, Susan, *Queen Elizabeth I* (London: British Library, 2003)
DORAN, Susan, *The Tudor Chronicles 1485–1603* (London: Quercus Publishing, 2008)
DUNN, Jane, *Elizabeth and Mary: Cousins, Rivals, Queens* (London: Harper Perennial, 2004)
ELTON, G.R., *England Under the Tudors* (Abingdon: Routledge, 1991)
FIELDS, Bertram, *Royal Blood: Richard III and the Mystery of the Princes* (Stroud: Sutton Publishing, 2000)
FLETCHER, Anthony & MACCULLOCH, Diarmaid, *Tudor Rebellions* (London: Routledge, 2016)
FRASER, Antonia, *Mary Queen of Scots* (London: Book Club Associates, 1994)
GUY, John, *The Children of Henry VIII* (Oxford: Oxford University Press, 2013)
GUY, John, *Elizabeth: The Forgotten Years* (London: Viking, 2016)
GUY, John, *My Heart is My Own: The Life of Mary Queen of Scots* (London: Harper Perennial, 2004)

HILTON, Lisa, *Elizabeth: Renaissance Prince* (London: Weidenfeld & Nicolson, 2015)

HUTCHINSON, Robert, *Elizabeth's Spy Master: Francis Walsingham and the Secret War That Saved England* (London: Phoenix, 2007)

HUTCHINSON, Robert, *House of Treason: The Rise and Fall of a Tudor Dynasty* (London: Phoenix, 2009)

JOHN, Judith, *Dark History of the Tudors* (London: Amber Books, 2017)

KESSELRING, K.J., *The Northern Rebellion of 1569: Faith, Politics, and Protest in Elizabethan England* (Basingstoke: Palgrave Macmillan, 2007)

LEVIN, Carole, *The Heart and Stomach of a King: Elizabeth I and the Politics of Sex and Power* (Philadelphia: University of Pennsylvania Press, 1994)

LOADES, David, *Tudors: History of a Dynasty* (London: Continuum Publishing, 2012)

MEYER, G.J. *The Tudors: The Complete Story of England's Most Notorious Dynasty* (Stroud: Amberley Publishing, 2015)

MULLER, Aislinn, *The Excommunication of Elizabeth I: Faith, Politics, and Religion in Post-Reformation England 1570-1603* (Leiden: Brill, 2020)

PLOWDEN, Alison, *Danger to Elizabeth: The Catholics Under Elizabeth I* (London: Book Club Associates, 1974)

PLOWDEN, Alison, *Elizabethan England: Life in an Age of Adventure* (London: Reader's Digest, 1982)

PLOWDEN, Alison, *The House of Tudor* (Cheltenham: The History Press, 2012)

REX, Richard, *Elizabeth: Fortune's Bastard?* (Stroud: Tempus Publishing, 2007)

REX, Richard, *The Tudors* (Stroud: Tempus Publishing, 2015)

RIDLEY, Jasper, *A Brief History of the Tudor Age* (London: Constable & Robinson, 2002)

ROUTH, C.R.N., *Who's Who in British History: Tudor England 1485–1603* (Mechanicsburg PA: Stackpole Books, 2001)

SEWARD, Desmond, *The Last White Rose: The Secret Wars of the Tudors* (London: Constable & Robinson, 2011)

SKIDMORE, Chris, *Edward VI: The Lost King of England* (London: Phoenix, 2008)

SMITH, Lacey Baldwin, *Treason in Tudor England: Politics and Paranoia* (London: Pimlico, 2006)

SOMERSET, Anne, *Elizabeth I* (London: Phoenix, 1997)

STARKEY, David, *Elizabeth* (London: Vintage, 2001)

STEDALL, Robert, *Elizabeth I's Secret Lover: Robert Dudley, Earl of Leicester* (Barnsley: Pen & Sword History, 2020)

STEDALL, Robert, *Mary Queen of Scots' Secretary: William Maitland, Politician, Reformer, and Conspirator* (Barnsley, Pen & Sword History, 2021)

WAGNER, John A. & WALTERS SCHMID, Susan (eds.), *Encyclopedia of Tudor England* (Santa Barbara CA: ABC Clio, 2012)

WEIR, Alison, *Elizabeth the Queen* (London, Vintage, 2009)

WHITELOCK, Anna, *Elizabeth's Bedfellows: An Intimate History of the Queen's Court* (London: Bloomsbury Publishing, 2013)

WILLIAMS, Kate, *Rival Queens: The Betrayal of Mary, Queen of Scots* (London: Arrow, 2019)

WILLIAMS, Penry, *The Later Tudors: England 1547–1603* (Oxford: Oxford University Press, 1998)

WILSON, A.N., *The Elizabethans* (London: Hutchinson, 2011)

WILSON, Derek, *The Uncrowned Kings of England: The Black Legend of the Dudleys* (London: Constable & Robinson, 2005)

WORMALD, Jenny, *Mary Queen of Scots* (Edinburgh: Birlinn Ltd, 2018)

Articles

BASING, Patricia, 'Robert Beale and the Queen of Scots', *The British Library Journal*, Vol.20, No.1 (Spring 1994) pp.65–82

BATHO, G.R., 'The Execution of Mary Queen of Scots', *The Scottish Historical Review*, Vol.39, No.127 (April 1960) pp.35–42

BEER, Barrett, L. 'John Stow and Tudor Rebellions 1549–1569', *Journal of British Studies*, Vol.27, No.4 (October 1988) pp.352–374

ELLIS, Steven G., 'Henry VIII, Rebellion, and the Rule of Law', *The Historical Journal*, Vol.24, No.3 (September 1981) pp.513–531

HIRSCH, Richard S. M., 'The Works of Chidiock Tichborne', *English Literary Renaissance*, Vol.16, No.2 (1986) pp.303–318

JAMES, M.E., 'The Concept of Order and the Northern Rising 1569', *Past & Present*, No.60 (August 1973) pp.49–83

KESSELRING, K.J., 'Mercy and Liberality: The Aftermath of the 1569 Northern Rebellion', *History*, Vol.90, No.298 (2005) pp.213–235

MANNING, Roger B., 'Violence and Social Conflict in Mid-Tudor Rebellions', *Journal of British Studies*, Vol.16, No.2 (Spring 1977) pp.18–40

RAPPLE, R. 'Writing About Violence in the Tudor Kingdoms', *The Historical Journal*, Vol.54, No.3 (September 2011) pp.829–854

SHAGAN, Ethan H., 'Protector Somerset and the 1549 Rebellions: New Sources and New Perspectives', *The English Historical Review*, Vol.114, No.455 (February 1999) pp.34–63

TENNEY, Horace Kent, 'The Trial of Mary Queen of Scots', *American Bar Association Journal*, Vol.17, No.5 (May 1931) pp.285–291

TIERNAN, R. Kent, 'Walsingham's Entrapment of Mary Stuart', *American Intelligence Journal*, Vol.34, No.1 (2017) pp.146–156

Other Resources

National Archives Currency Converter 1270–2017. The National Archives, accessed 31 July 2021, www.nationalarchives.gov.uk/currency-converter/#

Oxford English Dictionary Online. Oxford University Press, accessed 31 July 2021, www.oed.com/

Index

Peers are ordered by surname and then title e.g. Percy, Thomas, 7th Earl of Northumberland / Percy, Henry, 8th Earl of Northumberland

Abingdon, Edward 127, 131
Ackroyd, Peter 153
Acts
   Treasons Act 1534 79
   Act of Succession 1544 xiv, xvii
   Act Against Fugitives Over the Sea 1571 79
   Treasons Act 1571 79
   Act for the Queen's Safety 1584 99–100, 111, 116, 177
   Act of Union 1707 194
Alba, Fernando Alvarez de Toledo, 3rd Duke of 40, 58, 59, 65, 66, 68–69, 70, 73, 79
Allen, William 87, 104
Amin, Nathen 187
Anne, Queen 194
Anne of Cleves xiv
Arthur, Prince of Wales 1, 7, 13, 192
Arundel Castle 88, 90, 173
Arundel, Sir Charles 94, 95

Ashley, Kat xvii
Aske, Robert 15, 16–17, 18
Askew, Anne 93

Babington, Sir Anthony 53, 57, 82, 114–116, 118, 121–122, 123, 125–127, 130, 131–132, 134–135, 178, 179
Babington Plot xi, xii–xiii, xx, 37, 50–51, 53, 57, 68, 71, 82, 85, 94–95, 97, 100, 101, 110, 111–137, 165, 166, 168, 169, 170, 179, 182, 183, 190, 193, 194
Bacon, Sir Francis 140, 142, 157, 160, 179
Bailly, Charles 67, 68–69, 70, 76
Ballard, John 115, 120–122, 126, 127, 131
Bannister, Laurence 72
Barker, William 65–66, 72, 73
Barnard Castle 44
Barnwell, Robert 127, 131

217

Barton, Elizabeth, Holy Maid of Kent 140
battles
   Tewkesbury 1471 3–4
   Bosworth 1485 1, 4, 5, 6, 10
   Stoke 1487 5–6
   Sampford Courtenay 1549 22–23
   Langside 1568 67
   Gelt Bridge 1570 48
Beaton, James, Archbishop of Glasgow 87
Beaufort, Margaret, Countess of Richmond 10, 195
Bellamy, Jerome 132
Berkeley, Sir Richard 145
Bess of Hardwick 32, 114, 116
Bigod, Sir Francis 18
Blount, Bessie 139
Blount, Charles, 8th Baron Mountjoy 149
Blount, Sir Christopher 148, 159, 161
Boleyn, Anne xiii, xiv, xix, 1, 14, 15, 23, 24, 27, 139, 140, 161, 165, 166, 175, 192, 195
Boleyn, George, Viscount Rochford xiii
Boleyn, Mary xiii, 139
Bolton Castle 32
Bond of Association (*see Act for the Queen's Safety*)
Brandon, Charles, 1st Duke of Suffolk 15
Brandon, Frances, Duchess of Suffolk xviii
Break with Rome 2, 14, 15–16, 62–63, 153, 195
Brennan, Laura xviii
Brooke, William, 10th Baron Cobham 67, 77
Brooke, Henry, 11th Baron Cobham 147, 153
Browne, Anthony, 1st Viscount Montague 128
Browne, Thomas 72
Burgundy, Margaret Plantagenet, Duchess of 5, 6, 9, 10, 188

Carey, Catherine, Lady Knollys xiii, 32, 139
Carey, Henry, 1st Baron Hunsdon xiii, 43, 98, 122
Carlisle Castle 31, 32
Castelnau, Michel de 85
Catesby, Robert 102, 169
Catholicism xviii, 2, 14, 15, 17, 23, 26, 29, 33, 34, 36, 38, 41, 42, 51, 53, 54, 55, 57–58, 60, 61, 62, 64, 65, 66, 69, 70, 71, 72, 76, 79, 80–81, 82, 84, 85, 87, 88, 89–90, 91, 92, 93, 94, 95–96, 98, 101 102, 103–105, 106, 108, 109, 111, 113, 114–116, 118–119, 121, 122,

123–124, 126, 128, 129, 132, 133, 136, 165, 169–170, 172, 174, 175, 177, 178–179, 180, 181–185, 186, 189, 193, 196
Cecil, Sir Robert 42, 137, 140, 141–142, 143, 144, 145–146, 147, 148, 149–150, 153, 154, 155, 156, 158, 159, 160, 163, 168
Cecil, William, 1st Baron Burghley x, 34, 40, 42, 59, 61, 77–78, 137, 141, 150, 153, 186, 194
  and the Babington Plot 123, 127
  and the Northern Rising 30, 33, 36, 37, 40, 51, 168
  and the Parry Plot 103, 104–105
  and the Ridolfi Plot 58, 61–62, 65, 68, 69, 70–71, 72, 74–76, 77, 78, 80, 81
  and the Throckmorton Plot 90, 92, 93, 98–99
  relationship with Francis Walsingham 58–59, 177–178
  relationship with Mary Queen of Scots 32, 59, 67, 71, 74, 75, 79, 82, 151, 171, 177–178, 193
Charles I 3, 132, 154, 175, 194
Charles II 8, 175–176, 188
Charles V, Holy Roman Emperor 24
Charles VIII of France 9
Charles of Austria, Archduke 63
Charnock, John 132
Chartley Manor 71, 114, 115, 116, 117, 118, 121, 122, 123, 127–129, 133–134
Châteauneuf, Guillaume de L'Aubespine, Baron de 120
Chatham Dockyard 32
Chelsea Manor xv–xvi
Cheshunt Great House xv–xvi
Clifford, Henry, 2nd Earl of Cumberland 39
Clifford, George, 3rd Earl of Cumberland 128
Clinton, Edward, 1st Earl of Lincoln 25, 45, 50
Como, Cardinal 106
Constable, Sir Thomas 18
Cooper, John 84, 119–120
Cornish Rebellion 11–12
Coughton Court 84
Courcelles, Claude de 85
Court of Star Chamber 145–146
Courtenay, Edward, 1st Earl of Devon (1485 creation) 12
Courtenay, Edward, 1st Earl of Devon (1553 creation) xviii–xix, 24, 28
Cranmer, Thomas, Archbishop of Canterbury 14, 15

Cromwell, Edward, 3rd Baron Cromwell 149
Cromwell, Oliver 3
Cromwell, Thomas, 1st Earl of Essex 14, 15, 17–18, 34, 108, 168
Cuffe, Henry 148, 161
Cumnor Place 63
Curle, Gilbert 111, 127, 128, 135

Danvers, Charles 148, 159, 161
Darcy, Lord Thomas 16, 18
Darcy, Sir William 5
Davies, John 148, 149
Davison, William 152–153, 171, 174, 193
De Spes, Guerau 36, 61, 65–66, 78, 182
Denny, Sir Anthony xv–xvi
Desmond Rebellion 32–33
Devereux, Walter, 1st Earl of Essex 139
Devereux, Robert, 2nd Earl of Essex 136, 138, 139–142, 143, 144–148, 149–150, 152, 153, 154, 155, 156–157, 158, 159–160, 161, 162–163, 164, 184, 193–194
Device for the Succession 1553 xviii, 184
divine right 78, 142–143, 151, 175, 176, 177, 193, 195

Donne, Henry 132
Donne, John 132
Doran, Susan 33, 46, 57, 147
Douglas, Archibald 31
Douglas, James, 4th Earl of Morton xii, 66–67
Dudley, Ambrose, 3rd Earl of Warwick 45, 50
Dudley, John, 1st Duke of Northumberland 21, 22, 23, 26
Dudley, Robert, 1st Earl of Leicester xvii, xx, 28, 34, 50, 63, 95, 113, 137, 138, 139, 147, 160, 163, 164, 194
Dumbarton 73
Dunn, Jane 115
Dutch Revolt 70. 113, 174–175

Edward IV 4, 5, 7, 8, 152
Edward V 9, 101, 152
Edward VI xiii–xv, xvi, xviii, 2, 5, 14, 19, 21, 22, 23, 30, 35, 49, 50, 58–59, 78, 79, 137, 166, 184, 186–187, 189, 192, 195
Egerton, Thomas, 1st Viscount Brackley 144, 153, 159
Elizabeth I x, xi, xii, xx, 1, 2, 3, 26, 32, 35, 54, 63, 76–78, 85–86, 93, 97–98, 108–110, 120–121, 128, 136, 137, 139, 142–143, 155, 165–166, 168,

170, 174, 177, 178, 186–187, 189–190, 191–196
1559 Religious Settlement xx, 40, 62–63, 101–102, 103
childhood xiii–xv, 14
excommunication 62–63, 64–65, 114, 178, 179–183
succession xvii–xviii, 29, 30, 42, 63, 79, 85–86, 99–100, 133, 150–151
and the Babington Plot 111, 113, 114–115, 117, 119, 121, 122–123, 124–125, 126, 129, 130, 131–132, 135, 136
and the Essex Rebellion 138–139, 140–141, 143, 144, 145, 146–148, 150, 156–157, 158–159, 160–161, 162–164
and the Northern Rising 29, 33-34, 35–41, 42–43, 45–46, 47–51, 53, 55
and the Parry Plot 102, 104–105, 107–108
and the Ridolfi Plot 56–57, 58, 59, 61–62, 64, 65, 66, 67, 70, 71, 72–73, 74, 77, 78, 79, 80
and the Throckmorton Plot 83, 84–85, 87, 89, 90–91, 94–95, 97, 98, 100
and the Wyatt Rebellion xviii–xix, 3, 23–24, 26–28, 166
relationship with Mary I xix–xx, 2, 14, 24
relationship with Mary Queen of Scots xi, xii–xiii, xvii, xix, xxi, 14, 30, 31–32, 44–45, 51, 53–54, 56–57, 58, 59, 65, 68, 71–74, 75, 77, 81–82, 86, 91, 112, 117, 122, 128, 129–130, 132–133, 134 136, 150, 152, 153, 166–169, 171–172, 176–177, 183–184, 185, 186, 188–189
relationship with Thomas Seymour xv–xvii
Elton, G.R. 156
enclosure 2, 20, 28
Englefield, Sir Francis 90, 92
English Civil War 3, 132, 152, 154, 163, 194
Eric XIV of Sweden 63
Erskine, John, 1st Earl of Mar xii, 49
Essex Rebellion x, xii–xiii, xx, 138–164, 167–168, 169, 183, 184, 190, 193–194

Fawkes, Guy 169
Feron, Laurent 93

Fisher, John, Bishop of Rochester 79
Fitzalan, Henry, 12th Earl of Arundel 34, 69, 89
Fitzgerald, Gerald, 8th Earl of Kildare 5, 9
Fitzgerald, James, 8th Earl of Desmond 9, 10
Fitzgerald, Gerald, 14th Earl of Desmond 32–33
Fitzmaurice, James 32–33
Fitzroy, Henry, 1st Duke of Richmond 139
Flowerdew, John 20
Fotheringhay Castle 81, 129, 133, 134, 135, 171, 172, 173, 192
Framlingham Castle xviii
Francis II of France 75, 83, 132, 172
Francis, Duke of Anjou 63
Fraser, Antonia 176

Gage, Robert 132
Gardiner, Stephen, Bishop of Winchester 26
Gerrard, Sir John 156
Gifford, Gilbert 37, 115, 117–119, 120, 121, 122, 127, 169, 179
Glorious Revolution 1688 98
Gordon, Catherine 11
Gorges, Ferdinando 148, 149, 153, 154, 156
Gorges, Sir Thomas 127
Gregory, Arthur 118
Grenville, Mary 33
Grey, Henry, 1st Duke of Suffolk xviii, 24, 26
Grey, Lady Jane xv, xvii–xviii, 2, 14, 23, 24, 26, 28, 30, 86, 133, 158, 161, 175, 184, 187
Grey, Lady Katherine 30, 86, 133, 181, 192–193
Grey, William, 13th Baron Grey de Wilton 23
Grindal, William xvi
Guise, Henry I, Duke of 87, 88–89, 94, 95, 97
Guise, Mary of 172, 186
Gunpowder Plot 84, 102, 113, 136, 169–170

Halter, John 88–89
Hampton Court Palace xiv
Hardwick, Bess of (*see* Bess of Hardwick)
Hare, Hugh 104
Harwich 69, 73
Hastings, Henry, 3rd Earl of Huntingdon 43, 52–53
Hatfield House xiii, xvii, xix, xx, 26
Hatton, Sir Christopher 127, 134
Henry II of France 25
Henry III of France 87
Henry IV 151, 152

Index

Henry VI 152, 196
Henry VII xiv, 1, 2, 3–4, 5–7, 8, 9–10, 13–14, 20, 152, 186–187, 188, 192, 195
Henry VIII x, xiii–xiv, xv, xvii, xviii, xxi, 1–2, 14, 15, 16, 17, 18–19, 20, 21, 23, 25–26, 30, 34, 35, 36, 50, 62, 63, 64, 79, 81–82, 86, 93, 103, 108–109, 133, 139, 140, 153–154, 165, 168, 172, 175, 182, 187, 189, 192
Hepburn, James, 4th Earl of Bothwell 31
Herbert, John 149
Herbert William, 1st Earl of Pembroke 25, 103
Herle, William 68
Higford, Robert 72
Hilton, Lisa 162
Hopton, Cecily 96, 99, 101
Hopton, Owen 96, 101
Howard, Anne, Countess of Arundel 90
Howard, Charles, 1st Earl of Nottingham 147, 156, 159
Howard, Henry, Earl of Surrey 35, 64, 65
Howard, Henry, 1st Earl of Northampton 92
Howard, Katherine xiv, 161, 175
Howard, Philip, 13th Earl of Arundel 123

Howard, Thomas, 3rd Duke of Norfolk 17, 24, 35, 64, 65
Howard, Thomas, 4th Duke of Norfolk 33, 34–36, 37–38, 39, 40, 47, 49, 57, 58, 59, 61, 63–64, 65–66, 69, 70–71, 72–74, 75–77, 78, 80, 82, 92, 138, 170–171, 180
Hussey, John, 1st Baron Hussey 18
Hussey, Thomas 40

Iconoclasm 38
Ireland 4, 5, 8, 9, 10, 11–12, 32–33, 75, 138, 140, 141–142, 143, 144, 146, 149, 175
Isabella Clara Eugenia of Spain, Archduchess of Austria 148

James II 98
James IV of Scotland 9, 11, 63
James V of Scotland xii
James VI of Scotland (I of England) xii, 29, 30, 31, 32, 45, 49, 57, 60, 66–67, 81, 86, 87–88, 100, 116, 123, 133, 136, 147, 148, 156, 157, 173, 189, 194
Jesuits 104, 105, 115–116, 133
John of Gaunt 148
Jones, Edward 132

Katherine of Aragon xiii, xiv, 1, 13, 14, 17, 24, 172, 192
Kenninghall 34
Kesselring, K.J. 29
Kett Rebellion 2, 19, 20–22, 28, 166, 187, 189, 193
Kett, Robert 20, 22
Kingston, Sir Anthony 22
Knollys, Sir Francis 32
Knollys, Lettice 139
Knollys, William, 1st Earl of Banbury 153

Lee, Captain Thomas 158
Leicester's Commonwealth 1584 95
Leith 73
Leslie, John, Bishop of Ross 37, 58, 59, 60, 69, 70, 74, 76
Leveson, Sir John 154
Levin, Carole 140
Lincolnshire Rising 15
Lochleven Castle xii, 31, 189
London Bridge 13, 107
Lovell, Francis, 1st Viscount Lovell 5–6
Lumley, John, 1st Baron Lumley 69, 128
Lyttelton, John 148

Manners, Edward, 3rd Earl of Rutland 128
Manners, Francis, 6th Earl of Rutland 149, 162

Mary I xiii, xviii, xix, 2–3, 14, 19, 23–24, 25, 26, 28, 35, 42, 49, 50, 59, 61, 63, 75, 78, 109, 137, 166, 172, 175, 177, 182, 184, 186, 187, 191, 195
Mary II 98
Mary Queen of Scots x, xi, xiii, xx, 42–43, 44, 45, 47, 54, 55, 58, 60, 67, 75, 80, 81, 88, 96, 98, 100, 104, 105, 106, 114, 116, 136, 160–161, 165, 168–169, 176, 177, 178–179, 183–184, 188, 191, 194, 195
  and the Babington Plot 111–112, 113, 114, 117–118, 119, 120, 121, 122, 124, 127
  and Elizabeth I xi, xii–xiii, xvii, xix, xxi, 14, 30, 31–32, 44–45, 51, 53–54, 56–57, 58, 59, 65, 68, 71–74, 75, 77, 81–82, 86, 91, 112, 117, 122, 128, 129–130, 132–133, 134–136, 150, 152, 153, 166–169, 171–172, 176–177, 183–184, 185, 186, 188–189
  flight to England 28, 29–30, 33, 165, 170, 183
  and the Northern Rising 29, 30, 33, 36, 37, 41, 43, 45, 47, 51, 52–54

relationship with Duke of
  Norfolk 33, 34, 35, 39,
  57, 63, 65, 72–73, 75, 76,
  80, 180
and the Ridolfi Plot 56–57,
  59, 61, 64, 65, 66–67,
  68–69, 70, 71–72, 78, 82
succession 30, 33, 40, 41, 76,
  85–86, 99, 163, 180, 1814,
  182, 192–193
and the Throckmorton Plot
  83–84, 85, 86, 87, 89, 90,
  91, 92, 94, 97, 98, 105
trial and execution 51, 77, 78,
  81, 82, 111, 112, 132–135,
  137, 152–153, 157,
  159, 164, 165, 169–172,
  174–175, 188, 192, 196
Matilda, Empress 192
Matthieu, Claude 87
Mendoza, Don Bernadino
  de 87, 88, 92, 93, 96–98,
  120–121
Meyrick, Gelly 148, 161
Mildmay, Sir Walter 69
More, Sir Thomas 79
Morgan, Thomas 85, 92, 104,
  105, 115, 117, 119, 121, 127

Nau, Claude 111, 127,
  128, 135
Naworth Castle 45, 47
Neville, Charles, 6th Earl of
  Westmoreland 34–35, 37–39,
  40, 41, 45–46, 47, 49, 50,
  51–52
Neville, Edmund 105, 108, 109
Nonsuch Palace 143, 144
Northern Rebellion xii, 29–55,
  56, 58, 60, 61, 62, 64, 66, 72,
  73, 75, 111, 122, 167, 168,
  179, 180, 183, 190
Norton, Richard, Sheriff of
  Yorkshire 40, 41, 43–44, 45

O'Neill, Hugh, 2nd Earl of
  Tyrone 141, 142, 146

Paget, Charles 85, 87, 88–89,
  94, 95, 96, 97, 104, 105
Paget, Lord Thomas 89, 94–95
Parker, William, 4th Baron
  Monteagle 149
Parr, Katherine xiv, xv–xvi, 103
Parr, William, 1st Marquess of
  Northampton 21, 23
Parry, Sir Thomas xviii
Parry, Dr William 102–104, 105,
  106–107, 179
Parry Plot 102–109, 111, 170,
  179, 183, 190
Paulet, Sir Amyas 113, 114,
  115, 116, 117, 127,
  129–130, 171
Peasants' Revolt 1381 16
Percy, Sir Thomas 38
Percy, Thomas, 7th Earl of
  Northumberland 34–35, 36,

225

37, 38–39, 40, 41, 43, 44, 45–46, 47, 49–50, 51–52
Percy, Henry, 8th Earl of Northumberland 88, 89, 96, 100–101
Percy, Henry, 9th Earl of Northumberland 123
Phelippes, Thomas 112–113, 118, 120, 122, 124, 134
Philip II of Spain xviii, 2, 3, 24, 28, 42, 49, 59, 63, 65, 68–69, 73, 87, 88, 92, 94, 95, 97, 102, 111, 113, 121, 148, 174, 182
Pilgrimage of Grace x, 2, 14–19, 28, 36, 38, 40, 53, 72, 165, 167, 187, 189, 193
Plantagenet, Edward, 17th Earl of Warwick 4, 5, 6, 7, 8, 9, 13, 14, 187, 188
Plantagenet, George, 1st Duke of Clarence 4, 7
Plowden, Alison 139
Pole, Edmund de la, 3rd Duke of Suffolk xxi
Pole, Henry, 1st Baron Montagu xxi
Pole, John de la, 1st Earl of Lincoln 4, 5, 6–7, 13
Pole, Margaret, Countess of Salisbury xxi
Poley, Robert 37, 115, 126, 127, 169, 179

Popes:
  Pius IV 1559–1565 180
  Pius V 1566–1572 54, 57, 59, 62, 71, 87, 114, 179, 180
  Gregory XIII 1572–1585 87, 94, 104
  Leo XIII 1878–1903 49
Popham, John 153
Princes in the Tower 4, 6, 7, 8, 42, 101, 187, 188
Protestantism xii, xv, xviii, 2, 19, 24, 26, 29, 31, 33, 34, 38, 40, 41, 42, 51, 55, 57, 59, 61, 75, 80, 81, 82, 84, 98, 102, 113, 122, 123–124, 129, 132, 133, 136, 170, 177, 184, 185, 186, 189

Queenborough Castle 105

Radcliffe, Thomas, 3rd Earl of Sussex 37, 39, 40, 42, 43, 45, 46, 69
Radcliffe, Robert, 5th Earl of Sussex 149, 162
Raleigh, Sir Walter 84, 147, 153, 156
regicide 105, 124, 169
Regnans in Excelsis 1570 54, 62, 64–65, 114, 178, 179, 181–183
Renard de Bermont, Simon 26, 27

Index

Rheims 87, 104, 118
Rich, Penelope 149
Richard II 150–152, 196
Richard III 4, 5, 7, 8, 9, 145
Richmond Palace 194–195
Ridolfi Plot xii, 35, 51, 56–82, 83, 85, 109, 111, 138, 166, 168, 170, 171, 179, 182, 183, 190, 194
Ridolfi, Roberto di 36, 37, 56, 57–58, 60–62, 64–66, 68, 69–70, 72, 73–74, 75, 76, 78, 79, 80, 179
Robsart, Amy xvii, 63
Roncherolles, François de 87
Russell, John, 1st Earl of Bedford 22
Russell, Edward, 3rd Earl of Bedford 149, 162
Ruthven, Raid of 86, 88, 100

Sackville, Thomas, 1st Earl of Dorset 147
Sadler, Sir Ralph 43, 69, 73, 171
Salisbury Court 85
Salisbury, Thomas 132
Salutem in Christo 1571 74, 179
Savage, John 115, 121–122, 126, 127, 131
Scrope, Henry, 9th Baron Scrope of Bolton 48
Scudamore, John 126
Seething Lane 37, 61, 113
Seymour, Edward, 1st Duke of Somerset xvi, 19, 23, 58
Seymour, Edward, 1st Earl of Hertford 133
Seymour, Edward, 1st Viscount Beauchamp of Hache 86, 133, 181
Seymour, Jane xiii–xiv, xv, xvi, 1, 2, 192
Seymour, Mary xvi
Seymour, Sir Thomas xv–xvii
Shakespeare, William 150, 151, 152
Sheffield Castle 56, 71, 78–79, 83, 90
Sheffield Manor Lodge 90
Sidney, Sir Philip 138
Simnel Rebellion 3–7, 8, 9, 13, 14, 28, 186–187
Simnel, Lambert 2, 3, 4–5, 6, 7, 187, 188
Simons, Richard 4, 5, 6
Smith, Lacey Baldwin 102, 161, 184
Smythe, Thomas, Sheriff of London 154, 155
Somerset, Anne 45, 65, 142, 155
Somerset, Edward, 4th Earl of Worcester 153

Spanish Armada 26, 44, 51, 64, 65, 70, 81, 109, 111, 113, 130, 132, 136, 171, 174–175, 182
St James's Palace 25, 108
St Leger, Ursula 33
St Peter ad Vincula, Chapel of 161
Stafford, Edward, 3rd Duke of Buckingham xxi
Stafford, Sir Edward 95, 97
Stanley, Sir William 10
Stanley, Thomas, 1st Earl of Derby 10
Stewart, Esme, 1st Earl of Lennox 88
Stewart, Matthew, 4th Earl of Lennox xii
Stewart, James, 1st Earl of Moray xii, 32, 45
Stuart, Arbella 181, 192
Stuart, Henry, Lord Darnley 30, 74

Talbot, George, 4th Earl of Shrewsbury 17
Talbot, George, 6th Earl of Shrewsbury 32, 43, 69, 79, 114, 116
Tempest, Robert 40
Throckmorton Plot xii–xiii, 51, 68, 71, 82, 83–102, 105, 109–110, 111, 113, 115, 118, 120, 121, 166–167, 168, 170, 179, 182, 183, 190, 194
Throckmorton, Bess 84
Throckmorton, Sir Francis 57, 82, 83–85, 87, 90, 91–94, 95, 96, 97, 98–99, 101, 102, 175
Throckmorton, George 89–90, 92, 93, 96
Throckmorton, Margery 89, 90
Throckmorton, Sir Nicholas 84
Throckmorton, Thomas 89, 90
Tichbourne, Chidiock 115, 127, 130–131
Tilbury 26, 81
Tilney, Charles 127, 131
Tower Green xix, 26, 161
Tower Hill xvii, 13, 18, 23, 27, 77, 101, 161
Tower of London xvi, xix, 3, 4, 5, 8, 9, 13, 18, 23–24, 25, 26, 27, 28, 35, 47, 61, 64, 66, 68, 72, 73, 76, 92, 93–94, 95, 96, 99, 100–101, 117, 123, 129, 130, 137, 139, 152–153, 155, 157, 158, 159, 160, 161, 166, 174, 181, 187, 188, 191–192
Travers, John 132
Tresham, Francis 102, 169
Tudor, Jasper, 1st Duke of Bedford 3
Tudor, Margaret, Queen of Scotland 30, 63, 86, 133

Tudor, Mary, Duchess of Suffolk xviii, 63, 133
Tutbury Castle 32, 44
Tyburn 13, 15, 18, 45, 97, 158

Vere, John de, 13th Earl of Oxford 6
Vergil, Polydore 4, 6, 9
Villiers, George, 1st Duke of Buckingham 74

Walsingham, Frances 138, 145
Walsingham, Sir Francis x, 135, 137, 138, 149, 150, 151, 171, 174, 177
   and the Babington Plot xi, 112–113, 115, 116, 117–118, 119, 120, 122, 124, 125, 126, 127, 134, 137, 169
   and the Northern Rising 37, 50, 51
   and the Parry Plot 104, 106, 107–108
   and the Ridolfi Plot 58, 61–62, 65, 75, 76, 78, 80, 81, 82
   and the Throckmorton Plot 85, 86, 88, 89, 90, 92, 93, 94, 95, 96–99
   intelligence network 81, 89, 93, 95, 108, 109, 112–113, 115, 117–118, 120, 122, 126, 127, 134, 137, 141, 169, 178–179, 189
   relationship with William Cecil 58–59, 177–178
Warbeck Rebellion 7–14, 28, 186–187, 188
Warbeck, Perkin 2, 7, 8–11, 12–13, 187
Warnicke, Retha 124
Wars of the Roses xi, xiv, xxi, 1, 3, 6, 151–152, 192
Western Rebellion 2, 19, 22, 28, 166, 187
Westminster Abbey 8, 172, 194
Westminster Palace 13, 76, 107, 145, 146, 159, 169
Whitehall Palace 25, 26, 108, 149, 153, 154, 155, 162, 175, 194
William III 98
William of Orange (the Silent) 98, 102
Williams, Penry 154
Williams, Walter 93
Wilson, A.N. 41, 122
Windsor Castle 21, 47
Winter, Thomas 169
Wolsey, Thomas, Cardinal 34, 108, 168
Woodstock Palace xix, 27, 166
Woodville, Elizabeth 7
Wright, John 169

Wriothesley, Henry, 3rd Earl of Southampton 146, 148, 154, 155, 158, 159, 160
Wyatt Rebellion xviii–xix, 3, 23–28, 166, 167, 182, 191
Wyatt, Sir Thomas 24, 27
Wyatt, Sir Thomas the Younger xviii–xix, 3, 24, 25, 26, 27–28, 191

xenophobia 24, 25, 37, 42, 43, 81, 109, 148, 182

York House 144, 146
York, Elizabeth of 7, 195
York, Richard of Shrewsbury, Duke of 4, 8, 9–10, 11, 12, 13, 101, 187, 188